Dynamic Bodies

Dynamic Bodies

*A Framework
for Somatic Engagement
in Dance and Movement*

Elizabeth Limons Shea

Foreword by Harmony Jankowski

McFarland & Company, Inc., Publishers
Jefferson, North Carolina

This book has undergone peer review.

ISBN (print) 978-1-4766-8484-0
ISBN (ebook) 978-1-4766-5805-6

Library of Congress cataloging data are available

Library of Congress Control Number 2026000068

© 2025 Elizabeth Limons Shea. All rights reserved

No part of this book may be reproduced or transmitted in any form or by any means, electronic or mechanical, including photocopying or recording, or by any information storage and retrieval system, without permission in writing from the publisher.

Front cover image: *from left to right*, Kate Vermillion Lyons, Corey Boatner, Justin Sears, and Rachel Newbrough in Elizabeth Limons Shea's *Ascension*, at the Eskenazi Museum of Art, Bloomington, IN (author's collection, photograph by Freddie Kelvin).

Printed in the United States of America

McFarland & Company, Inc., Publishers
Box 611, Jefferson, North Carolina 28640
www.mcfarlandpub.com

For Mom and Dad

Acknowledgments

"I'm trying to tell you something 'bout my life...." The opening lyric to the Indigo Girls' iconic "Closer to Fine" runs through my consciousness as I complete the final writings of this book.[1] Undoubtedly, my life has been shaped by countless individuals who have provided support to both this project and to my broader journey as a dance artist.

Many teachers, mentors, artists, scholars, and colleagues have influenced my thought and actions over decades of professional practice. To all who have encouraged me to think and move more deeply, I express my sincere gratitude.

To my students—if I have taught you, you have taught me. As I journey further into my career as an artist/educator, these interactions grow more precious. I thank you for providing opportunities to mindfully assess my teaching and grow professionally and personally in this contemporary world.

Considering this manuscript specifically, there are several individuals who were all-important to the realization of this work. Research assistants Emma Hall and Megan Kudla provided essential support in gathering and classifying critical information, and the exquisitely written foreword and editorial coaching of Harmony Jankowski was integral to manuscript preparation and finalization. Likewise, the artistic talents of photographer Lindsay Osten and illustrator Abby Jones are showcased beautifully throughout the pages of this book. I extend a hearty thanks to these individuals for their indispensable work.

Co-authors Dr. John B. Shea (Chapter 2) and Dr. Frank Diaz (Chapter 4) provided crucial insight into relevant topics and current directions in their respective fields. John's research, which focuses on cognitive processes during the learning and control of purposeful movements, particularly his groundbreaking work in contextual inference, has led the field over many decades. Too, he has shared his passion for scientific inquiry with countless students globally, spurring new investigative directions in human learning and performance. A highly sought-after conductor and associate professor in the renowned Jacobs School of Music at Indiana University, Frank brings another perspective to somatic artistic engagement through his research in music education, which centers the contemplative sciences, particularly 4E cognition. Frank is also a master teacher of meditation, offering courses and workshops across the United States, furthering his dedication to mind/body theory and practice. I am grateful to both John and Frank for their contributions, which has elevated the discourse in these writings.

I would also like to thank the editorial staff of McFarland Publishing, specifically Layla Milholen, who shared their expertise so generously and patiently as I navigated this process during the Covid-19 pandemic and the caretaking and subsequent passing of my parents. Indiana University, my employer, too provided time and space so I might complete this manuscript, and I am thankful for these resources.

Finally, I thank my family for their unwavering support always. My parents, now gone, my husband, my son and stepchildren and their partners, and my grandchildren, have only offered encouragement and love throughout my sometimes-unconventional life as a dance artist/scholar/educator. My roles as a partner, mother, grandmother, and daughter, have been among life's most fulfilling, and for this, I am deeply grateful.

Table of Contents

Acknowledgments — vii
Foreword by Harmony Jankowski, PhD RYT — 1
Preface — 5

Part 1—A Theoretical Basis for Somatic Praxis — 9

1. Introduction, and Historical Context of Somatics — 11
2. Principles of Movement Learning: *An Overview* — 36
   Elizabeth Limons Shea and John B. Shea
3. The Flexible Nervous System — 60
4. Contemporary Theories of Learning, Performing, and Living — 85
   Elizabeth Limons Shea and Frank Diaz

Part 2—SomaLab: Efficiency in Learning; Expression in Performance — 109

5. What Is SomaLab? — 111
6. Building a Personal Practice — 134
7. Moving Together: *The Somatic Community* — 159
8. Somatic Dance-Making: *A Case Study* — 185
9. The Evolving Process: *SomaLab in Action* — 208

Concluding Remarks — 233
Chapter Notes — 235
Bibliography — 247
Index — 257

Foreword

BY HARMONY JANKOWSKI, PHD RYT

Try to remember the last time you typed something on a computer. Probably not difficult, as these machines often mediate our work, leisure, communication, and so many other aspects of our lives. Now try to recall what your body was doing, aside from typing. How were you sitting (not just where, but how)? How were your legs positioned? Two feet on the floor? Left crossed over right at the knee? Figure four? What about your spine? Your shoulders? How did the keys feel under your fingertips?

The specifics might be harder to recall, as so many of the activities we do each day we do by rote. If the body isn't signaling that something is off with unusual pain, we don't think about typing, or walking, or pulling on a sweater. The same becomes true for practitioners of yoga and other somatic modalities, and for movement artists of all varieties. We don't always think about the shapes and movement sequences that have become commonplace to us—and this isn't necessarily a bad thing—but we can add depth to our physical presence in our daily lives and in somatic and artistic practice when we build attentiveness to mind, body, and breath. In *Dynamic Bodies: A Framework for Somatic Engagement in Dance and Movement*, Elizabeth Limons Shea gives us a way to do exactly that. The book gives a thoughtful consideration of mind and body, and how they work with and upon each other, and proposes a framework that allows them to do so efficiently, expansively, and accessibly.

I first encountered Liz as a fellow mover in yoga classes; I was a graduate student, mom, and dancer seeking respite and recovery for my mind and body. As many yoga students and teachers will attest, people tend to favor certain areas of a studio, and Liz and I happened to tend toward a particular corner (perhaps because the class was heated, and we'd feel a very welcome draft whenever the door opened). Our pre- and post-class chats revealed that she was a professor of contemporary dance and I was writing a dissertation exploring shared conceptualizations of bodies, movement, and identity within modernist literature and modern dance. We started a conversation about movement, art, philosophy, teaching, and somatics that has persisted in different forms for more than a decade. I have often felt, when reading her book, as if we were continuing that conversation; I'm so excited for you, the reader, to begin a dialogue with Liz now.

I'm privileged to teach at the same yoga studio with Liz, and to frequent her classes, which invite students to commune with their physical and energetic bodies. These classes engage the intellect through precise cueing for mind, body, and breath that inspires awareness of the practice as it's happening. Put more simply, Liz leads classes that foster (and require) presence—she invites you to have a full bodymind experience, an experience infused with care and joy. As a teacher, she offers something more than a thoughtfully planned sequence; her guidance, through language, is specific, grounded in deep knowledge gleaned through life as a dancer, choreographer, teacher, and somatic and yogic practitioner. In practicing with Liz, I have found myself extending beyond my preconceptions about my own bodymind instrument. Her words nurture a mindful, abundant practice that far exceeds the attainment of proper alignment within sequence of poses.

Dynamic Bodies invites readers to share an experience not dissimilar to the kind she imparts in the studio. Somatic practices emphasize our relationship to our bodies, minds and senses and to the world around us. Liz doesn't simply remind her readers to attend to these relationships; rather she gives us a framework for doing so in SomaLab, and explains its rationale in detailed, well-researched prose. She makes the case for SomaLab's utility for all humans, laying historical, theoretical, and scientific groundwork in Part 1. The book attends carefully to how we learn movement digging deeply enough into cognitive psychology, kinesiology, and neuroscience to offer rich background, priming the reader, as in the way of a vigorous warm-up, for the work to come. Part 2 presents the SomaLab framework, describing its parts clearly and concisely before offering beautifully rich examples that will have the reader breathing deeply and visualizing even as they read. The book's final chapters promise to inspire readers to create through astoundingly beautiful, honest examples of how Shea has used the framework in the process of artmaking, and how she envisions using it within community spaces. SomaLab offers movement practitioners a rare framework that promises to hone their perceptive instruments, and to build mastery of a method for accessing a plurality of approaches to movement, rather than a single, codified technique. Through the tools and tasks offered in this text, Liz gives readers a point of access to the felt experience of practicing movement with her, as either a student or a fellow traveler.

Dynamic Bodies doesn't merely impart information; it engages its reader in the process of learning how they learn, though linked intellectual-emotional-social-physical activities, individually and in community with others.

Harmony Jankowski, PhD RYT, is a writer, an editor, a researcher, a project manager, and a yoga teacher whose wide-ranging interests span categories including various movement modalities, education research and infrastructure, somatics, and modernism. She lives in Bloomington, Indiana, with her family and too many dogs and cats.

Preface

This book comes from a deep place: a life joyfully invested in dance, movement, and thought. I have long been fascinated by the workings of the bodymind, and searched to uncover theoretical and experiential truth, witnessing along the way how the human condition is revealed through artistic investigations and embodied research.[1] The theory needs the practice and the practice needs the theory to move our experiences forward as movers and makers.

More specifically, this text focuses on the theoretical basis for somatic (addressing both the mind and the body) practice in dance and related movement arts. I also present a self-developed methodology, Soma-Lab® (hereafter referred to as SomaLab), which is broad in scope and invites creation within a framework defined by scientific discovery and first-person experiences. Necessity is veritably the mother of invention; as a dance artist, I developed this approach over many years of applying practical knowledge from performance, pedagogy, and making, as well as formal study in traditional and contemporary theories of learning and performance.

Our lives today are complicated, and those of dancers and movement artists are no exception. The explosion of social media and web-based viewing over the last decade has facilitated a broad sharing of form and philosophy. The new globalization of art making has brought artists closer together but also presents challenges. For example, learning many different movement forms can be time consuming if approached in a purely serial fashion; mastery of all seems near impossible. Likewise, expressive capabilities are muted without serious practice of the mind/body connection, where an individual's existence and empathy toward others' lived experiences inform their artistry.

The purpose of these writings is threefold: first, to provide a contemporary basis and rationale for somatic praxis; second, to offer a novel somatic methodology that is dynamic and reflects the complexity of the human nervous system; third, to further the conversation between theorists and practitioners. Part 1 begins by examining the origins and development of somatics from a socio-historical perspective and summarizes the current state of western somatic practice. Research based on existing theory in cognitive psychology and kinesiology follows, including motor learning paradigms, basic structure and function of the nervous system, and contemporary approaches to learning and performance, all in the context of their importance to major somatic constructs. Each of these independent but interconnected fields utilize differing vocabularies and research models; information is presented sometimes in more concrete terms and sometimes from a theoretical perspective. Part 1 provides critical scaffolding for understanding the why and how of somatic praxis.

Part 2 opens by introducing SomaLab, a framework for developing efficiency and expressive capabilities in the bodymind, and yokes knowledge and theory presented in Part 1 to a proposed system for somatic investigation. Information is framed to promote an understanding of how choices to construct the framework and identify tools and tasks were made and developed into practical applications. Subsequent chapters present examples for establishing movement praxis that are self- or leader-directed and can be offered in a variety of settings and to different communities, along with pedagogical and dance-making considerations. Knowledge gleaned in the laboratory, in the classroom, and in one's own bodymind informs these writings to include a holistic approach to movement and artistic investigation. Indeed, the entirety of these chapters documents the *process* of moving from theory to practice, serving as a metaphor for the SomaLab framework itself.

So, what is SomaLab, and why might the tools and tasks of this framework benefit movement artists? In basic terms, SomaLab facilitates the learning and performance of movement by deepening the practitioner's bodymind connection. This approach is designed to utilize the flexibility of the nervous system and promote efficiency in learning. By training the system, movers can work toward a plural instrument, where lived experiences and social-cultural considerations are centered. It is process-based and non-prescriptive, and it works to deepen and expand somatic experiences, not replace one way of moving with another.

To be clear, it is the pioneering work of many somatic investigators that has led us to this place. Some come from a perspective of artistic truth and beauty, while some follow the allure of human behavioral research. Each artist/scholar offers new insights and pieces to a complex puzzle that contributes knowledge to the planes of our existence. It is always intriguing to see the organization of minds laid bare as they offer their own individual approaches to how and why. This is truly the intersection of art and science.

And so, I offer you, the reader, the organization of my own mind as the why and how is presented. I hope it leads you to an inspired space, where mind and body move forward toward equanimity and wisdom.

Part 1

A Theoretical Basis for Somatic Praxis

1

Introduction, and Historical Context of Somatics

"Dance is for everybody. I believe that the dance came from the people, and that it should always be delivered back to the people."—attributed to Alvin Ailey

Introduction

What Is Somatics?

In one of his most insightful and well-known statements, iconic dance artist Alvin Ailey delivers a universal truth regarding the origin of human movement expression, and its purpose in our lives. We speak and know with the body; we innately communicate our innermost beliefs and feelings through action; we learn and understand with the totality of our physical instrument as it interacts with everything around us. This is the basis for somatic theory, study, and practice.

The *idea* of somatics is as old as the world; it encompasses the symbiotic relationship between life and earth and is the earliest representation of living organism and environment. At its very heart, the term *somatics* is associated with interrelationships between action and mind, mind and body, body and land, and land and its people. It is an integrative approach found in ancient philosophies of wholeness, health, and behavior, of interconnectedness and spirituality. Somatics holds that differing aspects of human behavior cannot be siloed from each other; rather, they are part of a complex system of interdependent mechanisms that, together, achieve individual wellness and fulfillment. When we define somatics in this way, the field becomes a *philosophy,* as opposed to a *methodology.* By abandoning the crusade to discover one set of movement patterns that can and *should* be adopted by all of humanity, we acknowledge the plurality of somatic practices and create space for all people to embrace first-person experiences.

The co-existence and shared importance of mind and body and the centering of movement in sensing and acting are key tenets of what today we call somatics. Thomas Hanna famously coined the term *somatics* in 1976, drawing from the Greek work "soma," meaning "body."[1] Contemporary western somatic techniques generally refer to body therapies, bodywork, movement awareness, and re-patterning systems devised by 19th- and 20th-century movement theorists.[2] Often, codified methodologies have not fully recognized the global lineage of modern somatic praxis, especially influences from Asia, Africa, and the African diaspora. Indeed, both philosophy and method have been appropriated in present-day somatic work; cultures that contributed mightily to the development of current praxis have not been named, recognized, and celebrated. Martha Eddy explains, "The whole system perspective is embedded in Afrocentric models, as reflected in the unification of mind-body and spirit, but more importantly the omnipresence of 'the circle,' the dance and communication formation that supports the communication in community."[3] Too, the interdependence of movement, music, speech and singing all work toward an embodied experience that is uniquely Africanist. In contrast, western-based movement systems tend to separate and disintegrate; so here we are with the work of reintegrating and putting everything back together that western society has pulled apart.

We now inch closer to defining somatics and arrive at both a philosophy that encourages holism in thought and movement, as well as a palette of practices developed by many great minds that reveal their commitment to, research of, and autobiographical approach to constructing praxis. This overarching somatic premise, accompanied by individuality in how the bodymind organizes, leads us to a rich and fertile field in which embodied knowledge accumulates. We make connections between ideas, contrast and compare, find similarities and differences, and distill information that guides us toward our own personal set of movement beliefs and values.

This chapter is by no means a comprehensive examination of the history of somatics and current practices; rather, it offers the reader an overview of various schools of thought that have influenced and continue to influence today's practitioners in their work. It is my intent that this overview will provide context and information as dance and movement artists develop their own philosophies and methodologies and share this work with others.[4]

Global Origins of Somatic Practice

Evidence of somatic thought is certainly apparent in antiquity throughout the globe and informs many societies and cultures today. The use of movement as a source of wellness and healing is integral to the guiding philosophies of ancient and indigenous peoples where the bodymind instrument is seen as interconnected. There has, without doubt, been a mass importation of this concept into contemporary somatic praxis without recognition or citation. In the absence of written materials, it's important to affirm the root of one's study and method when sharing somatic work.[5] Let's also distinguish between global bodymind practices *influencing* somatics, and these practices *as* somatics—both of which can be appropriate in this context.

Often overlooked are the unique philosophies germane to indigenous peoples from both the East and the West. For example, the First Nations people of North America envision the Sacred Circle of Life, an interconnectedness that extends to relationships between time, space, and living beings. The term *MSIT No'Kmaq*, which translates loosely to "All my Relations" in English, refers to the life-sustaining relationships between all elements of the universe, and to the idea of knowing. Holistic health and wellness are not possible without a life practice of these cyclical connections, especially with other people, fostering deeper spirituality and wisdom.[6] Wholeness, in body and spirit, where if any harm comes to either the other is affected, is another tenet of this complex philosophical system. Also related to contemporary somatic work is the First Nations people's approach to science, which is deeply phenomenological, and privileges first-person experiences in arriving at truth and knowledge. Indeed, Kaminski writes:

> Their [First Nations'] traditional practices boast amazing sustainability, ecological awareness and knowledge, and a strong scientific understanding of the earth, weather, cycles of the seasons, medicinal and food sources, marine foods and harvesting, and creating everything they need from nature's bounty. Before colonization, these practices and systems worked perfectly and in harmony with the world around them. They left a very light footprint upon the earth.[7]

Though it is a hallmark of many current investigative processes regarding somatic study, centering first-person experiences has roots in ancient practice, and is not a new approach to scientific inquiry.

Likewise, understanding the African worldview of an integrative life approach is essential when tracing the origins of somatic philosophy and methodology. Here, a binary division of mental and physical states does not exist; rather, the mind, body, and spirit work in complementary yet distinct ways to achieve optimal health and wellness.[8] African dance, especially, is an important tool for both the individual and the community, and the polycentric nature of movements in the art form reflects the complex relationships that exist both within (bodymind) and outside of (the land, nature, community) human beings. It's important to note here that while there is no one, singular form of African dance, but rather, many different styles that are particular to distinct peoples and cultures on the African continent, similarities exist (such as polycentricity) among these forms and are tied together by the Africanist worldview.[9]

Between the 16th and 19th centuries, many Africans were brutally enslaved, seized from their homelands, and forced to live in unimaginable hardship predominantly in North and South America, and the Caribbean. The African people used the art of dance as a healing force and to keep their culture alive.[10] Over hundreds of years these dances coalesced with Western forms, not only creating new styles globally throughout the African Diaspora, but also bringing the African worldview of holism, integration, and healing to other parts of world. This Africanist cultural vision was not strictly relegated to art; approaches to philosophy and science were also carried in the histories of bodies who were seized and annexed from the African continent. As culture directly reflects affinities exhibited by groups of individuals,[11] it logically follows that the Africanist rejection of dualism and division in scientific inquiry would migrate west, and the culture of belief would mingle with western empiricism. Indeed, dance artist Beatrice Capote (pictured in Figure 1.1), a specialist in Afro-Cuban dance, music, and culture, relays, "When I dance Yemaya, I holistically imagine the calm and the force of the water healing my soul. I connect to the elements of life, and I am reminded to empower my internal feminine energy exuding towards the external."[12]

Most certainly, influences from India, manifested through yogic thought and practice, are easily identifiable in many modern somatic systems. The word yoga, with etymological origins stemming from "yoke" or "join," indicates a symbiotic relationship between mind and body. To study yoga is to engage in growth, both through thought and action, and find a balanced relationship between the two. In *The Yoga of Breathing*, Richard Rosen shares that "practice has two poles—an active pole that entails intense and persistent exertion (abhyasa) and a passive one that encourages what yoga tradition calls samatva, an attitude of evenness or equanimity toward the world."[13] This idea of healing and wellness amid chaos and trauma is centered around the control of consciousness and building perceptive skills to influence action/reaction.

Yoga is an ancient practice that originated in Northern India and

1. Introduction, and Historical Context of Somatics 15

Figure 1.1. Beatrice Capote performing Yemaya, the Orisha or deity of the Yoruba or Lukumi traditions in Cuba, deriving from the IFA system of Nigeria, West Africa. Yemaya represents the mother of the fishes, the salt-waters, and ocean; she is a nurturer, a healer, and a protector (courtesy Beatrice Capote; photograph by bserafin photo).

is referenced in religious texts dating to approximately 5,000 BCE. Early teachings were decidedly philosophically and spiritually oriented, steeped in Hinduism. Patanjali's *Yoga-Sûtras*, written sometime during the 2nd century, is often considered the first text to outline methods that influence today's modern yoga. Physical postures, or asana, however, were not fully developed until much later, leading to what we know today as Hatha Yoga. The late 1800s and early 1900s saw the migration of yogic thought and practice west, developing into contemporary systems.

In addition to the basic tenets of yoga, which promote union and embodiment, and celebrate balance in the mind/body relationship, the deliberate use of breath, or *pranayama*, has greatly influenced somatic practitioners and performing artists alike. Conscious attention to breath is often the gateway of praxis in any body-working system and is certainly a cornerstone of yogic tradition. The very movement of the lungs as we inhale and exhale serves as a baseline for drawing attention to and processing the relationship between intention and action. The way breath is controlled, its effect on movement outcomes, however small, creates fertile ground for nascent embodied explorations. That the use of breath in today's somatic work stems directly from both ancient and modern yogic practice is clear, yet often unrecognized or credited. Too, the idea of achieving ergonomic alignment of the human skeletal system for health and efficiency of movement, codified in many body-working methodologies, has roots in Hatha Yoga.

Equally important, influences from Asia include Chinese martial arts, particularly the internal arts, which have strong connections to contemporary somatic praxis. These forms have roots in both Taoist and Confucian Chinese religious philosophy, each of which is grounded broadly in tenets of integration and harmony. Practiced worldwide, tai chi is one such internal martial art, finding popularity with non-combat practitioners beginning in the early 20th century. Although there are several schools of study, all forms of tai chi encompass aspects of martial arts (responding to outside force), health (effects of stress on the body and mind), and meditation (internal focus), each of which balances internal and external influences.[14]

Closely related, qigong is the practice of living and working with one's vital energy, or *qi*, housed in a framework of attentional breath and movement. Like tai chi, qigong has roots in Chinese martial arts and philosophy; both are ancient techniques codified for the modern world with wide-ranging global appeal. The goal of qigong is to reach a meditative mind-state, achieving balance in not only physical, but also emotional health. Pölönen, Lappi, and Tervaniemi recently studied the effect of qigong practice on flow (a deep, energized focus) and affect (emotion or mood), finding significant positive trends in both measures over a series of four sessions.[15] Empirical research delving into somatic-based work indeed continues to shed light on the ever-apparent complexities of the mind/body relationship and pushes past traditional understandings of information processing models (Chapter 2) toward embodied cognition (Chapters 4 and 5) in human movement and performance.[16] This and related work also bring to bear the role of mindfulness in emotional health, a perhaps less considered branch of somatic study.[17]

Japanese movement practices have also contributed significantly to modern somatic applications. Aikido evolved from ancient martial arts into an existent study of movement, breath, and mindfulness, and encompasses compassion, spirituality, and social touch. Moving meditation and conscious breath practice have long been an integral part of Japanese martial arts, dating from medieval Japan, where Samurai soldiers borrowed the Zen monks' mindful approach to stay focused during battle.[18] The ability to return to presence after experiencing a distracting thought is a hallmark of meditation and is not only a useful tool for spiritual and emotional health, but also for building neural plasticity and increasing the capacity for dual-task performance.

1. Introduction, and Historical Context of Somatics 17

Aikido additionally utilizes work with partners and social touch during training, another trait of codified somatic methodologies. This practice builds compassion and addresses spirituality; indeed, aikido is used in therapeutic settings with specialized populations. Lukoff and Strozzi-Heckler report robust programs of aikido offerings for veterans in Denver, Colorado; Cincinnati, Ohio; and Portsmouth, New

Figure 1.2. Marijke Eliasberg practices tai chi on the roof of her apartment building in New York, New York, at the height of the Covid-19 global pandemic (courtesy Marijke Eliasberg; photograph by Rebecca Oviatt).

Hampshire, and conclude that "Aikido training is a potentially therapeutic practice for some veterans coping with PTSD."[19] The pairing of certain movements with positive emotive states shares common threads with dance therapy, where movement works to make positive change through embodiment.

Evolving from the ancient art of jujitsu, judo is another Japanese martial art with close ties to current somatic praxis. After World War I, a young Moshe Feldenkrais (the Feldenkrais Method® of Somatic Education) living in Palestine practiced jujitsu as a means of survival on the streets. Relocating to Paris in 1933, he met judo's founder, Jigoro Kano, and began rigorous study of this new, internal art form.[20] Like aikido, judo focuses on an interconnectedness of the mind, body, and spirit and emphasizes an embodied approach to enlightenment while also putting forth the principle of "maximum efficiency, minimal effort" (a concept which would later form the groundwork for Feldenkrais' signature somatic program). Indeed, in *Higher Judo: Groundwork*, he writes, "The essential aim of Judo is to teach, help, and forward adult maturity, which is an ideal state rarely reached, where a person is capable of dealing with the immediate present task before him without being hindered by earlier formed habits of thought or attitude."[21] This idea of "adult maturity" has clear connections to the concepts of mindfulness and presence, ideas which thread through multiple somatic constructs, both eastern and western, ancient and modern.

Western Influence

In the 15th and 16th centuries, the Italian Renaissance revived an interest in the bodily aesthetics first embraced by Greek and Roman culture across Europe. Explorations in art and science revolved around human life on earth, shifting the gaze of creatives from spiritual realms toward flesh, bone, and breath. It was not until the late 19th and early 20th centuries, however, that a true focus on the physical body emerged. This divergence from an overarching umbrella of spirituality previously imposed by religious life and culture, and often associated with paganism of the past, would form the basis for contemporary western somatic thought. The concept that movement is expressive, healthful, and important for optimal human function began to take hold. The field of kinesiology was born around this time, in an attempt to bridge the gap between professional medical intervention and alternative methods of healing, such as self-care and wellness, including exercise and movement.[22] Likewise, the phenomenon referred to as physical culture began to spread

1. Introduction, and Historical Context of Somatics

throughout Europe, spurred very much by a warring continent, full of "badly knocked-about nations."[23] In Germany, physical training had an observable predilection toward nationalism, especially with regard to military education, while in Sweden, cures for the failed army intersected with aesthetic concerns; a search for the "body beautiful." Per Henrik Ling, the originator of Swedish gymnastics, developed a system that took root in Europe, spread west to America, and had a profound impact on somatic practice.

Ling's system of gymnastics was inclusive of mind/body/spirit models and promoted equanimity among this tripartite structure. Moving was for everyone and was considered essential to good health. A distinct harmony between physical strength and fitness, wellness and healing, and physical aesthetics was essential to his approach. In contrast, he deemed the competing system of German gymnastics unbalanced, with too much emphasis given to bodily accomplishments, as realized through competitions and exhibitions. After Ling's death, his disciples continued to promote his work, advancing, and redefining the system as physiotherapy, with American physician Charles Taylor publishing a booklet titled *The Movement Cure* in 1857.[24]

While gymnastics systems were redefining and refocusing physicality

Figure 1.3. An artist's rendition of women performing traditional Swedish gymnastics in the early 20th century (illustration by Abby Jones).

as a key component of the human experience, performing artists too were rethinking tools for coaxing expressiveness and truth from their trainings. The work of one such artist, French vocalist François Delsarte, had an indelible impact on both the body culture movement as well as the antecedents of early modern dance. First introduced in 1839, Delsarte's system for gesture training and classification was based on the idea that specific emotions generated corresponding places and actions in the body that were reliable and repeatable. The human instrument was incapable of producing movements that were untrue and falsely aligned with speech. Indeed, by employing this economical approach to behavior, body language served as a sort of built in "lie detector."[25]

Delsartism flourished in Europe and America and was widely practiced not just by arts professionals and those who embraced body culture, but by lawyers, ministers, politicians, and individuals whose trade was performative. Toward the end of the 19th century, many of Delsarte's disciples disseminated his methodologies while also establishing their own training perspectives. Genevieve Stebbins was one such revisionist, who broadened the original Delsartian regimen to include elements of Eastern yoga, Ling gymnastics, and breathing exercises, all practices which would provide the basis for her system of Harmonic Gymnastics. Stebbins embraced religion, mythology, and philosophy in her work and was a fierce proponent of un-corseted dress for women, as she considered the restrictive garments antithetical to health and movement.[26] We can see here a first small spark of artistic somatic praxis, where mind and body begin to work harmoniously toward mindfulness and artfulness in expression.

Another performing artist and educator who contributed to the cause was Swiss musician Émile Jaques-Dalcroze (1865–1950). Indeed, Dalcroze Eurhythmics (DE) is still offered today as a fundamental system for teaching music in many educational settings and is often regarded as a somatic practice.[27] Built on three principles which include rhythmic studies, aural training, and improvisation, DE utilizes movement in the study of music as a necessary and equal component that contributes to a deep and expressive understanding of both media. The concept of an inextricable relationship between music and dance, of course, as addressed earlier in this chapter, belongs to indigenous peoples, and is practiced widely today in many cultures. First-person experiences and sensations, too, are defining features of this work, even further linking it to contemporary somatic praxis. And, like SomaLab, introduced in Part 2 of this text, DE is more of a framework than a strict, codified system; it provides flexibility and welcomes additions from other voices.

1. Introduction, and Historical Context of Somatics 21

Thus far it is clear that the turn of the 20th century saw several converging and overlapping schools of thought addressing bodymind movement expression (along with many others unnamed in this short narrative) in Western Europe and the United States. But was there one unifying figure that moved the field forward, defining and distinguishing what we today consider to be "somatics" from other body-forward schemas? A good number of somatic scholars and historians credit Elsa Gindler as the matriarch of modern somatic praxis.[28]

Gindler (1885–1961) began her studies by practicing and teaching Stebbins' *Harmonic Gymnastics*, as taught to her by Hade Kallmeyer, in Germany. What Gindler found in this work was deeper than a Spartan approach to fitness or appreciation of physical capabilities, and more than a Delsartian affinity for true expressiveness. She defined gymnastic practices of the era to mean a training of one's total persona, mind, body, and spirit. As Gindler's movement research progressed, her work grew in scope and focus—the goal was no longer to achieve knowledge of methodologies by preordained measurable standards. Rather, her eye turned to the total training of the bodymind instrument by way of sensation, perception, incorporation—all terms so very familiar to modern era somatic practitioners. Gindler encouraged her students to find their own voices, thus sending forth thoughtful movement researchers, teachers, and specialists who broadened the field, carrying bits of their formal training into new personal landscapes of somatic ideas—another concept familiar to those in the field. Mullan importantly points out that Gindler ceased all teaching operations in 1933 as a way to protest and disengage from the Nazi propaganda that was required of all teaching institutions in Germany at the time. Others, including Rudolf Laban, did not follow suit, complying with Nazi regulations to continue their work.[29]

This discussion would not be complete without mention of Laban (1879–1958), whose approaches to movement have so greatly informed both dance and somatic worlds. A dancer, choreographer, director, physical educator, writer, and theoretician, he was widely regarded as "the founding father of expressionistic dance."[30] His legacy includes a system for analyzing movement utilizing movement flow, weight, and embodiment of time and space, a notation system for recording dance and movement (Labanotation), groundwork for the field of dance therapy, and a lineage of modern dancers schooled in "Der Freier Tanz."

Born in Austro-Hungary, Laban lived and worked in Munich and Berlin prior to World War II. In 1938, he relocated to the United Kingdom after refusing to join the Nazi party and facing termination from his government position. There are varying views regarding Laban's complicities and ties to the Third Reich among scholars—some paint him as a movement advocate who would sacrifice anything to move the field forward; others see evidence of Nazi sympathies, akin to those of his student/colleague Mary Wigman. Indeed, laws excluding Jews from all aspects of German society were fully enforced by 1933; Laban did not let these facts deter his work. Manning further contextualizes the conflict of dance in the National Socialist State between that of dance as art and dance as physical culture and correctly magnifies the "vanishing" of dance in the Third Reich.[31]

Today, Laban Movement Analysis (LMA) is one of the most widely practiced somatic systems in existence, and perhaps this provides a preliminary segue to a consideration of present-day somatic praxis. LMA utilizes the founding work of Laban, Irmgard Bartenieff (LMA is sometimes referred to as Laban/Bartenieff Movement Analysis), and other contributors to describe, understand, interpret, and document movement. A Certified Movement Analyst (CMA) is well-schooled in Laban's core approaches to body, effort, shape, space, and time, all employed in search of optimal bodymind integration and authentic expression. LMA is used by dancers, actors, directors, teachers, coaches, and scholars of human movement, such as anthropologists and psychologists, as well as those who seek wellness through total body engagement.

Before moving into a brief overview of current somatic and associated movement systems, consider that in the early 20th century, the development of what we today understand as somatics and the fledgling artform of modern dance emerged in tandem, like two adjacent roads that sometimes intersect, and sometimes diverge. The basic premises were there to be shared: admiration and acceptance of the authentic, physical body, elevated via the physical culture movement; a new, piqued interest in the workings of the mind, shaped by the transformative work of Sigmund Freud and Karl Jung; and a common interest in true expressiveness that could not be found in light and airy European ballet styles. Certainly, there are elements of class versus communal inclusion here too, with the early somatists advocating for physical education for everyone, and the early modernists producing authentic dances that were more aligned with humans' natural movement patterns. While these two fields have separate histories, they do share common ancestors, including American dancer Isadora Duncan, Laban's protégé Mary Wigman, and American dance educator Margaret H'Doubler.[32] And every good student of modern dance history has at least some working knowledge of the influence of Delsarte and Dalcroze on early expressive investigations. Indeed, today, many dance forms are associated with somatic philosophy and practice in both learning and performance.

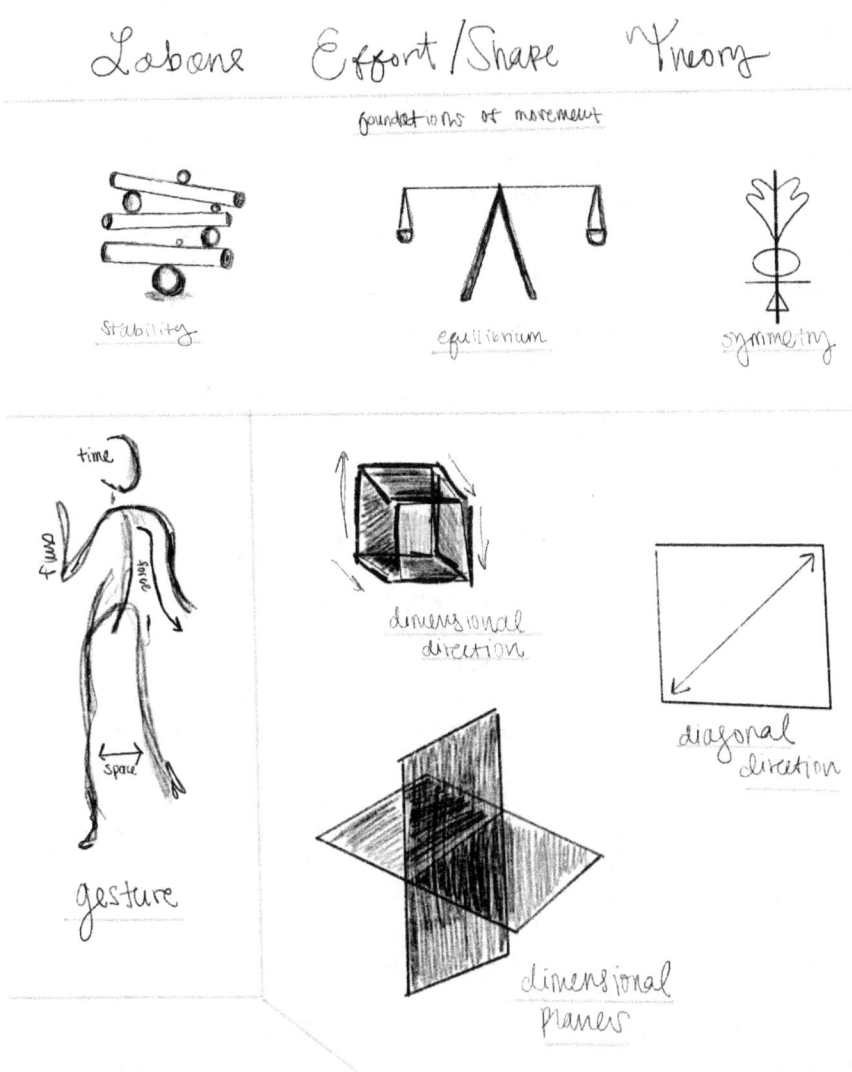

Figure 1.4. Laban's theories of effort/shape provide a framework for human movement (illustration by Abby Jones).

Contemporary Somatic Praxis

There are many, many contributors, cultures, and practices unnamed in this short, introductory survey meant to prime the landscape for an elemental understanding of somatic philosophy. My intention is to provide context, a lens through which to view how we've arrived at today's systems and methods and allow the reader to begin to find affinities to somatic and movement values. What follows is a short, noncomprehensive review of some of the major constructs offered and studied by somatic practitioners today, focusing on overarching philosophy and major characteristics of practical application. In their text *Somatics and Dance*, Brodie and Lobel identify four principles of somatic training; breath, sensing, connectivity, and initiation, which they find common to many frameworks for somatic investigation.[33] Assuredly, codified somatic practices are not only the vision of one individual, based on their own phenomenological experiences and particular worldview; they are also the sum of all that has come before, and bear the collective knowledge of many societies and cultures. The following overview aims to present this knowledge in a way that prompts critical analysis of somatic thought.

Laban Movement Analysis

Although Rudolf Laban and his work have already been introduced briefly, further examination of his philosophies is warranted, given the scope of his influence on today's somatic practice.

Laban proposed that the very principles of movement are founded upon stability, equilibrium, and symmetry, and that every gesture includes elements of space, time, force, and flux. As moving bodies, we constantly strive for balance on the continuum of our movement affinities. Laban's work centers spatial theory: he organized space in terms of dimensional direction, diagonal direction, and dimensional planes. Various avenues that connect direction while moving can form different shapes within the body, and the size of these shapes can shift within one's kinesphere—the space that surrounds a stationary body from core to periphery. Rhythm, time, and dynamics also intersect in Laban's movement language and notation, providing an organizational model for human movement. Today, Laban's principles are introduced to new generations via BESS: Body, Effort, Shape, and Space.

Alexander Technique

Frederick Matthias Alexander (1869–1955) was an actor from Tasmania who experienced voice loss during performance and sought his own solutions after traditional medical treatments failed. Finding success through his self-developed interventions, he brought the technique to London and New York in the early 1900s. His work is utilized by performing artists and world citizens who are interested in investigating a more efficient approach to movement in their professional and everyday lives.

Alexander's methodology centers a system of body re-education, postural alignment, and conscious mental control, where the body and mind are seen as a single unit, evinced by the terms "self" and "body/self." The "head-neck-back relationship" is foundational to the technique and integral to successful full-body alignment. Much of the training is done sitting or on a table to reduce the effects of gravity, and practitioners utilize a great deal of touch in guiding the body to healthy alignment. Like many somatic systems, Alexander Technique focuses on the unlearning of habitual movements that are incongruent with the healthful use of the human body, and sensation, perception, and mindfulness are key components in affecting change. However, there is no movement or set of movements that are a final goal; rather, the process of constant redefinition, of noticing the bodymind, guides the work.

Although not generally recognized by major insurance groups as a medical intervention, C. Stallibrass, et al. tested the effectiveness of Alexander Technique on Parkinson's patients. They found significant results utilizing the Parkinson's Disease Disability Scale questionnaire, Beck Depression Inventory, and Attitudes to Self-Scale following treatment against a control group and a second group that was treated with massage therapy.[34]

Ideokinesis

The idea of Ideokinesis was conceived by Mabel Todd (1880–1956), who in 1937 authored her seminal text *The Thinking Body*, a work that not only revolutionized current movement practice, but also would go on to influence future generations of somatic theorists. It was Lulu Sweigard and Barbara Clark, however, who further developed the methodology, with Sweigard naming the training with a term borrowed from piano teacher Bonpensière. The idea was the merging of thought and action, with imagery playing a prominent role in movement control.

The theory behind Ideokinesis shares common factors with information processing approaches (introduced in Chapter 2), where learning is a linear process. An *idea* initiates action, so it must be that thought can affect change. When you learn to observe, notice the body, a shift toward efficient movement and balanced alignment can occur. Much of the practice is done in a state of constructive rest, with tension reduced and kinesthetic awareness heightened. The process of re-patterning unhealthy habits happens through imagery, not repetition of new movement. As with many somatic systems, the work is not meant exclusively for elite performers but focuses on everyday movement for all human bodies.

Todd was always clear that Ideokinesis wasn't a medical treatment in the traditional sense, but an approach to movement education. The emphasis on imagery was an important step, another piece to the puzzle of the mind/body relationship.

The Feldenkrais Method

Dr. Moshe Feldenkrais (1904–1984), an Israeli scientist, founded the Feldenkrais Method which has been practiced since the mid–20th century. Like many somatic pioneers, he sought self-healing from a knee injury sustained during World War II after traditional medical treatments failed. A teacher and practitioner of judo, he used his knowledge of martial arts, engineering, and physics as a basis for self-study of bodily movement. He developed an approach that focused on a person's education of sensorimotor awareness; like Todd, he saw his methods as teaching as opposed to medical interventions.

Feldenkrais' praxes are offered in two forms. Awareness Through Movement® uses verbally guided movement explorations for student groups, focusing on perception, sensation, and mindfulness. Functional Integration® is available to individuals, and here, the teacher can focus more specifically on a person's habits and movement affinities. Through touch, specific solutions are discovered and employed for optimum learning.

Feldenkrais' methodologies have been the subject of some scientific study. Buchanan and Ulrich connected the somatic teachings to the then newly emerging dynamical systems theory (introduced in Chapter 4), arguing that attuning to movement behavior allows individuals to respond to new situations and environments with flexibility, and these behaviors can eventually transform into healthy habits.[35] Both dynamical systems theory and the Feldenkrais Method embrace the idea of multiple schemes working simultaneously to determine movement behavior, and always influenced by a person's lived experiences. Other researchers have applied the work as a treatment to specific populations, and Stephens and Hillier's review of literature makes a case for intervention.[36] They conclude that studies from 2005 to 2017 report positive results for balance and mobility improvements, especially in aging populations and those diagnosed with Parkinson's Disease. Pain management, too, is facilitated, as Feldenkrais participants learn to hold and maintain their bodies correctly and efficiently.

1. Introduction, and Historical Context of Somatics

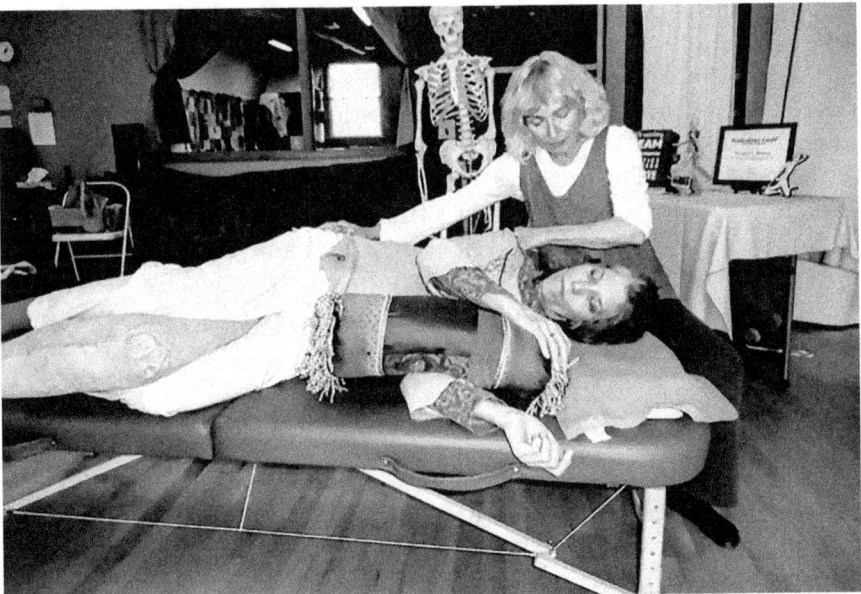

Figure 1.5. Feldenkrais practitioner Liz Monnier (in vest) works with a client, Laura Hillyard (courtesy Liz Monnier; photograph by Jarin Hart).

Rolfing® Structural Integration

Commonly referred to as "Rolfing" by practitioners, this system of myofascial manipulation was designed by Dr. Ida Rolf to improve skeletal alignment and the biomechanics of the body. Rolfing Structural Integration is a 10-session hands-on therapy that readjusts the body's fascia (connective tissue that unites bones, muscles, organs, nerves) so optimal bone alignment and joint structure is achieved. The work involves sensorimotor education as well, so the client gains physical awareness, allowing energy to move freely through the soma.

Ida P. Rolf, PhD (1896–1979), was a biochemist and the first woman to hold a research post at the Rockefeller Foundation. She was highly influenced by 20th-century postural training methods (i.e., the Feldenkrais Method) and by her lifelong practice of Hatha Yoga. She hypothesized that joint mobility aids fluid flow and benefits well-being, and vertical alignment is critical to the relationship of the human form to gravity. She additionally subscribed to the work of somatic psychotherapist Wilhelm Reich, who believed muscular tension and negative emotion were associated, and manipulation of muscles and fascia could release tension. Rolf began practicing in Europe in the 1940s and eventually brought her methods to the United States, founding the Rolf Institute of Structural Integration in 1971.

Like other somatic approaches, Rolf's methodologies are not considered prescriptive medical therapies, although the work has been the subject of scientific inquiry. Stall and Teixiera report significant results in the reduction of pain, anxiety, and depression following a 10-session "Rolfing" treatment for women suffering from fibromyalgia.[37] The author concludes that the physical manipulation of "Rolfing" allows for superior freedom of movement, and sensorimotor education provides a deeper understanding of individual pain and facilitates coping mechanisms.

Bartenieff Fundamentals

A star pupil of Rudolf Laban in Germany prior to World War II, Irmgard Bartenieff (1900–1981) developed a system of whole-body integration known as Bartenieff Fundamentals. She was a remarkable woman who was a dancer, choreographer, physical therapist, writer, founder of the American Dance Therapy Association, and partner in the development of Choreometrics (a system for analyzing and notating cross-cultural dance and movement). Bartenieff had a great understanding of the body and anatomy but seldom lectured in her classes; she preferred working directly with individuals and letting them discover movement and self-expression along the way.[38]

Bartenieff emigrated to the United States with her family in 1939, after the Nazi regime closed her dance company in Germany, thus bringing Laban's work to North America. She fused Laban's ideas of spatial construct with her physical therapy training, creating a unique approach to healing and wellness that expanded the field well beyond traditional exercises of isolated muscle groups. Although Bartenieff was not primarily a theoretician, the success she found in the application of this whole-body system to her work with polio patients and children with disabilities encouraged her to codify her system in the 1960s, referring to the work as "Bartenieff Fundamentals." She was a firm believer in discovering and learning through experiential practice.

Bartenieff also focused on active participation with her patients, helping them to embrace expressive movement and unite the mind/body system. A true somatic practitioner, she felt strongly that you could not treat disparate aspects of the human condition, and the whole of a person's instrument must be considered. She developed six fundamental patterns of total body connectivity: breath, core-distal, head-tail, upper-lower, body-half, and cross-lateral. These concepts are often foundational to

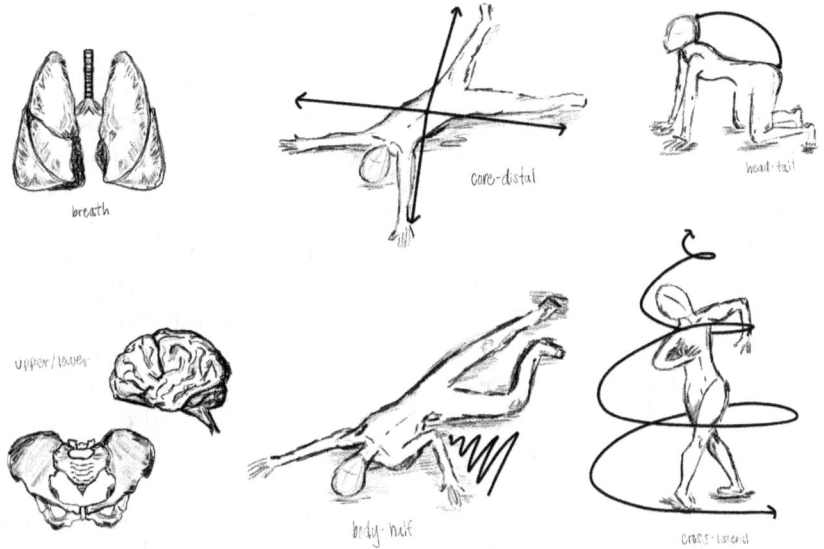

Figure 1.6. Bartenieff's six modes of body connectivity (illustration by Abby Jones).

dance training in major university dance programs and schools and are illustrated above in Figure 1.6.

In 1981, the year of Bartenieff's death, the Laban Institute of Movement Studies was renamed the Laban/Bartenieff Institute of Movement Studies. Her work, and that of her mentor Rudolf Laban, continues to educate and influence new generations of dancers, performers, movers, and health practitioners.

The Trager® Approach

This system of somatic education was developed by Milton Trager (1908–1997), an athlete and dancer. He served in World War II as a pharmacist's mate, and subsequently earned an M.D., completing a residency in psychiatry. The basis for the Trager Approach is Psychophysical Integration, a concept that purports the importance of the body-mind connection for healthful living. In 1980, he co-founded the Trager Institute with former student Betty Fuller, who was also instrumental in bringing Moshe Feldenkrais to the United States. Trager began his work in 1927 when he was just 19 years old and continued it until his death. He treated patients with cerebral palsy, muscular dystrophy, Parkinson's Disease, post-polio syndrome, and soldiers with battle fatigue.[39]

A session utilizing the Trager Approach begins with tablework, where the practitioner manipulates the client's body with gentle and painless movements, not pushing past resistance, and staying within normal ranges of motion. The participant becomes aware of holding patterns and is able begin to relax and release muscular tension, creating new patterns of bodily movement and statis. Mentastics®, coined by Trager as a combination of the words "mental" and "gymnastics," follows tablework, as participants explore, recall, and reinforce the work that was previously experienced through self-guided movements; here, a new orientation to gravity facilitates motion. Additionally, "hook-up" is tantamount to a successful Trager session as the patient enters a state of something akin to meditation which the practitioner mimics, enabling a shared bodymind experience.[40] This kind of kinesthetic empathy is indeed defined, discussed, and investigated in several later chapters of this book, and is an important element of the SomaLab framework.

A 2004 study conducted at the Department of Family Medicine at the Keck School of Medicine at the University of Southern California aimed to examine the influence of the Trager Approach on patients with chronic headaches. The design included two control groups (medication only and medication with healthcare attention), as well as a treatment group (medication and a Trager Approach session, once a week for six weeks). Both the treatment group and the control group that received healthcare attention demonstrated a decrease in headache duration, with the Trager treatment group showing the greatest reduction in frequency of headaches and the greatest increase in Headache Quality of Life. A 44 percent decrease in medication use was also noted in the Trager treatment group.[41]

Life/Art Process

A revolutionary icon of the postmodern movement in dance, Anna Halprin (1920–2021) not only influenced generations of dancers and dance-makers, but she was also the originator of the first movement-based expressive arts therapy program, founding the Tampala Institute with her daughter Daria in 1978. She studied dance at the University of Wisconsin and in 1938 attended the Bennington School of Dance (now the American Dance Festival) where she danced under the tutelage of Martha Graham, Doris Humphrey, Charles Weidman, and Hanya Holm. Her mentor, Margaret H'Doubler, highly influenced her eventual shift to somatic art and education, and away from codified dance techniques. Halprin developed teaching that emphasized functional anatomy of the body while identifying and working past habitual movements to reach authenticity and truth.[42]

While living in Boston, Halprin worked at the Winsor School where she began to adopt a creative approach to teaching dance. Concurrently, she observed the healing aspects of artistic movement through her employment at the South End Settlement House. Working with children who had experienced trauma informed her later work with adults, as she cultivated a process of recovery through movement. Halprin eventually relocated with her husband, architect Lawrence Halprin, to California, and in the late 1950s began to make dances highly influenced by space, design, and the environment. The Halprins' dance deck drew many famed movement artists and provided an impetus for ground-breaking work over several decades.[43]

Halprin's career is marked by her passion for engaging with both dancing and non-dancing bodies. She believed in the power of dance to heal—physically, emotionally, and psychologically. Life/Art Process uses an individual's own life experiences and employs movement, voice, drawing, performance, and reflection to explore one's inner landscape and promote health and wellness. Halprin dedicated the latter part of her life to working with terminally ill persons and weaved her treatment methodologies into artistic creations, prioritizing process and participation as opposed to performance for audiences.[44]

Continuum Movement®

A somatic practice founded by Emilie Conrad (1934–2014), Continuum Movement focuses on the biological basis of humanity, and emphasizes our natural, innate movement patterns instead of those absorbed through cultural mandates.[45] Conrad felt that Western life especially mechanized natural movement, taking people far from their primary state. She studied ballet and Dunham technique in New York and eventually became a dancer and choreographer for a folkloric dance company in Haiti, furthering her study and investigations into Afro-Haitian dance. Conrad's work with African Diasporic forms focused on the undulating movement of the body, which she felt was universal and connected all human beings to their environment and each other. She embraced the evolutionary origins of human biology, and believed water was our true home, but the eventual journey to land required a more functional adaptation to movement. Although humans are an organism in a continual state of flux and mutation, we carry the origins of our species in each cell.[46]

In 1974, Conrad created a protocol for people with spinal cord injury, where the fluid, primordial movement that serves as the basis for Continuum Movement aids in the creation of new motor patterns.

Without access to habituate physical action, new neural pathways are formed, facilitating a re-learning of natural movement, and leading to gains in function. Bonnie Gintis, Doctor of Osteopathic Medicine, in her 2001 writings, connects the underlying philosophy of Continuum Movement to the connection of fluid systems and lymphatic flow utilized in osteopathic study. She writes, "By refining our attention and intention to allow our fluctuating fluid nature to express itself, Conrad assures us that an exchange of information and nourishment will occur in our system that carries a divine and complex intelligence that is not limited by boundaries of our own thought process or of any treatment technique."[47]

Skinner Releasing Technique™ (SRT)

Joan Skinner (1924–2021) began dancing as a child under a disciple of Mabel Todd.[48] She continued her dance studies throughout high school and college, eventually becoming a performing member of the Martha Graham Dance Company, and later, of the Merce Cunningham Dance Company. It was during her tenure with Cunningham that she began to turn toward her dancing roots, investigating news ways of teaching and moving that incorporated imagery and deep states of relaxation.[49]

Upon retiring from the concert stage, Skinner began experimenting with her students at the University of Illinois, focusing on new methodologies that they described as "releasing," and the term was coined. She continued to codify and refine the technique, eventually offering teacher trainings by the 1980s. The basis for Skinner Releasing Technique (SRT) involves surrendering mind-body habits and patterns that cause tension and anxiety and replacing them with a free flow of energy that cultivates ease and efficiency. She described this intuitive approach to movement as "psychophysical unity," a state in which the mind does not control movement; rather, the body leads from a deeply natural, innate source.[50] Visualization and imagery are integral to the practice, and instrumental in discovering new neural pathways as a conceptual whole. Emslie points out that SRT does share commonalities with codified concert dance techniques, such as privileging posture and alignment and physical conditioning, as well as investigating dynamic range. However, creative processes, as opposed to rote repetition, are used to achieve movement goals, thus avoiding unnecessary tension and the development of poor movement habits.[51] Recently, the phenomenological aspects of SRT were used as a basis for research in affect and virtual reality, providing a structure for

1. Introduction, and Historical Context of Somatics

contemplating new thought patterns and encouraging the reception of novel information.[52]

Hanna Somatics

Although Thomas Louis Hanna (1928–1990) did not *found* the field of somatics, he is credited with naming the age-old field of study, which recognizes the undeniable connection between body and mind, sometime in the 1970s. Born in Waco, Texas, Hanna earned a PhD in philosophy and divinity and embarked on a successful academic career. While at the University of Florida, he began studying neurology and was later introduced to the work of Moshe Feldenkrais after moving to San Francisco. He participated in the first course in Functional Integration® in the United States, and by 1990, offered the first Hanna Somatics Education® program.

Hanna's somatic system centers around the concept of Sensory Motor Amnesia, a phenomenon where the mind has lost voluntary control over the body, resulting in the development and habituation of painful and inefficient movement patterns. The cure for Sensory Motor Amnesia is Sensory Motor Awareness, a process where physical changes are produced by regaining regulation of the voluntary sensory-motor cortex. This reconnection reverses chronic muscular contractions and restores ease of movement, allowing for improvements in posture, breathing, and repetitive stress injuries. In short, there is a rewiring of the brain's authority over the muscles, creating new neuromuscular pathways that encourage healthy functional movement (we will address structural, therefore functional, change in the nervous system in Chapter 3). Hanna was firmly committed to a phenomenological construct where first-person lived experiences carry value, as opposed to Western medical treatments, which are dominated by third-person perspectives.[53]

Hanna's methodology was greatly influenced by Alexander Technique, as well as by Feldenkrais' Functional Integration. A typical somatic education session begins with the patient becoming aware of involuntary patterns and muscular holding, followed by Kinetic Mirroring, a technique developed by Feldenkrais to initiate muscular contractions where there is no conscious control. However, pandiculation (purposeful readying of human/animal action through muscular engagement) is singular to Clinical Somatic Education and allows the patient to experience first-person sensation through self-initiated muscular awareness.[54] The idea of pandiculation shares similarities with the physical awareness (kinesthesia) element of the SomaLab framework.

Body/Mind Centering®

Bonnie Bainbridge Cohen (1941–) is the founder of Body/Mind Centering, a system of embodied study that integrates movement, sensation/perception, and consciousness. A lifetime movement artist, and originally trained as an occupational therapist, Bainbridge Cohen developed her own approach to somatic education, which is highly influenced by the work of modern dance great Eric Hawkins, dance therapy founder Marion Chase, Haruchika Noguchi, and many others.[55]

The underlying premise of Body/Mind Centering is the consciousness of tissues, nerves, ligaments, and fluids, all to the cellular level. Participants practice awareness of and experience sensation in basic neuro-cellular patterns which all vertebrate animals share, including reflexes and developmental responses to our interactions with environmental stimuli and constraints. Bainbridge Cohen's study and knowledge of human development and ontogenetic movement, including embryologic development, greatly informs the design of this work; she purports that our cells carry patterns and memories, and in exploring these primal roots we can discover the basic biology in our individual bodies. The practice of Body/Mind Centering can lead to more natural and authentic movement patterns, superior health, and the discovery of artistic truth.[56]

Conclusion

In tracing the origins of somatic practice and education from the earliest philosophers to the great minds of current day thinkers, we see concepts and theories that are rooted in the truth of our biology and human experience. So many overlaps and similarities exist between peoples, cultures, and practices, yet each is informed by the unique individuality of first-person lived experiences, perspectives, and the ways both societies and individuals organize function of the human organism. Much of this work is centered around a very old, yogic concept: how we are in the body, we are in the mind.

It should be noted that current somatic inquiry and praxis is not without criticism, or at the very least, qualifiers. De Giorgi raises important questions about the dogmatic presentation of theory, often without support from empirical research, and questions whether somatics is a field.[57] Ginot, Barlow, and Franko write that much of the foundational thinking and subsequent writings concerning somatics are wrought with "essentialism ... [and] ethnocentrism..." brought about by the underlying

1. Introduction, and Historical Context of Somatics

principle of a "universal body." They argue, compellingly, that somatic ideologies, especially those that constitute formal methodology, need to submit to transdisciplinary study that is inclusive of history, culture, gender, etc. They succinctly summarize the current state of somatic inquiry:

> Somatic discourses, therefore, must be read as performative discourses, situated in a precise context, and targeting thereby an equally precise efficacy. In this regard, somatic discourses do not stand apart from the practices that engender them. Their value is not universal but isolated, and their validity can only be measured by the effect they produce on a given subject, in his/her encounter with a given context. Somatic discourses constitute physical techniques, just as do the practices from which they emanate. [...] endogenous somatic discourses have a strictly performative function as techniques of the body, and their sole function is to contribute to the efficacy of somatic gesture.[58]

Perhaps by considering a perspective in which somatic work is seen as an *approach,* or as proposed early in this chapter, a *philosophy* that may have fluctuating value for different individuals and within different contexts, we can avoid dogma while pursuing qualitative and quantitative investigation into the complexity of the mind/body relationship. Indeed, moving into Chapter 2, we will focus discussions on movement learning and performance through the lens of literature in the field of motor learning. Here, we hope to gain some insight into the inner workings of the mind, and the body's response to situational environmental change, primarily through behavioral research.

In closing, it is worth considering the current state of western somatic praxis, as many 20th-century theorists have recently passed. Is this the end of an era? Will the work live on, and if so, how? What is next? Will movement as a tool for social justice enhance somatic study? Will generative and/or social somatics take firm root? Certainly, there is untapped opportunity here to affect global health and well-being, and lead movement artists toward greater agency and self-expression. We may be poised on the precipice of a great shift, but to get there we'll have to tear down old ways and aesthetics and build a new future that is yet unformed. How incredibly exciting.

2

Principles of Movement Learning
An Overview

ELIZABETH LIMONS SHEA AND JOHN B. SHEA

> *"He who loves practice without theory is like the sailor who boards ship without a rudder and compass and never knows where he may cast."*—Leonardo da Vinci[1]

Introduction

Chapter 1 explored, investigated, and discussed the history and philosophy of somatic practices, clarifying the necessity of human movement, and the relationship between artistic praxis and bodymind development. Over many centuries, even epochs, both individuals and societies have worked to organize and understand how and why we move; science and art coalesce to support states of feeling, acting, and being. Da Vinci's timeless words remind us that understanding the how and why can guide our somatic journeys and facilitate deep change and growth as artists.

As we begin our discussion of how the bodymind learns and moves, it is essential to consider the field of motor learning, which is largely concerned with observable and/or measurable changes in movement behavior resulting from practice over time. Research in this discipline generally falls within two categories: behavioral and neurophysiological. Behavioral investigations focus on practice conditions that lead to change in performance, while neurophysiological studies examine where in the nervous system change is occurring. Behavioral investigation can be further divided into task-oriented study, where only the action is considered, and process-oriented research, where the purpose is to study the cognitive mechanisms underlying performance. Motor learning is considered "relatively permanent"[2]—the old saying, "you never forget how to ride a bike" has scientific merit after all!

If motor learning has permanence, what about motor performance? Motor performance refers to a single task, or attempt, that is transient in nature, and may be affected by temporary internal and external factors, such as motivation, fatigue, the environment, current life circumstances, etc. Motor performance provides a snapshot of what is happening during the learning process but may not be a direct indicator of learning quality or quantity.

This important field of study provides valuable insights into how our bodymind takes in, processes, and uses information that results in action. As movement artists, a clear understanding of how we learn, how we change, how we perform in each moment can enhance our ability to move fully, somatically, expressively. To be clear, this is an extremely broad and introductory summary of research, principles, and paradigms that may be of interest to movement artists and shed some light on individual practices, preferences, and experiences.

Terminologies and Classifications

Let's begin by defining "skill," a term used frequently in movement learning research, and the primary focus of performers across movement disciplines. Whether the goal is a specific action, for example, jumping high, or a process, like the ability to improvise movement, the road to all skills is the same—practice. Likewise, all skills have similar characteristics: (1) a desired goal, (2) confidence that one can achieve the goal, (3) efficiency in energy expended, and (4) completing the goal in a desired amount of time. R.A. Magill adds that skill can be an indicator of quality of performance. In this use, skill is defined as a *qualitative* expression.[3] Hence, the word skill can be used to describe how well an individual accomplishes the goal of the task. Skills can also be classified as "open," which connotes an unpredictable environment, like in a group improvisational experience or jam, or "closed," referring to a set situation, for example, a performance for the stage, or a yoga flow sequence.

Movement can also be described temporally through the classifications "discrete," having an identifiable beginning and end (body isolation), and "continuous," exhibiting an unidentifiable beginning and end (walking, running). A third classification regarding time is a "serial response," which is a collection of discrete movements that comprise a whole. Devised choreography often falls into this category, as does classroom study in many somatic practices, such as dance genres, martial arts, and yoga.

Information Processing Model of Motor Behavior

Historically, theories of how humans learn and move have been influenced by information processing models of movement behavior, first introduced in the field of cognitive psychology. In this approach, the human mind is seen as a "processor" or computer—signals, or stimuli, come in (input), are stored and coded (processing), and then produce a motor response (output). During the processing phase, there are three distinct stages: stimulus identification, response selection, and response programming or initiation.[4]

If information removes uncertainty, then in an event that holds a great amount of "surprise" value (e.g., new input we have not experienced before), the processing time, or the time before the response, will be greater. This is known as Hick's Law.[5] When a movement or process is practiced, unknown outcomes are narrowed, and learning occurs. There becomes a greater compatibility between input and output, and not as much processing is required. So, the whole operation gets faster. You may have experienced this in everyday tasks, such as using new applications on your smartphone, or trying a recipe for the first time.

Memory also has an important role in information processing models. Here, memory is identified as "a place" where learned or experienced items are stored, ready for use later. The mechanism for accessing memory works as either recall or recognition. Recognition requires less effort or skill—consider recognizing a fact from this chapter thus far versus recalling a sentence verbatim—while recall necessitates more embedded knowledge. Memory can also be separated into "short-term" or "long-term," where short-term memory holds a few items temporarily, as opposed to long-term memory, which is characterized by a greater degree of permanence. Additionally, both "explicit" and "implicit" refer to different types of long-term memory, with explicit memory referring to the act of recalling specific facts, or sequences of events (details from your 16th birthday), and implicit memory alluding to processes you automatically seem

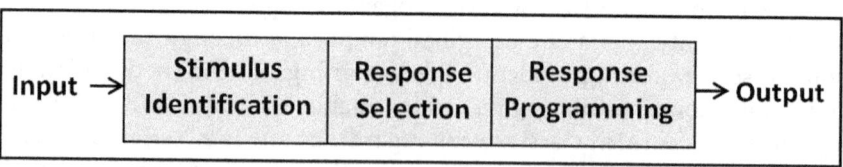

Figure 2.1. The three stages of movement planning, followed by response initiation (output) in information processing models (author's creation).

to know, like driving a car, or reciting the months of the year. The type of knowledge held in explicit long-term memory is termed "declarative," and "procedural" knowledge is the kind of information that resides in implicit long-term memory.

Furthermore, explicit and implicit memories are not mutually exclusive. For example, learning a motor task often requires learning "what" to do (explicit). However, with extended practice, explicit knowledge may eventually transition into "how" to perform the task (implicit) most efficiently, and with even more practice, performance may become automatic. At this latter phase of learning, explicit knowledge used during early learning may even be lost or inaccessible. An example of this is learning to tie your shoelaces, where young children often use a mnemonic tactic such as the "Bunny Ears Technique."[6] This technique utilizes as many as 11 steps to tie shoelaces. While children may verbally recite the 11 steps as they tie their shoelaces, adults rarely do. Adults quickly perform the task with little cognitive effort; few adults even remember this mnemonic method and may even have difficulty verbally describing how they tie their shoelaces without resorting to the physical action. This phenomenon of an explicit knowledge representation being transferred to an implicit knowledge representation is associated with practice over many years.

While information processing constructs are still widely considered and studied in the motor learning literature, alternative theories of human performance, such as 4E cognition and dynamical systems theory will be introduced in Chapter 4.

Attention and Performance

In 1890, William James defined attention as "the taking possession by the mind, in clear and vivid form, of one out of what seem several simultaneously possible objects or trains of thought. Focalization, concentration of consciousness are of its essence. It implies withdrawal from some things to deal effectively with others."[7] Indeed, some suggest that attention can be varied like a spotlight across the visual field, with the spotlight enhancing the efficiency of detection of events within its beam.[8] But what happens if two different beams are shone at the same time? Much of the investigation into how attention works in motor behavior has focused on attention as a resource, and what occurs when it is divided or distracted. Can human learners, movers, artists, attend to more than one performance parameter at the same time? And if so, is it optimal? Is it best practice?

Recent research suggests that we can, indeed, attend to more than one stimulus at the same time, especially if they access different resources.[9] For example, you may be able to listen to music and read a newspaper article simultaneously without much problem. But can you listen to an audiobook and read the same newspaper article without deficit? Another example may be having a conversation with a passenger while driving; often, this works just fine. But what about having a conversation with someone and reading your newspaper article? When the stimuli come from the same resources, in this case language centers, performance and/or learning may suffer. This is a multiple resources theory of attention, where attention is not viewed as a single capacity, but rather comprises multiple spaces that are designed to handle certain kinds of processing and action.[10]

This idea can be simply tested by putting theory into practice:

Circle your foot over the ground in a clockwise direction, as if you were drawing a circle on the floor. Now, with your hand over your knee draw another clockwise circle.

- *What happens? Is there ease in circling the hand and foot in the same direction?*

With a slight change, we create interference:

- *This time, circle your foot over the ground in a counterclockwise direction, as if you were drawing a circle on the floor. With your hand over your knee draw a clockwise circle.*
- *What happens? Is there now a sense of unease, or discomfort?*

Circling the hand and foot in different directions creates interference, and each action requires more attention for successful performance. With practice, can the bodymind learn to allocate its resources proportionately to secure successful performance? Or are we limited by neurological structures and capacities? We will see in Chapter 3 that the human ability to adapt is quite impressive.

Attention can also be categorized as "controlled"[11] or "automatic."[12] Controlled processing is described as slow, attention-demanding (in that other similar tasks interfere with it), serial in nature, and "volitional," meaning it can be easily stopped or avoided altogether. In contrast, automatic processing is fast, and non-attention demanding as other operations do not cause interference. It is parallel in nature, with various processes occurring simultaneously, and involuntary. Automatic attention might reference a skill that is highly practiced and is reproduced quite easily following a long period of learning, while controlled attention might be more indicative of early learning stages. Consider typing on a keyboard—for many individuals, this is an everyday task that does not require thought regarding where the fingers move to strike a particular letter or symbol. Now, recall learning to type—this was most likely a completely different experience, with lower speed and much higher error measures. With practice and subsequent learning, a skill can develop from controlled to automatic attention.

Anticipation, too, can play a role—how do performers respond when they know what to expect and are singularly focused on a habitual outcome, versus attending to many possibilities with no presumed conclusion? Indeed, interference plays an important role in practice and learning, one we will continue to discuss. This question also leads to an examination of selective attention, where, consciously or unconsciously, attention is focused on areas of the environment, as determined by the performer's prior experience with the movement at hand. Selective attention is categorized as intentional or involuntary; both refer to the allocation of attentive resources.[13] When attention is intentional, a choice is made to focus on a particular stimulus, for example, hearing a companion speak at a coffee shop but not processing the speech and language of others around you. If you hear a sudden, unexpected loud noise, attention is involuntary, and you are drawn, unwillingly, to locate the source. Involuntary attention is thought to be associated with the survival response typically displayed in "fight or flight" situations (see Chapter 3 for more discussion of the "fight or flight" response).

The idea of intention and attention is frequently discussed and considered in many bodymind practices. Yoga classes often begin with breathwork to reach a state of presence and create an intention that will guide the practice. In many movement arts experiences, there is a goal to the work, something practitioners are striving to achieve, and attention is an important part of a successful somatic event. While intention and attention are two different things, they are also closely intertwined, with one falling into deficit without the other. Both intention and attention are addressed in Part 2 as they relate to SomaLab praxis.

Sensory Contributions

Processing information has been at the heart of this chapter's discussion thus far, so an examination of the mechanisms that detect and gather data is crucial at this juncture. There are two types of information that we sense and process: *exteroceptive*, coming from outside the body, and *interoceptive*, coming from inside the body, or feeling from within. Proprioception is a type of interoception and gives us information about the position and movements of the body.

In hearing individuals, audition is a kind of exteroceptive sensation and can provide clues concerning actual movement performance.

However, for sighted individuals, vision acts as the primary sensory mechanism, contributing data regarding the environment, moving objects, and the body's own movement. Visual details attract attention before other forms of input, a phenomenon referred to as visual capture, and supersedes other forms of information, described as visual dominance. Vision, too, can be focal, or central; focal vision is highly linked to consciousness. When you see an object, your recognition memory works to identify it, give it a name. In a sense, focal vision tells you "what" you are looking at. Peripheral vision complements this process by adding cues regarding the environment, for example, "where" the object is, and usually works unconsciously; it is specialized for movement control.[14] In other words, central (focal) vision is responsible for resolving fine details, and peripheral vision plays an essential role in motion detection, spatial orientation, and locomotion. Knowing that central and peripheral vision serve different purposes helps us understand how information is processed in movement-based situations. For example, in performing a devised choreography, the "what/who" provides cues about the movement itself, while the "where" becomes important for staging and design.

Vision also has proprioceptive properties, providing environmental cues and contributing knowledge about where the body is in space. In their seminal work on movement and balance, Lee and Aronson found that vision contributes to afferent (traveling to the central nervous system) information in the "moving room experiment."[15] This study cleverly utilized a three-sided room (the floor was stationary), which could be moved forward or backward. Subjects were asked to maintain a static posture while facing the front wall, and the wall was moved back and forth by small amounts. The researchers measured postural sway (unconscious, small, correctional movements enacted to maintain balance), and found that in adults, moving the wall forward only a few centimeters resulted in backward lean, while moving the wall backward resulted in a dramatic forward lean. Children who participated in the study showed a total loss of balance.[16] This is fascinating work, and has obvious implications for skilled movement practice, especially where balance is a key factor in performance.

Other proprioceptive receptors and structures provide knowledge of our bodymind instrument, such as the position of joints, tension in muscles, and the spatial orientation of the body. For example, the vestibular apparatus (inner ear) detects the orientation of the head and is sensitive to this positioning with respect to gravity. Like visual proprioception, the inner ear is heavily involved in maintaining posture and balance. Consider motion sickness, an unpleasant occurrence where dizziness, nausea, and vomiting occur due to a mismatch between visual and vestibular sensory information, so passengers who are flying, driving, and sailing may be affected. Reading while traveling can also cause motion sickness, as the eyes sense limited motion, while the inner ear detects a high degree of movement. Turning or spinning can also cause this phenomenon, as visual focus and subsequent sensory input cannot keep up with the amount of information acquired by the vestibular system. This problem may be addressed using "spotting" when executing a series of turns, such as when a dancer performs a pirouette and precedes the rotation of their body by quickly turning their head and focusing on a spot in the environment. Once the body turns and aligns itself with the spot in the environment on which vision is focused, the "spotting" process begins again, and the dancer avoids dizziness.[17]

In addition to the inner ear apparatus, receptors in joint capsules (structures that surround synovial joints in the body) communicate joint position, while muscle spindles (receptors found in most muscles) provide information regarding muscle stretch as part of proprioception. These spindles are connected in parallel with muscle fibers and can be innervated by both efferent (moving away from the central nervous system) and afferent (moving toward the central nervous system) motor neurons. The role of the muscle spindle is to relay information about the dynamic stretch of the muscle; as stretch increases, output from spindle also increases, additionally contributing information concerning limb position. Research by Polit and Bizzi,[18] preceded by

Figure 2.2. Stevie Oakes, front, and Adriane Fang complete turns in performance (author's collection; photograph © 2018 Yi-Chun Wu).

Feldman's work,[19] led to a proposed mass-spring model for muscle control, where the muscle spindle pre-shortens to the length it should be when the limb arrives at a specified location. When the limb reaches this location, and the muscle spindle achieves a specified length, the muscle contraction and movement of the limb stops. In a sense, then, according to the mass-spring model and similar equilibrium-point models, the muscle spindles serve as both feedback and feedforward control systems.[20] Here, we see the results of practice at the structural level, allowing the body to know when it has achieved a specific point in space.

Another proprioceptive structure is the Golgi tendon organ, located in junctions between muscles and tendons. It, too, provides information about the tension (force) in the muscle and prevents overstretch and rupture by inhibiting motor responses. Finally, cutaneous receptors govern the important sense of touch. Located on skin, they are sensitive to pressure, heat, chemical stimuli, and pain. The fingertips have the greatest concentration of cutaneous receptors, making them very important in the manipulation of objects, and impeding the amount of data gleaned from the fingertips can seriously hamper both speed and accuracy. Have you ever attempted to complete a task with gloves on that is usually performed without? Perhaps texting? Are you a musician who sometimes plays an instrument outside in cold weather?

Central Contributions

Chapter 3 presents a detailed investigation of the human nervous system with the intention of examining changes in structure and function following praxis. In the context of movement behavior, the role of the central nervous system (CNS) is important as an intermediate processing center of information as subsequent action is planned. The integration of signals from proprioceptive receptors, and delivery of accurate kinesthetic information to efferent nerves, is crucial to successful motor performance. Open and closed-loop systems offer one explanation for how movement is controlled by the brain.

A closed-loop system provides feedback regarding performance of an action and updates the system for future movement attempts. In a closed-loop system, there are four components that work together to produce movement:

- The *executive* system makes decisions about movement planning.
- The *effector* system carries out the commands of the *executive* system.

- *Feedback* provides information to the *executive* system about the body in space.
- The *comparator* works as an error detection mechanism using feedback.

A closed-loop model is heavily dependent on feedback for error corrections; the process is linear in nature. Thus, it is time-consuming and most appropriate for slow, long-duration, and continuous movements. A closed-loop circuit also relies heavily on a comparator, or frame of reference, and thus poses a problem for learning a new movement—there is no measure yet of correctness at the outset of practice.[21] Additionally, there is also the question of how fast, discrete movements are controlled.

Referencing the latter point, open-loop systems explain the process responsible for movements requiring speed and that are short in duration.[22] This model is based on movement without the possibility of an outer feedback loop and requires little attention to the movement itself. The idea is that for every response, there is a motor program that is recalled and produced when a stimulus is introduced. That is a lot of motor programs! Both open and closed-loop theories require the use of large amounts of storage space from the CNS, leading researchers to create other models of human learning and performance.

In response to the limitations of both open and closed-loop systems, Schmidt proposed a "schema" theory of motor learning and control.[23] This approach suggests that groups of similar movements, even if they are novel, are controlled by a general motor program that can be adapted to specific situations. So, let's say you have experience in jumping with both legs extended, but you would like to jump with one leg flexed at the knee. Under the schema theory, the CNS retrieves the general motor program for jumping and the executive commands are adapted to produce novel movement.

Speed-Accuracy Trade-Off

Another prevalent phenomenon in the motor learning literature with great implications for both everyday tasks and highly skilled performance is the speed-accuracy trade-off. Many planned movements require either speed, accuracy, or a combination of both. Laboratory research has shown with consistency that as speed increases, accuracy decreases, and as accuracy increases, speed decreases. Fitts mathematically described and predicted this relationship in spatially oriented movements. This description has been extensively tested across laboratory and real-world tasks and has been found to be wide-ranging, so much so that it's often referred to as "Fitts's Law."[24]

Fitts's Law has typically been used to describe information processing in visual-motor tasks for which the target or goal is a specified location. But questions regarding the role of sensory information other than vision in the performance of these tasks has recently been addressed. Hatfield, Wyatt, and Shea augmented traditional speed-accuracy laboratory research with an auditory cue (a beep) to inform subjects of successful task completion.[25] They found that the auditory cue significantly reduced the difficulty of the task, improving performance. Hatfield et al. theorized that the addition of the auditory cue allowed performers to shift their attention to planning their next movement, thus introducing the role of multi-sensory integration into speed-accuracy trade-off paradigms. Furthermore, this finding may have practical application for movement performed to music or specified rhythms. It suggests that timing and accuracy of movements to spatial locations may be improved when the endpoint is paired with an auditory cue, which can be present in musical scores and other types of sensed rhythms.

We have examined the effects of changes in speed regarding visual-spatial tasks, but what about temporal accuracy? In many instances, the accuracy of movement time is important to performance, i.e., the synchronization of one body into another when practicing contact improvisation or tap dancing to a devised musical composition. In both cases, anticipation of when events occur is key to successful performance. Here,

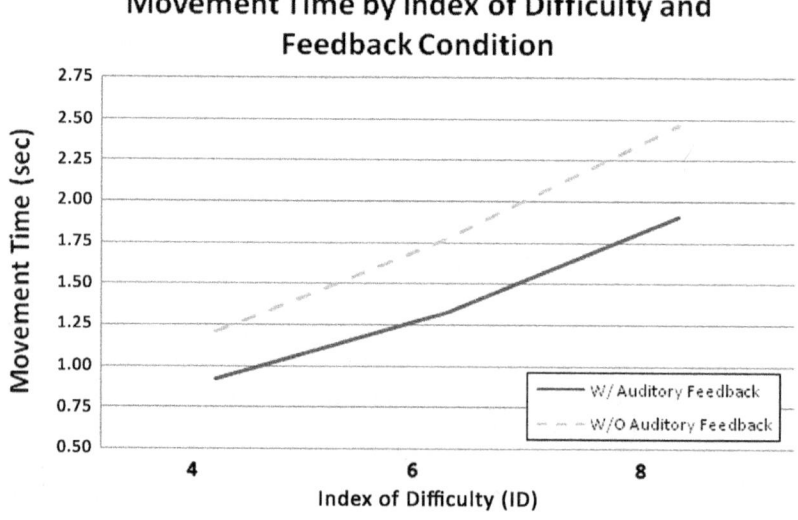

Figure 2.3. Hatfield et al. found that auditory cues facilitated performance when added to a traditional Fitts Tapping Task (author's creation).

we have the inverse of Fitts's Law, where performing an action faster actually provides more time for information processing, so there is more time to anticipate a response. In other words, as speed increases, so does accuracy. Think about dancing a series of novel movements together sequentially. In early learning, there is a lot of sensing and processing of information happening all at the same time to get the order, timing, and other details correct, so the next action in line may be late. After a period of practice, you can perform each element a little more smoothly, leaving additional time before the next movement in the sequence, resulting in a higher degree of accuracy. In fact, many dancers experience a deficit in timing (too fast) after a sequence becomes highly practiced due to automation and efficiency. For example, in devised works that movers have been performing for long periods of time, it becomes essential to re-enter some phase of research and investigation, thus activating the processing of information, and recreating earlier stages of learning. It's that sweet spot between novelty and rehearsal where artistry lies, and the persistent search for growth adds layers of understanding and expression in action.

Learning versus Performance

At this juncture, a discussion regarding learning versus performance is timely, as we prepare to discuss conditions of practice. Does performance provide a true window into the quantity and quality of learning? Or does performance represent an ephemeral moment, a snapshot that is part of a much larger picture? This question has challenged and continues to challenge movement researchers in creating valid and reliable experimental designs—investigations in behavioral science can often leave the clinician with unanswered questions. For artists and educators too, this inquiry is critical.

The definition of movement learning as relatively permanent is the basis for the distinction between learning and performance variables. A single performance measure, or observation, can be examined to give us information at a specific point in time and place, but to see true learning, performance over time is more indicative of end processes. Data can be plotted to offer a visual demonstration, but do these graphic shapes mirror the internal structural differences between experimental groups? Do they demonstrate internal processes?

The answer to this question is sometimes yes, and sometimes no. This is just as true in laboratory environments as it is with qualitative research and anecdotal observation. There are visible effects in performance that do not always directly correspond to internal learning processes. Ceiling and floor effects (performance plateaus with no obvious possibility for improvement) are one such example. These artificial barriers prevent performance from improving and reliably demonstrating the total amount learned. In laboratory studies, this could be due to the simplicity of the task or the sensitivity of the measure. In observations based on lived experiences, overt external progression is not always indicative of complex internal processing. A learning plateau, too, is something all teachers and practitioners experience some time in their careers; as one reaches higher levels of mastery the work can become more demanding, with those last details requiring more time, energy, and dedication. A small improvement for elite performers may require an equal or even greater amount of these measures as a large improvement for less experienced performers. Real life complex movement requires playing the long game; small victories and losses are all part of the journey to a larger goal. And, there are a plethora of other internal and environmental considerations, such as bodily fatigue or illness, or a change in the physical space for practice or performance. Understanding the difference between performance, which can be temporary (or not), and learning, which is more lasting, is important as we embark on a discussion of conditions of practice.

Conditions of Practice

Examining how practice is structured, and what effects practice schedules may have on movement, is one of the most important, and fascinating, elements of the motor learning field. Almost a century of study has shown that there are clear praxis scenarios which favor long-term retention, and those which support superior immediate performance. Critical to this discussion is the difference between performance variables and learning variables as discussed in the previous section; performance variables often have short-term effects on performance, while learning variables have long-term or relatively permanent effects.

Massed and Distributed Practice

In discussing conditions of practice, we should recognize that a single, optimal distribution of practice and rest periods does not exist, and that this choice will depend on the skill as well as many other factors specific to an individual. This is an important qualifier as we introduce massed and distributed practice. While a well-designed laboratory experiment can shed much light and understanding on movement behavior, especially when

2. Principles of Movement Learning

effects are replicated over time, the very controls that provide reliability and validity also diminish the chaos present in real world operations. Knowledge of the task at hand, as well as first-person lived experiences, changing environments, and other psychosocial and/or cultural contributors are all essential components of decisions regarding practice schedules.

In the literature, massed practice is defined as sessions in which the amount of practice time is greater than the amount of rest between trials, and distributed practice occurs when the amount of rest between trials equals or exceeds the amount of time of the trial itself. Consider learning a short movement phrase during a dance class. You can practice it over and over, with only short rests, let's say 10 times, or take longer rests between each repetition, still practicing 10 times. Which condition do you think favors performance, and which learning?

Overall, massed practices can result in superior immediate performance, while distributed practice leads to greater retention. Although initially unintuitive, it makes sense if you think about it. Holding the amount of practice constant, anything that takes more time could ultimately yield greater dividends. But what is happening during the time of non-practice, the rest between trials? One phenomenon that occurs in massed practiced schedules is reminiscence, or spontaneous recovery after a rest; there is no forgetting of the task between trials in performance measurements. Interestingly, in studies where massed-practice groups are

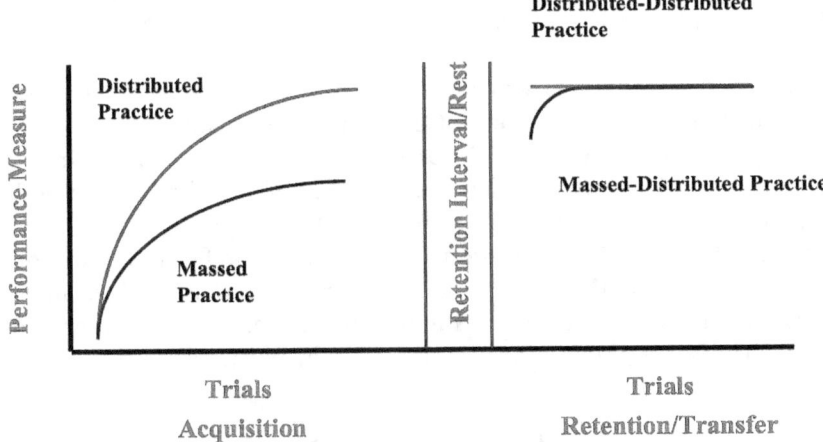

Figure 2.4. An illustration of the Adams and Reynolds paradigm, where the difference between massed and distributed groups typically disappears in studies where massed-practice groups are transferred to distributed practice after a rest (author's creation).

transferred to distributed practice after a rest, the difference between the formerly massed and distributed groups typically disappears, a phenomenon known as the Adams and Reynolds paradigm.[26]

Variability of Practice

Variability of practice is another critical factor in both performance and learning. Studies in this area show that rehearsal of several different versions of tasks belonging to the same movement class will result in greater generalizability (or performance of new tasks of the same movement class) than the practice of one or some limited number of tasks. For example, if you rehearse a series of five jumps, as opposed to just one jump, even though they differ in form, you are more apt to have success when learning a novel jumping sequence. This body of research provides theoretical support for the SomaLab framework, as introduced and discussed in Part 2, where developing the flexibility of the nervous system is an important process, and, in fact, often more efficient and effective than the serial learning of disparate skills.

Earlier in this text, when discussing central contributions, "schema theory," proposed by Richard Schmidt,[27] described one way of accounting for the human brain to process large amounts of material. In this construct, a generalized motor program is responsible for groups of movements that are similar in nature, i.e., turning has one motor program, jumping another, and accuracy in timing yet another. This same principle can be applied to explain success in learning using variability of practice schedules.

In essence, the schema forms a response from a generalized motor program that "covers" a variety of movements with some related characteristics. Schema memory is informed by elaborative and distinctive processing facilitated by the elements of the related skills. This could be interpreted as a development of process, or flexibility. Anyone who has practiced movement improvisation knows that you do feel more comfortable, and can respond easily and efficiently, with experience. As the movements are not devised, the process in which a mover becomes expert, and here, variability in praxis and approach, is highly desirable.

Contextual Interference

One of the most enduring, and intriguing, phenomena in the motor learning literature is contextual interference. While initially unintuitive, much like massed and distributed practice, a more thoughtful examination of the paradigm aligns with the complexity, and efficiency, of the human nervous system. The results of these experiments also provide substantial insight into human behavior and have fueled great conversation regarding how we learn. Indeed, addressing the resurgence in motor learning research in the 1980s, Lee and Carnahan write:

> The most important contribution arose from the publication of one paper by Shea and Morgan (1979) on contextual interference, which not only resulted in an explosion of follow-up studies within kinesiology, but in many other research areas, such as psychology, neuroscience, and various applied disciplines.[28]

Contextual interference refers to a learning situation where interference or difficulty during the acquisition of some number of skills leads to enhanced retention and/or transfer. A typical experimental paradigm testing these effects utilizes two conditions: low contextual interference, or blocked practice, and high contextual interference, or random practice. In blocked practice, a prescribed number of tasks (let's say three) are rehearsed in a systematic order, and all trials on one task are completed before the first trial on the next task is introduced. For example, a practice schedule with tasks A, B, and C looks like AAA, BBB, CCC. Alternatively, a random practice condition rehearses the same three tasks unsystematically with a seemingly chaotic offering of the same three tasks, something like A, B, C, A, C, B, A, C, B. The amount of practice on each skill and the time between rehearsals is held constant. Performance is measured both during the initial blocked and random practice schedule, and then later, after a rest period; the second performance test shows the degree of retention.

Typical results of these experiments are somewhat surprising but are reliably replicated time and time again: the blocked condition performs better during practice than the random condition, but later performance during a retention test is better for the random condition than for the blocked condition. Shea and Morgan were the first researchers to demonstrate these results, utilizing retention tests after 10 minutes and then again after 10 days.[29]

Shea and Morgan also introduced a transfer element into their experimental design. Here, subjects were tested on their performance of a novel task (one they had not practiced) in addition to retention. Again, the random group performed better than the blocked group. This finding could be aligned with the idea that "process" can be practiced and developed. More specifically, the random practice subjects learn to identify and compare similarities between previously practiced and novel tasks to enhance performance. In other words, they were quick to incorporate new, but related, skills into their already

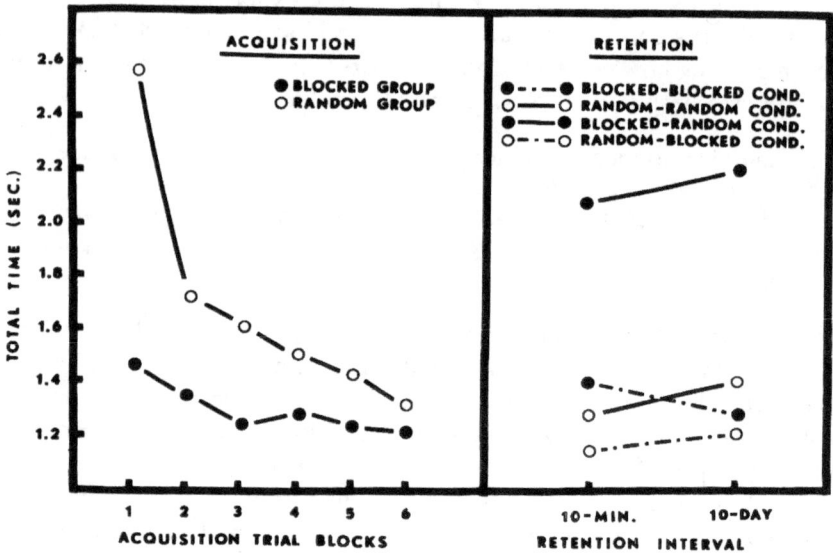

Figure 2.5. Original data from Shea and Morgan demonstrating the effects of contextual interference (author's creation). John B. Shea, and Robin Morgan, "Contextual Interference Effects on the Acquisition, Retention, and Transfer of a Motor Skill," *Journal of Experimental Psychology: Human Learning and Memory* 5, no. 2 (1979).

established retrieval networks and were better at it than blocked practice subjects.

What kind of insight into movement learning and the nature of human behavior can this experimental paradigm offer? Several theoretical constructs provide inferred explanations for the contextual interference paradox. One theory hypothesizes that forgetting plays a key role in context effects.[30] Another explanation for the effects of contextual interference that also features forgetting is elaboration. Shea and Zimny proposed that because forgetting occurs with random practice condition learners, they make cross-task comparisons and associations with previously learned information.[31] One could also construe this as support for the idea of sense-making, introduced as part of 4E cognition in Chapter 4. The idea of retroactive interference, where new learning interferes with the memory of previously learned material, has also been proposed as an explanation for superior retention by high contextual interference rehearsal groups.[32]

The contextual interference paradigm is just one example of the complexity of human behavior, and poses many questions for artists, educators, scientists, and lay people. Do we need situations that are specifically structured, so we expend enough effort to do our work, and find connections between information and experiences? Are we effortful, curious creatures? Are there limits to our learning, where new knowledge and old compete for space and attention from our central nervous system? Most importantly, how do we design learning and performing situations that best utilize our gifts and tendencies, that push us to delve deeper, developing our innate capabilities as human movers?

Augmented Feedback

The topic of feedback is likely the oldest studied in the field of movement learning and performance and still has an enduring presence in the field. The reason for this great interest is that feedback seems to be essential for learning to take place,[33] and movers are dependent on information regarding their performance during practice to show improvement over time. Technological advances, for example motion capture analysis and brain imaging instruments, have spurred new areas of inquiry and data analysis.

Feedback is critical to learning and performance and provides accuracy regarding outcome. As discussed earlier in this chapter, intrinsic feedback is traditionally referred to as afferent data from proprioceptors. This section addresses extrinsic, sometimes called enhanced or augmented feedback. Verbal cues provided by a leader or teacher are examples of augmented feedback, as are films and videotape, and they can be both precise and prescriptive. Knowledge of Results (KR), which informs the learner of their success relative to a goal is another example of augmented feedback, as is knowledge of performance (KP), which addresses the relationship of kinematics (motion of objects) to the movement pattern used. Variability in performance may decrease in the absence of KR, but the learner often becomes more consistent around their own habit, which may be incorrect. To illustrate this idea, recall a movement that felt "right," correct, and comfortable in your own body, but you were later informed by a teacher or leader that in fact your performance was not consistent with the movement form, or wasn't safe. As you try to change your performance, proprioception tells you that your efforts are off target. It takes much time, practice, and feedback to effect change once you've established a habit.

Knowledge of results functions chiefly as a motivator, a reinforcer, and a source of information. Research has also shown that KR does have dependency producing properties; the use of mirrors when teaching movement that requires a specific aesthetic or form is a prime example. Movers can easily become so accustomed to seeing their bodies in the mirror that they experience deep discomfort when this tool is removed.

Thus, inquiries surrounding the deliberate administration of KR become significant. For example, empirical research indeed demonstrates that a higher frequency of KR increases performance but is detrimental to learning (as measured by retention) as illustrated in Figure 2.6.

Furthermore, instantaneous KR, or information received immediately following performance, has also been shown to degrade learning, perhaps by interfering with "subjective evaluation,"[34] or the efforts of the learner. Too, the accuracy of augmented feedback is also important, as increased accuracy of KR leads to greater learning, but the benefit becomes smaller and smaller if the KR is too exact. Again, there seems to be a pattern of laboratory results that support the importance of effortfulness in learning. An individual must do some kind of work on their own for learning to be meaningful.

What happens when knowledge of results is withdrawn, and the learner must generate their own error information by using feedback

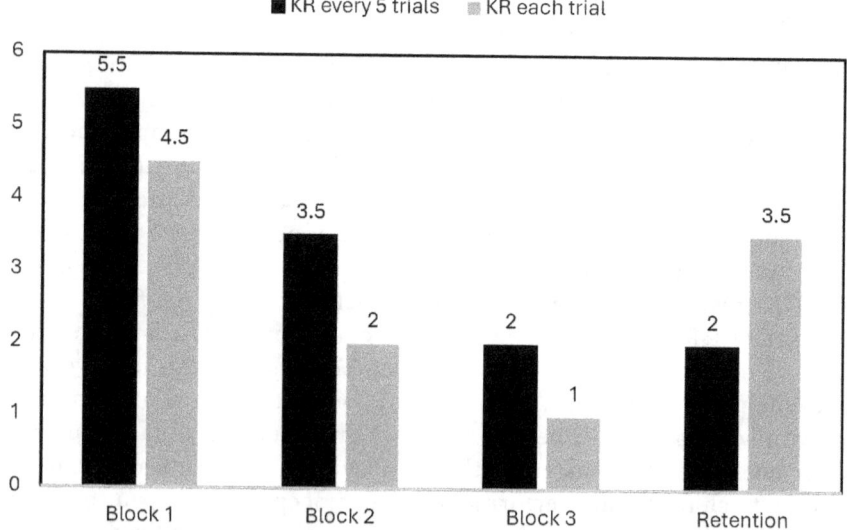

Figure 2.6. Like contextual interference effects, a higher frequency of KR increases performance, but impedes learning, as measured in errors (author's creation).

2. Principles of Movement Learning 55

compared to an internal representation of the correct response? The process of generating one's own error signal is called subjective reinforcement,[35] and is developed when a learner has had sufficient time to create their own error detection mechanism. Using your own first-person experience as a learner and mover, think how continued outside information informs your own practice, especially if you are an elite performer. Do you need augmented feedback to delve deeper? Or can you develop more fully using subjective reinforcement? What if your professional work necessitates performing repeated movements consistently over long periods of time, like a dancer in a Broadway show, or a professional company—do you tend to stray from the original form without an outside eye?

Thus far, the scheduling and temporal elements of delivering knowledge of results have been addressed, but not the content. Feedback can be described in four ways:

- Program Feedback
- Parameter Feedback
- Visual Feedback
- Descriptive and Prescriptive Feedback

Program feedback is information regarding the fundamental pattern of movement, or the beginning and ending actions relative to other movements (sequencing). Think of learning a movement phrase, and a leader commenting that the last two elements have been reversed, or there is a specific body sequence that should be followed to achieve a particular action, like shifting your weight first to one foot before standing on one leg. After program performance is consistent, feedback related to parameter modifications can be delivered. This might be information about how much force should be used and is generally used to refine movement. Visual feedback can also be beneficial to learning and performing, such as watching recordings of performance or using mirrors (but not too much!) to attend to nuanced body adjustments. The key here is not to overload individuals with information, as only a few adjustments can be expected on a subsequent performance. Other kinds of material offered to learners can be descriptive, where errors made during performance are reported, and prescriptive instructions allow for ways to correct errors or enhance movement. Experienced teachers and practitioners know that none of these feedback mechanisms is more important than the another; rather, they all work together toward reaching movement goals.

Feedback is an important topic for both performers and leaders and is a key element of the SomaLab framework, assisting practitioners working toward integrating many types of knowledge and influences into movement praxis as they seek growth, development, and expertise in their respective fields.

Retention and Transfer

More on Memory

The study of retention and transfer in motor skills is fundamentally linked to the study of memory. In fact, retention and transfer experiments are conducted with the aim of discovering the nature of memory. To review, earlier in this chapter memory was conceptualized as a "place" where information is stored for later use. Note that the word "place" is used metaphorically, as memory is a hypothetical construct. We don't know exactly what constitutes memory in a physical sense; it is more like a distributed neural system. Recent investigative findings have identified memory as groups of brain cells that were operative when the memory was shaped. The hippocampus, located in the medial temporal lobe of the brain

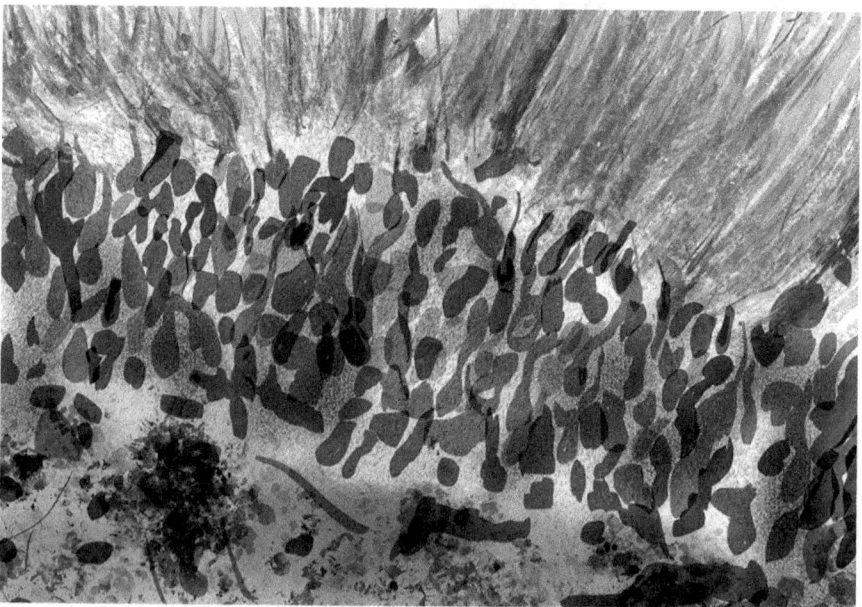

Figure 2.7. What does a memory look like? Physically, a memory is groupings of cells present when the memory was formed. Frances Collins, "What a Memory Looks Like," NIH Director's Blog, last modified November 21, 2019. https://directorsblog.nih.gov/2019/11/21/what-a-memory-looks-like/ (illustration by Abby Jones).

2. Principles of Movement Learning

(see Figure 3.3, Chapter 3), is heavily involved in storing these cells, and when called upon, is active in retrieval as well.[36] Remembering, the process of retrieving information from memory, can be studied through behavioral research, as can the process of "storing" or "encoding" information in memory.

Sometimes, retrieval from memory fails, typically for two reasons: the information is no longer present in memory, which is referred to as being no longer "available," and, information may be present in memory ("available"), but the act of retrieval is not sufficient to access it. In that case, the information is deemed not "accessible."

Retrieval can be classified into three sub-categories. Direct retrieval occurs when a memory is directly accessible and is typical of highly practiced skills where performance is automatic. A second type of retrieval is indirect, in which other associated information or cues are necessary to recover information. Lastly, retrieval may be reconstructive, such as when the performer may access an incomplete or partial set of actions and then fill in the missing units. Have you ever forgotten a piece of a choreographic sequence as you prepare for a rehearsal, but are able to retrieve it by working with known movements before or after? And what happens when you simply can't remember, when information is neither available nor accessible? Forgetting occurs and is inferred from lived experiences, or in the laboratory, performance on retention tests. It is helpful if these tests are designed to be informative regarding the nature of the forgetting that has taken place.

Delving further into theoretical memory constructs, we find that conceptual frameworks fall into two broad categories: first are the traditional "box" theories, and second are the "levels of processing" theories.[37] Box theories are named by their visual representation of three separate storage compartments: short-term sensory storage (STSS), short-term memory (STM), and long-term memory (LTM).

In this paradigm, short-term sensory storage is where incoming, unprocessed information first resides. Although the capacity of STSS is described as limitless, data is only available for a very short time, the equivalent of 250 milliseconds. In contrast, Short-Term Memory has a much smaller capacity (approximately seven items), and information is available for 15 to 20 seconds without rehearsal. With longer periods of practice, an action can be passed on to long-term memory where it is permanently stored. In this model, LTM is not constrained by limits.

Another approach to conceptualizing memory is a "levels of processing" construct, where after information enters the system via short-term sensory storage, ensuing retention reflects the extent or level of meaningful processing. Here, movements derive meaning from previous experiences, which make them more memorable. In addition, if an action is compared or contrasted with other similar movements, this elaboration further deepens memory connections. Elaborative processing facilitates the development of multiple associations or retrieval routes by which movements are remembered.

Finally, skill retention differs among types of movements. For example, continuous tasks (no distinct beginning or ending, like walking and running) are remembered quite easily while discrete movements are more susceptible to forgetting. It is possible that these tasks have a large verbal-cognitive component, which is more easily forgotten than the motor components.

Transfer

The last movement learning principle introduced in this chapter is transfer, defined as the generalizability of learning to the extent that practice on one motor skill, or set of motor skills, contributes to the performance of other, related tasks. Research in this area can be informative about which elements of a movement, once mastered, are integral to learning and performance of other like movements. Categorizations of transfer include proactive and retroactive. Proactive transfer "works ahead in time" to influence performance of a future skill, in other words, previously learned movement aids in learning new movement behaviors. Conversely, retroactive transfer "works backwards in time" to influence performance of an earlier learned skill; so, previously learned, and practiced movements benefit from new knowledge and information. Direction of transfer is also a consideration. For example, positive transfer occurs when learning and performance of a skill is facilitated by previous movement experiences, while negative transfer manifests itself when prior praxis interferes with and degrades new learning. For negative transfer to occur, skills are typically not only dissimilar, but quite opposite. Finally, zero transfer describes situations in which both previous and new learning have no effect on each other.

There are also different types of transfer that can influence motor behavior. Inter-task transfer occurs between two different movements like, for example, jumping and leaping. Varying the conditions of a singular task is intra-task transfer, like driving two different cars, or performing a devised dance work on the proscenium stage and then al fresco. Practicing part of a movement and then incorporating it into the whole is part-whole transfer. Think about learning the footwork for a time step, and then adding the upper body, or creating a movement score and then performing it.

An important principle to note when examining the effects of transfer on movement behavior is that motor transfer is small, especially when considering two different kinds of movements. The more similar the skills, the greater the influence of one upon the other. That said, motor transfer has real-world implications beyond movement praxis. The use of simulators and virtual and augmented reality in training programs are examples of movement transfer that can potentially create efficiency and cost savings in professional and personal environments. This is a clear example of the importance of laboratory research, the results of which can often feel remote and isolated. However, there are real-world, significant applications of research paradigms to human living that can greatly increase the quality of our everyday lives. This is the bridge of theory to practice, scientific inquiry to dissemination, all to the betterment of human living.

Conclusion

This chapter provides a brief overview of both historical and current approaches to how human beings learn to move, how learning is retained, and what conditions and practices are integral to successful performance. The story of movement behavior is complex, fascinating, and at times, unknowable. In Chapter 3, we dig deeper into the intricacies of our nervous system, seeing how change at the structural level occurs, and the story begins to take shape. All the while we remember that the individual path of each artist is guided by their own unique bodymind, as well as the totality of surrounding environmental influences.

We (the authors) recognized, in constructing this chapter, that several theories and experimental designs revolve around the idea of effort; in other words, it seems that many explanations for contextual interference effects, knowledge of results protocols, practice schedules, etc., are linked to the idea that both the amount, and type, of work we engage in as learners and movers is important. Conditions where rote production is promoted over more meaningful engagement are simply not as successful. This generalization, indeed, tells us something regarding the richness of our human experience, and the importance of integration and holism in our movement lives.

3

The Flexible Nervous System

"When you have a change in function, you have a change in structure."—Jill Bolte Taylor, PhD[1]

Introduction

Chapter 1 presented the *idea* of somatics and the history of peoples and systems that utilize the mind/body connection to promote health and wellness, as well as artistry and expertise in communication and expression. The success of these systems is both empirical and anecdotal; recognizing the bodymind as one entity and rejecting the dualism of mental and physical processes is the cornerstone of somatic practice. Chapter 2 introduced us to how people learn movement behaviors, carefully considering the sequence of sensing, perceiving, processing, and acting.

The relationship of the body to the mind is bridged by the nervous system, an indelible and complex network that connects neurons to muscle and converts ideas into action. The nervous system is also flexible, meaning it has great propensity toward change. Each life experience, each rehearsal, each practice period leaves its mark— and a measurable difference. As neuroanatomist and author of *My Stroke of Insight* and *Whole Brain Living*, Jill Bolte Taylor, so succinctly points out, the structure and function of the bodymind are inextricably linked.

This chapter provides a basic introduction to the structure and function of the nervous system, fostering a layman's understanding for the betterment of somatic application. Increased insight into the workings of the human instrument can only deepen the work, and support novel and distinct investigation.

Basic Brain Facts and Information

As our discussion commences, it's important to define several key structures and terms. The most fundamental unit of the nervous system is the neuron, or nerve cell, which is integral to brain communication. The space between two neurons is a synapse, and neurotransmitters facilitate the exchange of information between nerve cells. At the synapse, the initiating neuron instructs the receiving neuron to fire, or not, therefore propagating or terminating a signal. When neurons fire, information moves through the nervous system much in the same way the heart propels blood through the body.[2] The human brain contains around 86 billion neurons[3] and weighs approximately three pounds. Even though this small structure accounts for only 2 percent of our body weight, it uses approximately 20 percent of our resting metabolic rate to maintain function.[4] The brain is constantly active and responsive, even during sleep.[5] A more detailed examination of neurons, synaptic activity, and brain anatomy follows later in this chapter.

Another important term, albeit imaginary, is the neuroaxis. This line runs from the base of the neck to the top of head; it originates in the brain stem, travels to the diencephalon, then on to the limbic structures, and finally terminates in the prefrontal cortex. In folk-psychological terms, structures near the base of the neuroaxis are considered more primitive, or automatic, while more complex and sophisticated processes associated with cognition are located higher up. Consciousness and deliberateness are also aligned with the top of the neuroaxis, while impulsive actions, or those thought

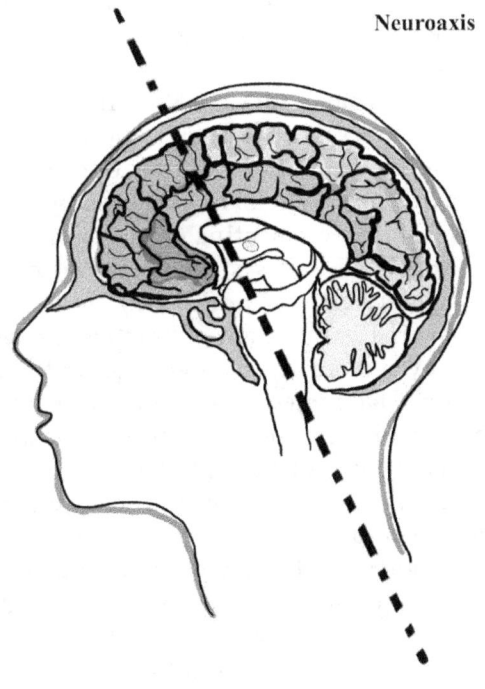

Figure 3.1. The neuroaxis provides a visual representation of differing levels of function in human behavior (illustration by Abby Jones).

to be ruled by emotions, stem from lower levels. The idea of the neuro-axis implies a bottom-up development, simple to complex, uncontrollable to controllable architecture of the brain. However, let's not discount the importance of structures located at the base of the axis, as they are crucial to the utilization of higher function areas.[6]

What Is the Brain? What Is the Mind?

At first glance, it is tempting to use the terms "brain" and "mind" interchangeably, but they mean different and specific things. The brain makes the mind—it is the physical structure at the center of the nervous system—while the mind, shaped by our lived experiences, is birthed from the physical structure of the brain. Too, the brain is the point of genesis for psychological experiences or states, and neural activity. This activity fosters interactions between multiplex networks of neurons, forming memories and guiding behaviors, thus creating the mind. Truly, one cannot exist without the other; the mind cannot do its work without the physical structure of the brain and consciousness is dependent on a healthy, functioning unit.[7]

Furthermore, the mind "thinks," and the brain responds to "thinking" in observable ways, creating neural pathways in its wake. In his original 1949 publication of *The Organization of Behavior: A Neuropsychological Theory*, Hebb links the biology of the brain to the abstract idea of the mind, a connecting of neuroscience to psychology of sorts. The cyclical, closed-loop system of neurons firing, connections forming, and subsequent behavior reinforcing these pathways lays the groundwork for learning as the result of practice. However, the flexible nervous system is even more capable—changes in thought processes can create new pathways, facilitated by a set of neurons firing on different sets of neurons, or in different places. Hebb's publication provided scaffolding for the idea that neurons firing together create pathways, and this circuitry can be altered in both positive and negative ways by changes in thought processes—because the mind shapes the brain.[8]

Maguire et al. provide some evidence for this thesis in their 2000 study, "Navigation-Related Structural Change in the Hippocampi of Taxi Drivers."[9] Using Magnetic Resonance Imaging (MRI), researchers saw concrete changes in the hippocampi (larger volume) of London taxi drivers compared to the non-taxi-driving control group, suggesting that the physical structure of the human brain can be altered with function (i.e., practice, learning). Furthermore, there was a correlation of time spent driving a taxi to hippocampal volume within the driving group. The investigators concluded that healthy human adult brains demonstrate plasticity when confronted with specific environmental conditions.

Neuroplasticity

Very broadly, the taxi drivers in this study display neuroplasticity, or the ability of the brain to make functional and structural changes in response to the environment.[10] In other words, the brain responds to our situational needs continuously throughout life, evolving with each lived experience[11]; neurotransmitter synthesis and release are altered in response to increased neural activity that contribute to structural alterations and subsequent behavioral changes.[12]

There are two forms of neuroplasticity: structural plasticity, and functional plasticity. Structural plasticity manifests as physical modifications in brain structure resulting from practice and learning, and from new experiences introduced by changing environments. Alternatively, functional plasticity occurs when there is a sort of role shifting within the brain. For example, if there is damage to one area of the brain, like stroke or other traumatic injury, other areas may be able to overtake the work of the damaged area.[13]

The brain structure also evolves through synaptic pruning, a process in which neurons and synaptic connections that are not being used and reinforced are eliminated.[14] Think about cutting away stems that are not thriving from your favorite rosebush so new, stronger growth can emerge. We can view synaptic pruning in evolutionary terms as survival of the fittest—what the brain needs to grow and prosper is maintained and strengthened, while what is not needed or used is discarded. This pruning is also partly responsible for a young brain's ability to mold and change, as there are extra synapses available to be used or reassigned as needed.[15] Indeed, the critical period hypothesis, which researchers propose as an optimal period in children and adolescents where the environment for learning is most favorable, is a behavioral outcome of plasticity in youth.[16]

Neuroplasticity is not only evident in healthy brains as the result of focused learning and repeated lived experiences but can also be observed after injury and trauma. Stroke affects almost 800,000 people each year in the United States alone and can leave victims with diminished language capability. While language is typically lateralized to the left hemisphere, Crosson et al. found that patients who were treated for aphasia (the loss of the ability to understand and/or express language) recruited the brain's right hemisphere during word production.[17] This transfer, or ability for one part of the brain to reorganize and take over tasks from another when

Figure 3.2. Pre-professional contemporary dance students engage in new learning with K. Meira Goldberg, center, flamenco performer, teacher, choreographer, and historian (author's collection).

information is not available, or, organic damage occurs, is yet another example of the flexibility of the human nervous system.

Neurogenesis

The creation of new neurons is termed neurogenesis. While scientists previously determined that human brains were not capable of growing new nerve cells, recent evidence suggests that neurogenesis can, indeed, occur in some areas of the brain, particularly in the hippocampus and the olfactory bulb.[18] For example, investigators found that some individuals experience a decrease in nerve cell regeneration due to stress or depressive episodes. However, following antidepressant therapies that increase the synaptic levels of neurotransmitters, or even due to other internal bodily changes, subjects were able to return to the original basal rate of neurogenesis.[19] This study, and others, support the idea that, while the human brain is affected by negative environmental factors (in this example, stress and depression), those changes need not be permanent.

As this brief introduction concludes, we are now ready to embark on more specific study of our neural structures, and function, beginning with the central nervous system.

The Central Nervous System (CNS)

The nervous system comprises two main parts: the central nervous system, which includes the brain and spinal cord, and the peripheral nervous system, a complex network of nerves that lies outside of the central nervous system. First, let's examine the CNS, beginning with the brain.

Brain Neuroanatomy and Function: An Overview

The largest section of the brain is the cerebrum, which is located at the front of the skull. The cerebrum is divided by a fissure into two hemispheres that are similar in size and appearance but provide different functions. The left hemisphere is associated with language, speech, reading, and writing. The right hemisphere guides a different set of functions, such as abstract reasoning,[20] facial recognition and emotional cuing,[21] and musical appreciation.[22]

The right and left hemispheres of the cerebrum also control opposite sides of the body, a phenomenon termed contralateral control, where the right side of the body is governed by the left hemisphere, and the left side the right hemisphere. To clarify, although there is factual data that the two hemispheres of the cerebrum have deliberate and separate functions, it's important not to attach too tightly to the "left-brained or right-brained" idea. Although some activities are clearly lateralized, the human brain is plastic; it can and will change in important ways when called upon. Likewise, overstating that one region or network is solely responsible for specific actions, i.e., emotional responses, is an oversimplification. It is more accurate to consider that different areas of the brain collaborate to produce and modulate emotion. The brain is like a symphony, a mosaic, where a combination of different sectors creates the human experience.

Moving on, the corpus callosum is a structure that connects the two hemispheres of the cerebrum and facilitates communication between the two halves. This important structure, characterized by an extensive network of nerve fibers, is crucial to hemispheric communication, and bisecting this important bundle of nerves results in compromised neural activity. In fact, a procedure known as a corpus callosotomy, where a band of fibers is severed, can be used to treat severe seizure disorders when medications are ineffective.

Covering the outermost layer of the cerebrum is the cerebral cortex. The cortex is responsible for processing most of what we experience in life, including sensory information, emotion, voluntary movement, language, personality, learning and memory, reasoning, and problem solving. Sometimes referred to as "gray matter," it contains an abundant number of neuron cell bodies that appear gray in color, while "white matter"—collections of axons that are white due to the presence of myelin—is found deeper within the brain. The cerebral cortex also appears "wavy" due to bumps and grooves called gyri and sulci. This intelligently designed pattern increases the surface area of the brain.[23]

The cerebral cortex is additionally separated into four lobes, known as the frontal, parietal, temporal, and occipital lobes. The frontal lobe controls planning, short term memory, and movement control,[24] as it contains the primary motor cortex.[25] The somatosensory cortex resides in the parietal lobe, which governs somatic sensation[26] and provides information regarding spatial awareness.[27] Hearing and deeper structures associated with memory and emotion are controlled by the temporal lobe, while the occipital lobe is responsible for vision.[28]

The prefrontal cortex is the section of the cerebral cortex that guides planning, goal setting, personality, decision-making, and social behavior and covers the anterior portion of the frontal lobe.[29] This is the home of human executive function, or higher cognitive thought, such as task-relevant actions that are essential to reaching a planned goal; it involves both the inclusion and exclusion of assigned outcomes.[30] It is this executive function that truly distinguishes human behavior from that of other mammals.

Connecting to both the limbic system, which regulates emotions, and the prefrontal cortex is the anterior cingulate cortex (ACC), which lies in the center of the brain's frontal lobe.[31] This dual connection potentially aids in the integration of emotion and cognition and has a role in planning and motivation. Too, the insula, a buried part of the cerebrum that separates the temporal and frontal lobes,[32] is thought to fill a diverse range of roles, including emotional and body awareness.

Another important brain structure is the hippocampus, which is embedded deep in the temporal lobe, and is part of the limbic system (a more detailed discussion of the limbic system follows). The hippocampus is largely involved in learning and memory, particularly episodic memory,[33] which involves retrieval of previous life events used to direct current behaviors.[34] Likewise, it is important in the transfer, but not storage, of new, explicit memories to long-term memory.[35] Recall from Chapter 2 that explicit, or declarative memory, is defined as the retention of voluntary and specific events, while implicit memory develops from unintentional behaviors.

Our understanding of the hippocampus's role in memory originated from a patient referred to as H.M., who had his hippocampus removed due to uncontrollable seizures in 1953. In 1955, scientists William Beecher Scoville and Brenda Milner began studying the patient and nine others like him. Post-surgery, H.M. suffered from anterograde amnesia and was not able to form new memories. To clarify, while the subject was unable to configure novel explicit memories, the ability to retain implicit memories (i.e., riding a bike, daily care, and grooming) remained intact.[36]

Researchers have also investigated the role of the hippocampus in spatial navigation. Revisiting the Maguire et al. study that measured gray matter volume in the brains of taxi drivers, the researchers specifically found increased volume in the hippocampi of the subjects, supporting the thesis that the hippocampus is involved in spatial cognition and navigation.[37]

We also know, that as part of the limbic system, the hippocampus is important in emotional regulation and processing[38] and dampens or inhibits the stress response.[39] Finally, recall that the hippocampus is one of the brain structures that can form new neurons into adulthood (neurogenesis).

Also part of the limbic system is the amygdala, an almond-shaped (amygdala derives from the Latin "almond") collection of nuclei located deep within the temporal lobe. There are actually two "amygdalae," one in each cerebral hemisphere. This structure governs our emotional states and has an evolutionary role of protection.[40] Humans experience anger, fear, anxiety, or any intense emotion when the amygdala is stimulated, thus contributing to the "fight or flight" response.[41] When damage to the amygdala occurs, the result may be a mellow, flat affect.[42] Additionally, damage to this structure can compromise the ability to recognize facial expressions such as fear, indicating the role of the structure in social cognition and judgment.[43] Indeed, Sripada et al. found that alcohol consumption hampered amygdala activity, reducing stress and anxiety by interfering with fear and threat processing.[44] Researchers have also observed hyperactivity in the amygdalae of clinically depressed individuals relative to healthy subjects.[45]

The amygdalae further support the interaction of memory and learning with emotion and emotional memory[46] and are especially important in learned fear. For example, if a child has been stung by a bee, the presence of the insect alone is enough to generate unpleasant emotions; when we experience pain resulting from a specific stimulus, later, the stimulus alone can cause fear. Furthermore, the amygdala is particularly responsive to negative stimuli[47] and is primed to respond to potentially harmful or unfavorable environmental situations. Receiving input from many different sensory inputs, the amygdala integrates both external and internal stimuli to help us arrive at a "gut feeling" or subjective instinct regarding a particular situation.[48]

Bridging the midbrain to the forebrain is the diencephalon, which contains both the thalamus and the hypothalamus and part of the pituitary gland. The thalamus is a sensory (except for olfaction) and motor relay station and sends important information to the cerebral cortex.[49] The central location of this structure perfectly positions it for this role—sitting above the midbrain, the thalamus can connect to all areas of the cortex as well as the limbic structures, assuring a significant role in learning and memory.[50] The thalamus is also associated with the regulation of consciousness[51] as well as sleep and circadian rhythms.[52]

The hypothalamus links to the pituitary gland and integrates somatic and visceral information to produce a response when fluctuations in the body are detected.[53] So, when sensory input indicates a change that needs to be addressed, the hypothalamus activates, thus promoting homeostasis in important states such as body temperature, blood composition, and energy levels. This autonomic maintenance occurs without our conscious knowledge, but can also elicit a behavioral response, i.e., eating when our stomach growls and we feel hungry. Another example is the hypothalamic control of body temperature—when the unit senses the body is too hot, the hypothalamus causes you to perspire, cooling as the sweat evaporates, and conversely, when you're cold, the hypothalamus sends signals to your muscles to produce shivering, which warms the body. Associated body functions also include influences on circadian rhythms and sex drive.[54] The hypothalamus also contains neurosecretory neurons that communicate the needs of the soma to the pituitary gland, which releases hormones in response. This yoking of the brain to the body via the pituitary, in essence, positions the hypothalamus as the main connector between the nervous and the endocrine systems. It's important to note that while the hypothalamus is a "ruler" of sorts, it operates with the information provided by the body, which is influenced by environmental and psycho-social factors.

Let's circle back to the all-important pituitary gland, another "ruler," as it controls the function of many other endocrine glands. No larger than a pea, it is divided into two lobes: the posterior and anterior. The posterior lobe can release oxytocin (the "love hormone") and vasopressin (controls salt concentration and blood volume) while the anterior lobe of the pituitary synthesizes and secretes many hormones that regulate the endocrine system and is under the control of the secretory hypothalamus. Together, the hypothalamus-pituitary-adrenal (HPA) axis is important in stress response, as it controls cortisol release from the adrenal cortex when stressful or harmful situations are detected.

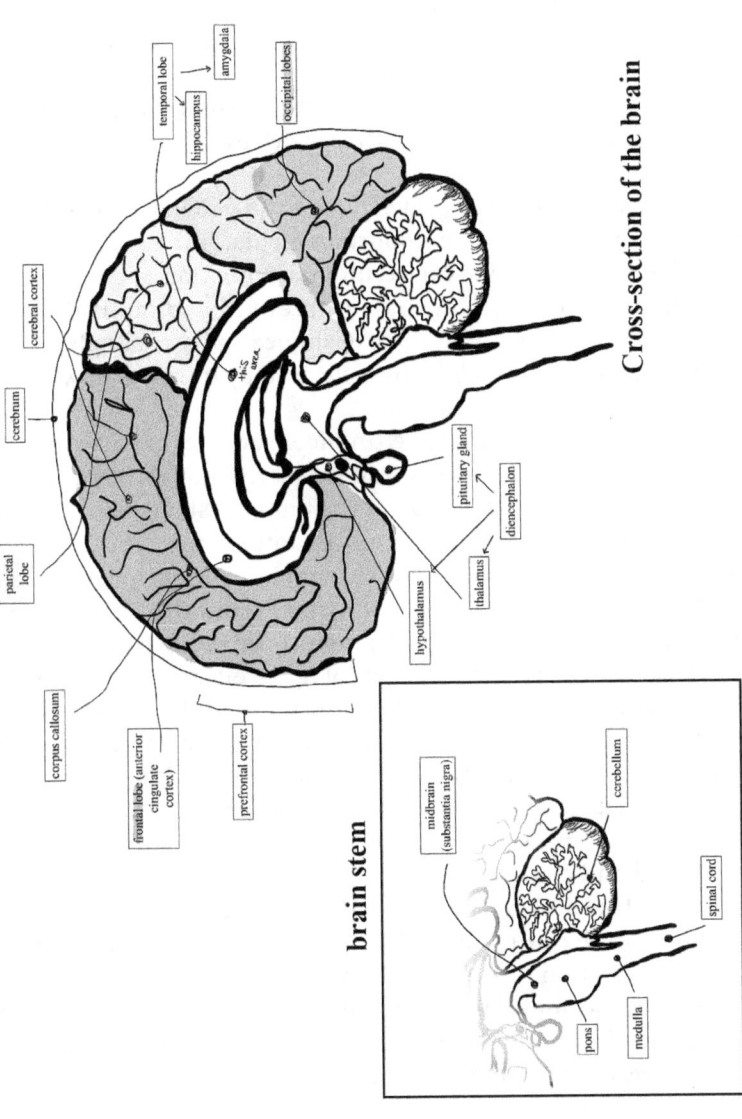

Figure 3.3. A cross-section of the human brain that displays the location of major anatomical structures in the central nervous system (illustration by Abby Jones).

Also found in the diencephalon (in addition to the thalamus, hypothalamus, and pituitary gland) is part of the basal ganglia, a collection of distributed cell groups (as opposed to a single structure) that are involved in purposeful movement, including motor learning and control.[55] The nuclei select and initiate appropriate actions and guide execution, influencing the quality and correctness of motion.[56]

With important connections to the limbic system,[57] emotions also fall under the control of the basal ganglia, as do reward and motivation, including the prediction of rewards.[58]

To perform these functions properly, the basal ganglia depend on the successful release of dopamine, an important mediator in movement production. Low levels of dopamine can result in dysfunction, including cognitive, emotional, and motivational issues[59]; reward and motivation are closely intertwined with dopamine. One example of a basal ganglia disorder is Parkinson's Disease, which is characterized by tremors, slow movement, and difficulty initiating action.

Current research shows that the limbic structures are involved in emotion, motivation, memory, stress, and sleep.[60] Although there is some debate about which structures constitute the limbic system, generally, the list includes the amygdala, hippocampus, hypothalamus, and cingulate cortex, and sometimes the basal ganglia.[61] To review, the amygdala is associated with fear, anxiety, and emotional memory and the hippocampus with memory and emotion. The hypothalamus is linked to the autonomic nervous system, which regulates the physiological effects of emotion and communicates with the rest of the body, while the cingulate cortex guides cognition and emotion. Interestingly, the limbic system has a close relationship to the olfactory system, and processes sensory input regarding smell while also influencing our emotional response to odors.[62]

Moving down from the cerebrum is the brain stem, which connects to the spinal cord and consists of the midbrain, pons, and medulla. The brain stem supports functions that are vital to survival, such as breathing, heart rate, temperature control, digestion, and sleep.[63] It is broadly considered a type of information relay station between brain and spinal cord.[64]

Anatomically, the midbrain sits just below the diencephalon and controls auditory and visual information, including movements of the eye. A structure of interest housed here is the substantia nigra, which contains dopaminergic neurons and is also considered part of the basal ganglia.[65] Referencing our previous discussion, Parkinson's Disease is caused by the loss of dopaminergic neurons in the substantia nigra.

The pons too serves as a relay station of sorts, sharing movement information between the cerebrum and the cerebellum.[66] It is also involved in the regulation of breathing, namely respiratory control (volume, rate).

Figure 3.4. Dance for Parkinson's participant Glenn Balbua, right, engages in a community class, led by teaching artist Carly Liegel, left, at the Joffrey Ballet, Chicago, Illinois (courtesy Carly Liegel; photograph by Carolyn McCabe).

In other words, its function is to adjust the quality of breath as opposed to initiating a breath.[67] In addition to its role in regulating REM sleep,[68] the pons also contains cranial nerves important in facial movement and sensation.[69]

The third of the brain stem structures is the medulla oblongata, which connects the pons and spinal cord[70] and communicates information from the latter to the brain. It is involved in vital autonomic functions, specifically respiratory and cardiovascular operations.[71] Along with the pons, it too plays a critical role in respiration, controlling breath rhythm and driving the muscles responsible for inspiration and expiration.[72] All three structures of the brain stem together control not only autonomic functions crucial to survival but are also important to threat assessment and reaction, i.e., pulling back your hand after touching a hot stove.

Sitting close to the brain stem at the base of the cerebrum is the cerebellum, which has extensive connections to both the cerebrum and the spinal cord.[73] Cerebellum is Latin for "little brain," and though it is small, it contains just as many neurons as the entire cerebrum. In contrast to the cerebrum, however, the left side of the cerebellum controls the left side of the body, and the right side controls the right side of the body, exhibiting ipsilateral control, as opposed to contralateral like the cerebrum.[74] A major function of this structure is to control walking, balance, standing, and other complex motor tasks, and it is heavily involved in motor learning and guiding the body's range of movement.[75]

Completing the central nervous system is the spinal cord, which attaches to the brain stem and allows communication between the brain and the body via spinal nerves. Just like the brain, the spinal cord is composed of gray matter and white matter. These spinal nerves connect with the gray matter of the spinal cord via the dorsal root, which brings sensory information into the spinal cord, and the ventral root, a motor nerve, which carries information away from the central nervous system to organs, muscles, skin, joints, etc.[76] Spinal cord injuries result in paralysis as those nerves can no longer communicate with muscles (or skin, joints, etc.) to initiate movement; these cells cannot regenerate after injury and do not exhibit the same degree of plasticity as those in the brain.

Reflecting on this brief introduction to the various structures and function of the central nervous system, we indeed see support for the idea that brain areas are more "collaborators" than "sole creators" and that many are involved in learning and motor control. It is fascinating to discover that behavioral changes resulting from learning and performance situations presented in Chapter 2 have organic origins; change does, indeed, happen at the structural level. The same can be said for the peripheral nervous system, next in our discussion.

The Peripheral Nervous System (PNS)

If we think of the central nervous system as the control center of the bodymind, the peripheral nervous system is, then, its delivery service. The peripheral nervous system includes all nerves and ganglia (collections of neurons) that lie outside of the brain and spinal cord and relays information to and from the CNS. As mentioned previously, sensory, or afferent nerves, carry messages from the body back to the central nervous system, while motor, or efferent nerves, send signals to the body from the CNS. The terms afferent and efferent describe the direction the nerve axons are headed. The PNS is further separated into two main parts, the somatic nervous system, and the autonomic nervous system.

The Somatic Nervous System (SNS)

The somatic nervous system is responsible for the voluntary control of our bodies, and consists of nerves that innervate the skin, joints, and muscles; it also dictates skeletal and muscular action. This is the part of the PNS that we utilize when we consider mindful, purposeful movement. The SNS is broken down further into sensory and motor axons. Sensory axons collect information from muscles, joints, and skin, carrying information to the central nervous system, while motor axons send signals to initiate muscle contraction.[77] For example, an executive decision (CNS) is made to have an afternoon snack. The SNS carries the commands to walk to the refrigerator and move the body to prepare something to eat.

Autonomic Nervous System (ANS)

In contrast, the autonomic nervous system, also known as the visceral nervous system, manages involuntary function. As the name suggests, this portion of the peripheral nervous system regulates activities that are automatically controlled, e.g., blood pressure and digestion. The ANS is largely controlled by the hypothalamus and keeps the body operating without conscious knowledge via innervation into the internal organs, blood vessels, and glands. While the somatic nervous system commands our skeletal muscle, the ANS governs all other body systems.

This regulation commences with the ANS relaying sensory information regarding visceral function to the central nervous system. Motor neurons then initiate an appropriate response, such as muscular contractions in the intestines, heart, and blood vessels; the ANS also responds to information from glands. The cycle involves two kinds of synapses—the preganglionic neuron that connects to the central nervous system, and the postganglionic neuron which attaches to the effector organ. The postganglionic neuron is what directly causes a visceral reaction (secretion, contraction, relaxation etc.).[78]

The Sympathetic Autonomic Nervous System (SANS)/ Parasympathetic Autonomic Nervous System (PANS)

The autonomic nervous system is further divided into the sympathetic and parasympathetic nervous systems, both of which are the subject of a great deal of contemporary discussion. The sympathetic autonomic nervous system is associated mostly with states of arousal, especially the "fight or flight" response, which activates when humans detect a threat to bodily safety. This intense response is short-term and unmaintainable; it is characterized by increased heart rate, slowed digestion, increased blood glucose, and sweating. The ganglia of the sympathetic nervous system run along the vertebral column (preganglionic axons originate in the thoracic and lumbar regions) and communicate with spinal nerves and internal organs.[79]

The parasympathetic autonomic nervous system has a very different function, in that it facilitates rest and digestion, immune responses, and energy storage, keeping the body at statis, with a long-term, business-as-usual approach. It normalizes heart rate and blood pressure, and monitors digestion. Much of the innervation of the PANS comes from the vagus nerve, a cranial nerve originating at the medulla, but also from preganglionic axons extending from the brain stem and sacral region; the postganglionic cell bodies lie near the target organ or tissue.[80]

Stimulation of the vagus nerve has certainly become a topic of keen interest in discussions surrounding stress regulation and relaxation. A recent *New York Times* article, "This Nerve Influences Nearly Every Internal Organ. Can It Improve Our Mental State, Too?," details some "at-home" methods for vagus nerve stimulation including holding your breath or submerging your face in cold water. To be clear, these methods

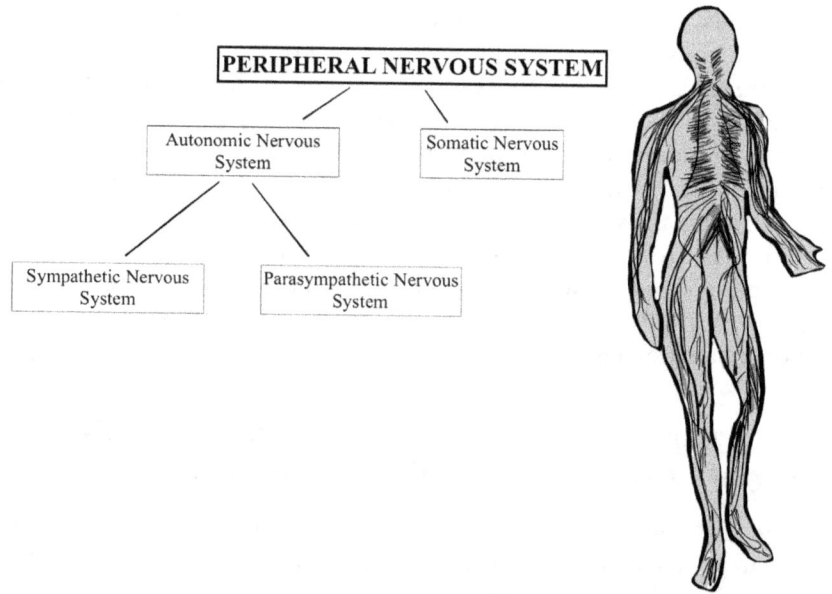

Figure 3.5. The Peripheral Nervous System (PNS) lies outside of the brain and spinal cord and is organized into the Autonomic and Somatic Nervous System (illustration by Abby Jones).

haven't been studied empirically or extensively, although the author suggests these practices are not harmful. The article additionally provides clinical background on current research investigating vagus nerve stimulation: "Researchers who study the vagus nerve say that stimulating it with electrodes can potentially help improve mood and alleviate symptoms in those who suffer from treatment-resistant depression, among other ailments."[81]

The sympathetic and parasympathetic nervous systems stimulate many of the same organs and have reciprocal effects on those systems. For example, heartbeat is controlled by an internal pacing system, but the SANS and PANS innervate the heart and can control actual rates, with the PANS slowing it down, and the SANS speeding it up. It is no surprise that humans perform optimally when these two systems work in harmony. While sympathetic activation sometimes suffers from a negative reputation, it serves an essential purpose, allowing us to perform well during critical moments. Parasympathetic activation prevents mild anxiety or excitement from distorting systemic balance. The SANS facilitates performance, while the PANS maintains our homebase. We need them both: "Happiness, love, and wisdom aren't furthered by shutting down the SNS, but rather by keeping the autonomic nervous system as a whole in an optimal state of balance."[82]

The enteric nervous system (ENS) is another division of the autonomic nervous system that resides within the digestive system, more specifically, in the lining of esophagus, intestines, pancreas, stomach, and gallbladder. Although it operates largely independently, the ENS does take some cues from the ANS—both the sympathetic and parasympathetic divisions can essentially override the daily workings of the enteric nervous system during periods of stress or rest.[83] The ENS contains approximately 100 million nerve cell bodies, and second to the brain, is the largest collection of nerve cell bodies in the human body.[84] Furthermore, the gut-brain axis (GBA) links the central and the enteric nervous system, connecting the emotional and cognitive centers of the brain with peripheral intestinal functions, monitoring and integrating gut function.[85]

The Somatic and Autonomic Nervous Systems Revisited

Having considered how each branch of the peripheral nervous system works independently, it is now important to contrast and compare the two classifications. There are some key differences in both structure and function—first, the result of autonomic nervous system activation is typically widespread, and less specific than somatic nervous system activation. Additionally, the SNS is excitatory only and exclusively commands skeletal muscle, while the ANS is excitatory *and* inhibitory, and governs all other tissues and organs. Regarding structure, somatic nervous system motor neurons lie within the CNS, while autonomic system motor neurons reside outside the CNS.[86]

"Fight or Flight"

We have previously discussed how the autonomic nervous system responds to harm, initiating the "fight or flight" response, but more specifically, how does the sympathetic autonomic nervous system react? Here, when the body is under stress, whether it be emotional, psychological, or physiological, epinephrine and norepinephrine are released, causing physiological symptoms such as increased heart rate, respiratory rate, blood pressure, dry mouth, and pupil dilation; digestion slows, or ceases.[87] The release of cortisol from the adrenal cortex also elevates glucose levels, resulting in increased energy, and suppresses the immune system. There is strong involvement of the amygdala, which "sounds the alarm" so to speak, and the hippocampus, which is involved in recalling prior life events and forming new memories. This combination of limbic and endocrine activation enabled by the nervous system results in widespread physiological effects.[88]

As this response cascades, there is less cognitive control, or involvement from the cortex. Qin et al. studied the effect of psychological stress on activities that require working memory and utilize the prefrontal cortex; healthy adults were asked to complete a task while viewing either a stress-causing or neutral movie. Analysis of functional magnetic resonance imaging (fMRI) showed working-memory related prefrontal cortex activation was reduced in the experimental group, supporting the hypothesis that resources typically used in executive function are diverted during times of stress. The researchers further propose that this reallocation of resources may indeed be an important survival tactic and allow the autonomic and endocrine systems to do their jobs.[89]

And how do components of the central nervous system and endocrine system work in concert with the somatic nervous system during a stress response? As previously discussed, the amygdala is primed for threat detection and fear, alerting the hypothalamus which, in turn, stimulates the adrenal glands to release the hormones epinephrine and cortisol, causing a physiological response—it is the hypothalamus that activates the sympathetic chain. The amygdala additionally communicates with the hippocampus, allowing the recall of similar stressful experiences during a current or future incident. These mechanisms, though seemingly primitive, are an important part of the evolution of the human nervous system, working to keep the bodymind safe from harm. However, overt, and persistent activation of the sympathetic division, like chronic stress, can have widespread, negative effects on the brain and various other systems, resulting in anxiety and depression as well as gastrointestinal, immune, cardiovascular, and endocrine problems.[90] Hence, regulating stress is critical to healthy human function.

Many somatic methodologies and systems foreground activating the parasympathetic chain, primarily through breath control, and there is empirical research to support this practice.

For example, Chang, Liu, and Shen varied participant's breathing to either 8, 12, or 16 breaths per minute. They found the slowed breathing (eight breaths per minute) increased vagal (parasympathetic) activity, modulating autonomic cardiovascular regulation.[91] Another group of researchers found similar results over a three-month period, where healthy subjects practiced either slow breathing or fast breath cycling.[92]

The benefits of meditation, too, are likely fostered by attention to the

Figure 3.6. Alex Clair, front, and fellow somatic practitioners engage in breathwork as they shift attention from cognitive thought to sensory engagement (courtesy Stefanie Nelson; photograph by Rachelle Saker).

breath, in concert with other factors such as a focus on relaxation and thought redirection, which causes a parasympathetic response. Brand et al. found that in healthy adults, both immediate and longer-term meditation practice resulted in decreased cortisol levels, as well as superior sleep quality and higher scores on mindful measures.[93] Hölzel et al. also reported significant changes in the brain following eight weeks of Mindfulness-Based Stress Reduction (MBSR) treatment. They found an increase in gray matter volume in the hippocampus, posterior cingulate cortex, temporo-parietal junction, and cerebellum, all brain regions associated with learning and memory processes and emotional regulation.[94] While experienced somatic practitioners have long known the benefits of breath training on human bodyminds, these conclusions are often formed from anecdotal evidence. Understanding the actual structural changes in the nervous system resulting from such training adds an extra layer of knowing and understanding to the work.

Somatic (Bodily) Responses to Nervous System Activity

Intuitively, we know that the human body reacts to nervous system activity, and these reactions produce distinct sensations that are easily felt and noticed. We have all experienced a racing heartbeat when we're frighted, or "butterflies in the stomach" when we feel nervous or anxious. There is an established pattern of increased heart and respiratory rate due to the involuntary response of the autonomic nervous system in fearful and stressful situations.[95] Here, the sympathetic nervous system releases norepinephrine, which acts on various organs, more specifically the adrenal medulla. The adrenal medulla, in turn, produces adrenaline, leading to increased heart rate, respiratory rate, and blood pressure. The sympathetic nervous system is hyperactivated and directs somatic responses by sending information to the cardiovascular system. The body's response is not only felt, but measurable via heart rate variability (HRV), which is a marker for autonomic nervous system activity and indicates stress. When the bodymind experiences fear, anxiety, or trauma, the heart beats faster, and the time between beats, or HRV, decreases.[96] Cardiac vagal tone (vagal nerve activity) is also measured using heart rate variability, and often decreases during stressful situations.[97] If heart rate variability decreases, there is also a lessening of vagal tone, and a decrease in contributions from the parasympathetic nervous system—recall that the vagus nerve is the primary communication highway for the PNS.

Back to those "butterflies" we all experience on occasion—there is a firmly established relationship between the gut and the brain, with stress and anxiety often resulting in gastro-intestinal symptoms such as abdominal pain, diarrhea, and nausea.[98] The gut-brain axis is the conduit for bidirectional communication between the two sets of structures, so gastro-intestinal (GI) function is linked to cognitive and emotional brain centers.[99] In other words, the brain influences the gut, and the gut influences the brain. It has already been established that internal and external stressors to the soma can cause upset in the GI tract. Given the two-way gut-brain axis, might gastro-intestinal issues that originate organically influence human emotional states? Lurie et al. studied the effects of antibiotic exposure on subjects' risk for compromised emotional states. They found that recurrent antibiotic use (antibiotics often produce GI difficulties) was indeed associated with an increased risk of depression and anxiety, supporting the argument for equanimity in the network.[100] The mind and the body are truly inseparable.

Building Blocks

Having completed a brief survey of major nervous system divisions and classifications, including structure and function, this chapter will conclude with an examination of its smallest units, specifically nerve cells and neurotransmitters.

Neurons

Neurons were introduced earlier in this chapter as cells that facilitate communication between different areas of the brain, as well as between the brain and other parts of the nervous system. There are three basic types of neurons: sensory neurons, which carry information from the skin and other organs back to the brain; motor neurons, which send signals to muscles and glands; and interneurons, which are responsible for exchanges between neurons.[101] Additionally, a more distinct type of motor neuron is the mirror neuron, which activates when an individual performs movement, as well as when one person watches another move. The mirror neuron system has obvious and specialized connections to somatic practice, and to the movement arts, supporting the importance and empirical existence of body experiences in the wholeness of human function. Tortora explains how the mirror neuron system plays a critical role in movement therapies:

> These discoveries provide a means of explaining the deep visceral ways in which we gain insight into our patients when we move with them and witness

them during nonverbal dance and movement oriented therapeutic explorations. The mirror neuron system provides the means by which two partners use perceptive and proprioceptive experiences to match and complement affect and feeling tones in order to come to know the psychological state of the other.[102]

Indeed, the concept of movement, or kinesthetic, empathy is a critical element of the SomaLab framework presented in Chapter 5 and is integral to building flexibility in movement praxis.

In terms of structure, a neuron looks something like a tree (see Figure 3.7). Dendrites extend up from the soma, or cell body, while an axon reaches downward, ending with the axon terminal, which serves as the site of a synapse. Axon terminals synapse with the dendrite of another cell, thus moving information forward, or stopping it, depending on the command.

At the center of the nerve cell is the soma (cell body), which is identical in structure to other cells that reside in the body. It houses organelles, including a nucleus, which carries genetic material; mitochondria, which are responsible for energy production; and the endoplasmic reticulum, which is responsible for protein production, all of which perform specific functions to keep the cell alive and healthy. The soma is essentially the "meat" of the cell and is critical to supporting the work of the neuron.

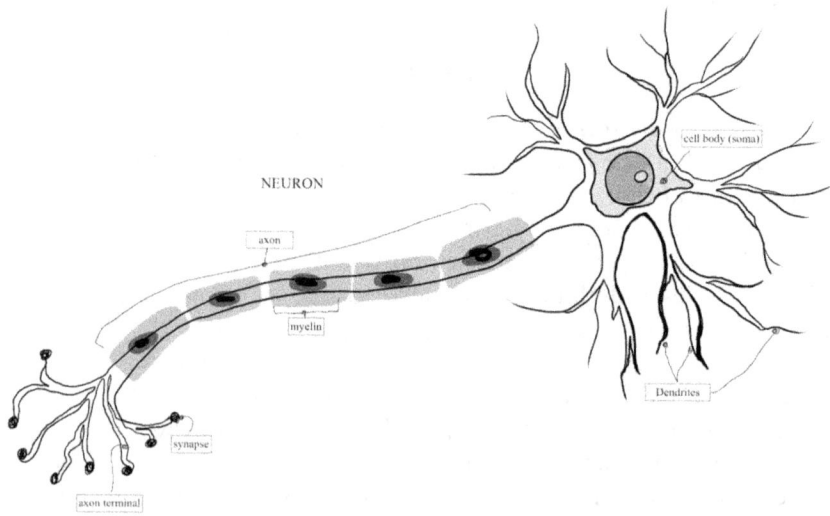

Figure 3.7. As referenced in the text, a neuron somewhat resembles a tree. Information is exchanged via synaptic sites, at the end of neuron structures (illustration by Abby Jones).

The axon appears as a line, or wire, which can be long or short and runs between the soma and the axon terminal, carrying information. Axons are covered in myelin, which increases the speed of transmission; more myelin means greater velocity and a faster message, or action potential. Additionally, the greater the diameter of the axon, the quicker information is transmitted. Indeed, a shortage of myelin has important implications in disease; for example, multiple sclerosis (MS) is a demyelinating illness. At the end of an axon lies the axon terminal, which concludes at the site of the synapse, or place where information is shared with other neurons and cells in the form of neurotransmitters. Also branching off from the soma are dendrites, which receive neurotransmitters from other neurons, either exciting the nerve cell to propagate a message or stopping an action potential from continuing.

Synapses, the small spaces between an axon terminal and a dendrite that are essential to communication between nerve cells, can be classified further as presynaptic—the axon terminal of the cell where a message begins—and postsynaptic—meaning the dendrite or soma of another cell receiving information. This information typically originates in the form of an electrical impulse (action potential) that starts at the soma, then travels through the axon, and is transferred to a chemical signal (neurotransmitter). More specifically, synaptic vesicles (think of small bags of neurotransmitters) that dock at the axon terminal release neurotransmitters into the synaptic cleft, defined as the area between the presynaptic and postsynaptic membranes. The postsynaptic membrane contains receptors for neurotransmitters, which, in turn, cause a change in the membrane and initiates another electrical signal. To summarize, an electrical signal causes a chemical response, which initiates a new electrical signal, thus moving communication forward through the network.[103] And what happens to unused neurotransmitters after secretion? The answer is reuptake, a process where chemicals are reabsorbed back into the axon terminal, a type of recycling so to speak.[104] In fact, depression is often treated using Selective Serotonin Reuptake Inhibitors (SSRIs), pharmaceuticals which block the reabsorption of serotonin, thereby increasing levels of available serotonin in the brain.

As mentioned, an action potential is a message that travels down an axon causing a release of neurotransmitters from the axon terminal; it is the "electrical" portion of neuron-to-neuron communication, and the frequency and pattern of action potentials is critical to this exchange. More specifically, an action potential is generated via an intricate dance between sodium and potassium—an influx of sodium into the cell causes a depolarization, and if the degree of depolarization reaches a certain threshold, an action potential is generated. Conversely, if the cell does not reach this threshold, no electrical signal is generated.[105]

Glial Cells

Glial cells are another kind of cell in the nervous system, which are not neurons but provide important support to nerve cells. They are located in both the central and peripheral nervous systems, acting as facilitators to neurons that clean, connect, protect, and communicate, and also generate myelin. Different kinds of glial cells perform different functions; for example, microglia reside in the brain and spinal cord and as immune system cells, respond to injury and infection, and regulate brain development. Astrocytes are plentiful in the CNS and provide structural support and promote synaptic cleaning/clearing, and oligodendrocytes are the myelin producers of the CNS. Schwann cells are the myelin producers of the PNS and are vital to maintaining axonal health.[106]

Neurotransmitters

We have already touched on the role of neurotransmitters in the neural network as chemical messengers that are released based on conditions and goals, and it should come as no surprise that different types of neurotransmitters have differing functions. For example, gamma-aminobutyric acid (GABA) is a primary inhibitory neurotransmitter, in that it stops nerve transmission.[107] Benzodiazepines, e.g., Xanax and alcohol, are GABA receptor agonists, hence their sedative, calming effects.[108] In general, here, a receptor agonist binds to a cell and mimics an endogenous substance.

Conversely, glutamate is a neurotransmitter with primary excitatory properties, in that it promotes nerve transmission. It plays a key role in learning and memory, more specifically, in long-term potentiation (LTP) and long-term depression (LTD), which at the synaptic level, are processes that support learning, memory formation, and plasticity.[109] LTP strengthens synapses, and allows for lasting signal transmissions between neurons, while LTD weakens synapses, depressing communication. Both processes are heavily involved in mediation of sensory information, emotion, motor coordination, and cognition.[110]

Dopamine is a much-discussed neurotransmitter that is involved in reward, motivation, attention, and learning, and plays a key role in addiction:

> That such structures are subject to dopamine-dependent LTP and LTD encourages the hypothesis that these mechanisms are involved in behavioral conditioning. Whatever the mechanism, brain dopamine seems to stamp in response—reward and stimulus—reward associations that are essential for the control of motivated behavior by past experience.[111]

Dopamine is also important in maintaining consistency in movement. Recall that the symptoms of Parkinson's Disease, which is characterized by tremors, slow movement, and difficulty initiating movement, are linked to a depletion of dopamine in the basal ganglia. In fact, treatment for Parkinson's Disease involves drugs that increase dopamine levels.[112]

Another well-known neurotransmitter is serotonin, which is critical in mood regulation and therefore a target for treatment of many mood disorders, like depression. As previously discussed, serotonin-selective reuptake inhibitors (SSRIs) curb the reuptake of serotonin back into the presynaptic cell, therefore allowing excess serotonin to remain in the synaptic cleft, increasing the amount available for use.[113] The modulation of eating and food intake is affected by this neurotransmitter in that serotonin levels in the hypothalamus spike when eating, cementing a relationship between food and mood. Accordingly, drugs that increase serotonin levels can act as appetite suppressants.[114] Indeed, the primary source of serotonin in the body is a subtype of cells located in the intestines,[115] further strengthening the argument for the brain and gut connection.

Acetylcholine, a neurotransmitter heavily involved in learning and memory, is particularly germane to our understanding of bodymind processes. Increased levels of this chemical are associated with memory and comprehensibility,[116] and the loss of cholinergic neurons in the hippocampus correlate with memory disorders, including aging-related dementia.[117] Acetylcholine also enables muscle contraction and voluntary movement in the somatic nervous system.[118] It is found in all motor neurons in the spinal cord and brainstem and facilitates synaptic transmissions at neuromuscular junctions, or where neurons meet muscle,[119] and is utilized by both branches of the autonomic nervous system.

Let's also revisit epinephrine and norepinephrine, neurotransmitters that work in concert during a stress response. Norepinephrine is the primary neurotransmitter in the sympathetic nervous system and is released by the postganglionic neurons when the SANS is activated, having widespread effects.[120] Norepinephrine signals epinephrine release when facing "fight or flight"; it is additionally involved in the regulation of attention, arousal, and sleep-wake cycles.[121] Norepinephrine-containing neurons are least active during rest, but encourage responsiveness in neurons of the cerebral cortex during robust sensory stimuli.[122] When norepinephrine signals the release of epinephrine, or adrenaline, from the adrenal medulla,[123] we see strong physiological reactions such as increases in heart rate, blood pressure, and respiration, as well as increased blood flow to muscles, and dilated pupils. Digestion is also inhibited.[124]

Lastly, let's consider endorphins, neurotransmitters that are essentially endogenous opioids, and have similar chemical properties to opiates. Endorphins are associated with pain reduction, positive moods, and pleasure—think love, sex, food, laughter, and exercise.[125] To illustrate,

Manninen et al. studied the effect of social laughter on endogenous opioid release. Using a positron emission topography scan (PET), an imaging tool that detects cellular activity to track an opioid receptor ligand, they demonstrated a significant effect for endogenous opioid release in the experimental (laughter) group, arguing that laughter can be a powerful way to form social bonds within communities. Furthermore, they postulate that the calming effects of endorphin release during social activities promote affiliation and bonding between individuals.[126]

This discussion of the smallest units of the nervous system, neurons and neurotransmitters, is important in understanding the organic origin of somatic experiences, and the root of the mind/body connection, right down to the cellular level. These micro-structures and chemicals perform a crucial, complicated dance in maintaining the stability, and the viability, of our bodymind instrument.

Conclusion

If this chapter illustrates anything, it is the wonder, the beauty, the efficiency, and the flexibility, of the human nervous system:

> Thus it is not accurate to think of a mental process as being mediated by a chain of nerve cells connected in series—one cell connected directly to the next—for in such an arrangement the entire process breaks down when a single connection is disrupted. A more realistic metaphor is that of a process consisting of several parallel pathways in a communications network that can interact and ultimately converge upon a common set of target cells. The malfunction of a single pathway affects the information carried by it but need not disrupt the entire system. The remaining parts of the system can modify their performance to accommodate the breakdown of one pathway.[127]

It seems that the concept of the nervous system as collaborative and communal is critical to its plasticity—perhaps its structure and function are an organic precursor to human interactions and relationships, providing insight into the unique social needs and practices of our species.

As we move forward investigating human movement and artistic expression through the lens of somatic study, our next step is to yoke organic function with learning theory in forming complex, all-encompassing approaches to behavior that are inclusive of first-person experiences. In Chapter 4, we will consider the totality of learning, performing, and living by examining three contemporary models of human behavior as we prepare to segue to theoretical application of somatic praxis in Part 2.

4

Contemporary Theories of Learning, Performing, and Living

Elizabeth Limons Shea and Frank Diaz

> "You would never admit that you were doing your art as spiritual practice. But there was a certain point where I realized, you know, life is short. If there is a relationship between my practice and my artwork, why not? Why should one thing be over here and the other thing be over there? Why can't that impulse be unified?"—Meredith Monk[1]

Introduction

Thus far in our journey into the human bodymind, we have framed somatics in the context of historical and contemporary philosophies, investigated behavior from a movement learning perspective, and understood that practice results in real structural change within our nervous system. As we conclude Part 1, the final step is to incorporate this knowledge into a dynamic framework for how human beings navigate their movement, artistic, and daily lives. This chapter explores three multi-dimensional and multi-faceted contemporary approaches: 4E cognition, dynamical systems theory, and the OPTIMAL theory of motor learning. The wisdom of visionary musician and movement artist Meredith Monk foregrounds the complexities and interconnectedness of art making and living, reflecting the importance of these interactive theories in the story of human behavior.

4E Cognition

Performing artists navigate a complex world filled with meaning and social interactions. From the simple act of mirroring a partner's movements to the intricate choreography of a group performance, or from learning to play a lone melody to improvising with a jazz ensemble, we are constantly engaging with others and our environment in ways that shape our understanding and experience. This process of collaborative meaning making, or participatory sense-making, lies at the heart of the enactive approach to cognition, where the mind is not a passive receiver of information, but an active participant in creating meaning.

The enactive perspective is part of a broader movement in cognitive science known as 4E cognition, which emphasizes the embodied, embedded, extended, and enactive nature of the mind (recall from Chapter 3 that the mind is the sum of our lived experiences as they impact the brain) and examines how the interaction of the bodymind and the environment shape consciousness. This approach challenges traditional computational and representational views of cognition, such as information processing explored in Chapter 2, and instead posits that cognition is deeply rooted in our bodily interactions with the world and with others. Importantly, this perspective not only reshapes our understanding of the individual bodymind but also offers new insights into the dynamics of learning, development, and social interaction in the context of dance, movement, and music.

We'll begin by investigating the broader landscape of 4E cognition, exploring its theoretical foundations, empirical support, practical implications, and history, tracing the roots of 4E from the early critiques of computationalism to the emergence of embodied and enactive frameworks in the 1990s. We'll also consider various perspectives that highlight the role of the body, the environment, and social interaction in shaping cognition generally as well as in artistic settings more specifically. Central to this discussion is the enactive concept of participatory sense-making, a theory which emphasizes the collaborative nature of the environment and the bodymind in understanding the world, particularly social behaviors.

Delving more thoroughly into the 4E approach, we explore the practical applications of 4E cognition in domains such as dance and music education, therapy, and interactive performance technologies. By grounding cognition in the lived, embodied experience of individuals and their social contexts, the 4E approach offers a broad framework for understanding and supporting the rich diversity of human bodyminds. Insights from philosophy, psychology, neuroscience, and the arts, converge as we form a deeper appreciation for the complex and inherently meaningful nature of behavior and its inextricable connection to the world and others through artistic expression.

Historical Context

As presented in Chapter 2, the idea that the mind is computational was introduced in the mid–20th century, working in ways similar to how computers process information using abstract rules and symbols. Influential examples of this movement include Chomsky's theory that children learn language using built-in mental rules to organize words into grammatical sentences,[2] and Marr's theory that our brains construct 3D images of the world by running algorithms on 2D input from the eyes.[3] These ideas align with functionalism, a philosophical view that mental states are defined by their functional roles rather than by the specific physical components involved, just as a piece of computer software performs the same task regardless of the hardware on which it runs.

However, embodied cognition theorists argue that the mind is heavily influenced or even fundamentally shaped by the physical body it inhabits. More radical approaches, grouped under the "4E cognition" label (embodied, embedded, extended, enactive), claim that cognition cannot be fully explained without reference to the body's interactions with the environment. For instance, Varela, Thompson, and Rosch argue that thinking emerges from the ongoing interaction between brain, body, and world, rather than being a process confined within the head.[4] While they differ in specifics, embodied cognition theories collectively suggest that traditional "mind as computer" views fail to capture the crucial roles played by the body and environment.

As we explore the 4E cognition framework, it may be helpful to consider how it augments and departs from traditional computational models. The latter approaches emphasize symbolic processing at an abstract level as the core of cognition, with everything else being subservient to these mental processes. In contrast, the 4E framework expands the scope of what is considered relevant to cognition. The first E, embodied, incorporates factors outside of neural networks, such as the physical form, into explanations of what influences or constitutes the mind, thus *bodymind*, a term that is used consistently throughout this text to indicate the inseparable and embodied nature of human behavior and existence. The second E, embedded, adds physical and social phenomena as integral to cognitive processes. The third E, extended, takes this further by considering these factors as building blocks of the cognitive system itself. Finally, the fourth E, enactive, views the entire agent-environment system as an open, dynamic network characterized by co-regulation, constraints, and action-perception feedback loops, encompassing even higher-level cognitions such as meaning making. While this characterization simplifies the complex relationships among these dimensions, it provides a useful tool for understanding how the 4E framework challenges and enriches traditional computational accounts of cognition (see Figure 4.1).

The roots of embodied cognition can be traced back to the late 1970s, with theorists like Hubert Dreyfus and J.J. Gibson questioning the idea that the mind operates like a computer. Gibson proposed that perception is not about building detailed inner models of the world but about picking up useful information directly from the environment through active exploration.[5] However, it was not until the 1990s that embodied cognition gained significant traction as a research program, sparked by influential works such as Andy Clark's *Being There*, which argued that thinking is fundamentally tied to action and shaped by the resources in our environment.[6] This idea has important implications for movers and performing artists, suggesting that performers' understanding of their own movements and sounds, as well as those of their peer performers and audience members, is not based on abstract mental representations but on the direct perception of bodily cues and environmental properties. Subsequently, embodied approaches have made inroads into virtually all areas of cognitive science.

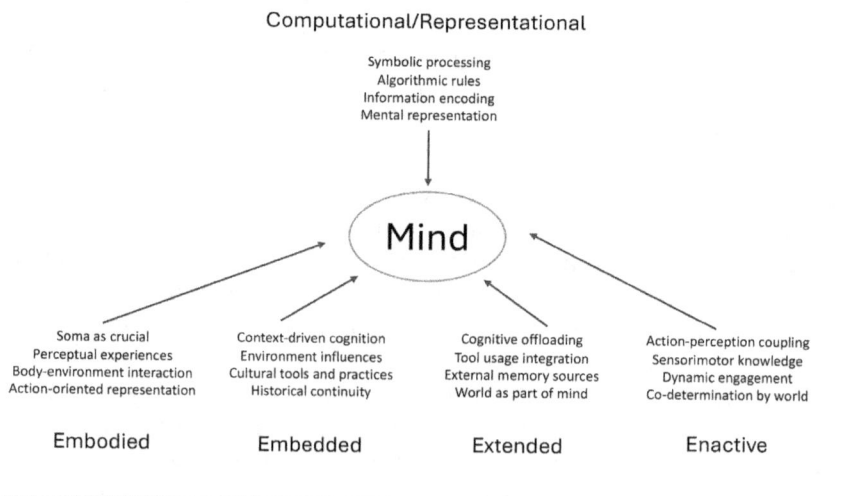

Figure 4.1. A visual representation of 4E cognition (author's creation).

Embodied Cognition: Key Concepts

In their overview of embodied cognition, Shapiro and Spaulding identify three key themes that characterize this approach: conceptualization, replacement, and constitution.[7] These themes provide a useful framework for understanding the various ways in which embodied cognition departs from traditional cognitive science.

Conceptualization suggests that our bodily experiences shape the very concepts we use to understand the world. This notion is exemplified in the work of Lakoff and Johnson, who argue that our conceptual systems are grounded in embodied actions.[8] They claim that abstract concepts are understood through metaphors that are associated with more concrete, bodily domains. For instance, we might understand the concept of "balance" in movement not only in terms of physical equilibrium but also in terms of the balance between tension and release, or between individual expression and group cohesion. This suggests that the structure of our bodies and the nature of our physical interactions with the world play a crucial role in shaping our cognitive processes at a fundamental level. Indeed, conceptualization informs a key task in the SomaLab framework described in Chapters 5 and 6, aptly named "conceptually-guided prompts," and is the basis of the Individual Movement Inventory, a tool that facilitates individualized movement learning (see Figure 5.3, Chapter 5).

The second theme of embodied cognition, replacement, subverts the traditional computational view of the mind even further. Researchers in this area, influenced by the work of Gibson and the field of ecological psychology,[9] argue that cognition should be understood not in terms of internal mental representations but in terms of the dynamic interaction between a person and their environment. Brooks, for example, developed robots that could navigate complex environments without relying on internal models or representations. Instead, the robots' behavior emerged from the real-time interaction of their simple sensorimotor capacities with the environment.[10] This approach suggests that the basis for artistic cognition lies not in the mental representation of movement or sound patterns but in the real-time, adaptive interplay between the performer's body, the artistic material, and the surrounding space.

Lastly, constitution is central to the embodied cognition framework, asserting that the body and environment are not merely influences on cognition but are part of the cognitive system itself. Clark and Chalmers famously argue for the extended mind thesis, theorizing that cognitive processes can go beyond the individual to include tools and artifacts in the environment.[11] They provide the example of a notebook used by an individual with memory impairment, arguing that the notebook plays a role functionally like biological memory and should be considered part of the person's cognitive system. In the context of dance and music, this idea suggests that elements such as the dance floor, the musical instrument, and even the audience can become part of the performer's cognitive system, shaping, and constraining the possibilities for movement and expression. The concept of constitution is also supported by work in dynamical systems theory (discussed later in this chapter) which models cognition as emerging from the complex, real-time interactions of brain, body, and environment.[12]

We find strong evidence for the embodied nature of cognitive processes in empirical work investigating behaviors in the performing arts. For example, in the realm of music, studies have demonstrated that musicians' body movements play a crucial role in shaping their sound and expressive intentions. Wanderley et al. found that clarinetists' ancillary body movements, such as swaying or nodding, were closely related to their musical phrasing and expression.[13] Studies have also shown that dancers' physical movements can shape their emotional experiences and vice versa (this is the basis for dance therapy). For instance, Winters found that participants who embodied postures associated with anger identified the emotion of anger more frequently compared to those who merely observed others embodying the same postures.[14]

These findings and others underscore the importance of bodily states,

Figure 4.2. Musicians Dorian Jackman, left, and Brian McNulty exhibit attentional body language as they focus carefully on a remaining dancer's movement on stage waiting for their final cues (author's collection; photograph by Jeremy Hogan).

sensorimotor processes, and embodied experiences in shaping our cognitive and affective engagement with artistic expression. They suggest that the creation, performance, and reception of these art forms are not purely abstract processes but are deeply rooted in our embodied interactions with the world and with others. As noted previously, the concept of embodiment is critical to the SomaLab framework explored in Part 2, which presents direct applications to movement learning and performance.

Embeddedness and Extended Cognition

The dimension of "embeddedness" within 4E cognition refers to the effect of physical and social environments on mental processing and behavior. A concrete example is the influence of a musical instrument's physical structure on a performer's technique and expressive capacities. Practicing on a violin, with its relatively short and narrow neck, imprints a very different set of tactile cues and resultant neural networking than practicing on a double bass, with its much larger neck. Approaches to these instruments, including socially derived expectations about appropriate posture and other expressive elements, would also vary based on whether they were played in a symphony orchestra or a country-western ensemble. Moreover, the acoustics of the performance space and expressive feedback loops between performers could all be considered as causal factors in the perceptual-cognitive-behavior loops that constitute "minds" in this context. This dovetails with ideas of transfer of motor skills presented in Chapter 2, where although similar skills, in this case stringed instruments, can transfer more easily than dissimilar skills (for example, from violin to flute), the playing of each carries with it a unique and meaningful set of behaviors, in essence, its own "mind."

Two often-cited works that lend empirical support to the concept of embeddedness in 4E cognition include Hutchins' *Cognition in the Wild*[15] and Martin and Schwartz's study on children and calculating fractions.[16] Hutchins presents a detailed case study of navigation aboard a U.S. Navy ship, arguing that cognitive processes are deeply embedded in the social and material contexts in which they occur. He introduces the concept of "distributed cognition," suggesting that human knowledge and cognitive processes are not confined solely within the individual mind but are distributed across individuals, tools, and artifacts within the environment. We could imagine that members of a dance or music ensemble display distributed cognition. Furthermore, Martin and Schwartz found that children significantly improved their ability to calculate fractions when they physically manipulated pie pieces compared to when they merely observed them, thus increasing learning through sense-making facilitated by touch.

Building on the theoretical and empirical foundations of embedded cognition, the dimension of extended cognition takes the interactivity between the individual and environmental elements even further, arguing that cognitive processes can move beyond the limits of a person's physical boundaries. While embedded cognition emphasizes how our cognitive processes are influenced and facilitated by our immediate physical and social contexts, extended cognition theory posits that concrete elements in our environment do not just influence cognitive processes—they become part of them. This theoretical shift is exemplified in the work of Clark and Chalmers,[17] who articulate a vision of the mind that extends into the environment, incorporating external devices directly into the cognitive system. Just as Hutchins observed that cognitive tasks such as naval navigation involve complex interactions between humans and tools, extended cognition suggests that these tools are not merely aids but constitute cognition itself.[18]

In considering movement and performing artists, these frameworks suggest that the artifacts used in artistic creation and performance, such as musical instruments, dance shoes, digital technologies, and performance sites become an integral part of the performer's cognitive system. This perspective questions traditional notions of the mind, encouraging us to reconsider what comprises cognitive processes and where they occur, blurring the lines between the bodymind and its environment.

Support for the extension of cognitive processes beyond the brain and into the environment can be found in scholarship focused on the use of external devices and technologies. As mentioned earlier, Clark and Chalmers propose that cognitive processes can reach beyond the boundaries of the skull, and into the environment. They illustrate this idea with the hypothetical case of Otto, an Alzheimer's patient who relies on a notebook as a memory aid, arguing that the notebook plays a role functionally like that of biological memory.[19] Similarly, Sellen and Harper explored how digital calendars and notes extend our memory and planning capabilities.[20] Other researchers have investigated how spatial arrangements in the environment influence problem-solving tasks, showing that the arrangement of physical objects can significantly alter cognitive outcomes.[21]

Further evidence for extendedness arises within studies on the use of large interactive displays, which can encourage collaboration through shared helping and coordination, creating expressive, lively interaction.[22] Additionally, Smith et al. found that toddlers' own bodily actions, such as bringing objects close to their face, can significantly influence their visual experiences during group play, potentially simplifying the learning environment by reducing ambiguity and directing attention. Here, the body and its interaction with the environment play a crucial role in shaping cognitive processes in early development.[23]

Enaction: Cognition as Interaction

The last of the 4Es is the "enactive" dimension. Building upon the foundational concepts of embodied and embedded cognition, enaction further explores the dynamic interplay between individual and environment, proposing that cognition arises through ongoing interactions with the world. This approach, pioneered by scholars such as Varela, Thompson, and Rosch,[24] emphasizes that cognitive processes are not merely brain-based but are fundamentally intertwined with corporeal actions and environmental contexts. Enaction suggests that our understanding of the world is informed by our sensory-motor experiences, which involve active exploration and manipulation of our surroundings. This perspective is well-illustrated in studies of perceptual learning, where the act of touching and manipulating objects leads to richer cognitive and perceptual experiences, showing that cognition extends beyond neural responses to include the body and its interplay with the physical world.[25] Regarding the performing arts, enaction suggests that an individual's understanding of their own movements, sounds, and those of others is formed through their sensorimotor experiences, which involve exploration and manipulation of the body in space and time.

The enactive approach is further supported by research in dynamical systems theory, explored in more detail later in this chapter, which views cognitive systems as complex and adaptive. This view aligns with theories suggesting that cognitive processes acclimate and evolve in response to real-time environmental changes, challenging the conventional notion of static cognitive states.[26] For instance, consider the concept of "sense-making," where we understand and make meaning from events and individual lived experiences. Here, enaction is exemplified through the participatory dimensions of cognition observed in social contexts. Studies have shown that cognitive processes such as decision-making and problem-solving are significantly influenced by social interactions, and individuals create meaning through shared actions and mutual engagement, reflecting the interdependent nature of human thought processes.[27] A key example of this premise is demonstrated in dance-making praxis, where the choreographer has strong, interdependent artistic relationships with movement collaborators (see Chapter 8 for a case study of somatic dance-making) and creating a dance is a mind-building exercise for all parties. This notion is central to the enactive approach, as it emphasizes the inherent connection between humans and their world. Sense-making is not a passive reception of information, but an active, embodied engagement deeply rooted in our autonomy and evolution. For enactivists, cognition is not about representing an external world but creating a reality through actions and perceptions.

In the context of social interactions, sense-making takes on a participatory dimension, where individuals engage in a shared process of meaning generation. This "participatory sense-making" involves group regulation of actions and intentions, leading to the emergence of novel, mutually constructed domains of meaning that are not reducible to individual cognitions.[28] Social contexts, such as group movement experiences, musical ensembles, or teacher-student relationships, exhibit participatory sense-making, as individuals who engage in these activities often partake in a shared process of meaning generation. This perspective highlights the intersubjectivity of human cognition, suggesting that our understanding of the world is deeply shaped by our embodied, affective, and cultural engagements with others, also a pillar of the OPTIMAL theory of motor learning presented later in this chapter.

Empirical support for participatory sense-making can be found in studies of social coordination dynamics, a framework which examines how people create and extinguish bonds with each other. For instance, consider research on the "perceptual crossing paradigm," a virtual reality experiment designed to study how people recognize others through online interactions. These experiments have shown the mutual regulation of actions in a virtual environment can give rise to co-created meanings and the recognition of social contingencies (reactions to others' behaviors), even in the absence of complex linguistic or cognitive abilities.[29] Furthermore, the enactive notion of sense-making is tied to the concept of autonomy (also a tenet of the OPTIMAL theory). For an individual to maintain their identity and successful existence, they must continually manage their interactions with the environment, further defining sense-making as a process that supports stability; certain interactions are seen as beneficial to one's autonomy, and others are detrimental.[30] This aspect of sense-making highlights continuity between life and the bodymind, suggesting that cognition is not just a neutral process, but a meaningful activity rooted in maintaining human viability.

The enactive approach to cognition has important implications for our understanding of learning and development for movement artists. By emphasizing the role of active exploration and sense-making in cognitive processes, enactivism questions established views of learning as the passive acquisition of knowledge. Rather, it suggests that learning is an embodied and interactive process in which individuals construct meaning through their ongoing engagement with the world and others. This is not dissimilar from observations made in the conclusion of Chapter 2 regarding the critical nature of effortful, engaged learning. So, the enactive understanding of sense-making, particularly in its participatory and autonomy-preserving dimensions, offers an intelligent framework for understanding the embodied, interactive, and meaningful nature of cognition. By grounding cognitive processes in the dynamic between the bodymind and environment, and by emphasizing the mutually created nature of social understanding, enactive models expand conventional views of the mind, opening new avenues for investigating the complex dynamics of human cognition and intersubjectivity.

To summarize, the 4E cognition framework offers a rich set of ideas that can be applied to a wide range of movement and artistic praxis, including education, therapy, and performance. By grounding cognition in the embodied, embedded, and interactive dimensions of human experience, this framework provides an ecologically valid and individual-oriented foundation for designing learning environments, therapeutic interventions, and technologies that support artistic development and well-being.

More specifically in the domain of dance and music education, the 4E perspective highlights the importance of designing practice environments that provide opportunities for hands-on exploration, social interaction, and co-construction of meaning. This might involve the use of movement and music improvisation, collaborative projects, and specific learning experiences that allow learners to engage artistically in authentic, real-world contexts, as well as maintain agency over their own actions—all part of the SomaLab framework.

The 4E approach may also have important implications for dance and music therapy, particularly in the context of mental health and well-being. By emphasizing the role of embodiment and social interaction in the constitution of cognitive and affective processes, the 4E framework suggests that therapeutic interventions should target not only the individual's internal mental states but also their embodied and interpersonal dynamics. This might involve the use of body-oriented therapies, such as dance/movement therapy or music therapy, which aim to promote healing and self-management through the exploration of bodily sensations, movements, and expressive qualities.

In the realm of movement and the performing arts, the 4E perspective offers a framework for understanding the complex, dynamic nature of artistic cognition and creativity. By highlighting the role of the body, the environment, and social interaction in informing cognitive processes, 4E advocates for a view of performance as not merely a matter of executing pre-determined plans or expressing inner mental states. Rather, it is an emergent, interactive process that arises from the real-time, adaptive interplay between the performer, the artistic material, and the audience. This view has important implications for the design of performance technologies, such as interactive sound and light systems, as well as for the development of improvisational and collaborative performance activities.

As we look to the future of movement and performing arts studies, the 4E cognition framework offers a promising avenue for further research and exploration. By continuing to investigate the complex, multiscale dynamics of embodied, embedded, extended, and enactive cognition in artistic contexts, we can deepen our understanding of the nature of the expressive bodymind and its place in the world. This understanding, in turn, can help us to develop new theories, practices, and technologies more attuned to the richness and diversity of the human artistic experience. Next, we'll examine dynamical systems theory, a related theory of human learning, performance, and living, which also has great potential for expanding our understanding of the complexities of human behavior.

Dynamical Systems Theory (DST) and Movement Behavior

Over the past few decades, dynamical systems theory (DST) has strongly influenced human movement scientists studying motor learning, control, and development.[31] Borrowed from mathematics, DST can be described as a quantifiable measure of synchronization patterns between and within a system over time. Here, the patterns are dynamic, either coalescing or exhibiting variability.[32] While more traditional models of skill acquisition seek to limit fluctuations in performance, DST considers constant change necessary for the healthy function of an individual. As constraints appear within an environment, movers respond with a task-specific approach, arrived at through a complex interaction of knowledge, input, and status.[33] When a movement problem is presented, the system needs to remain flexible and open to react to variations in incoming information. DST's emphasis on interactivity with the environment and variable response to stimuli offers an important contribution to the theoretical scaffolding we're building; the SomaLab framework that comprises Part 2 focuses on developing a nervous system responsive in the moment and not reliant solely on rote learning. Scholars have previously recognized this connection, for example, Batson adeptly highlights the importance of dynamical systems in the work of Feldenkrais, and related principles in Rolfing, Alexander Technique, and Energy Medicine.[34]

Newell and Vaillancourt propose that environmental constraints play a key role in the dynamic organization of motor responses, and interact with the individual, the task at hand, incoming perceptual information, and a representation of the proposed action to influence activity following a stimulus.[35] This model centers constraints, including changes in the environment and incoming information, as opposed to the individual's existing memory framework. In effect, like 4E cognition, it is a shift from putting the individual and their cognitive/memory structures at the center of the motor behavior and making them more of a complicit player within systems of action and performance. The flexible and dynamic human organism is constantly alert, with all systems in play, in meeting the goals of the central command, and adapting movement plans to match pre-determined intention.

Davids et al. point out that both the stability provided by human beings, and the environmental changes that require flexibility are necessary for optimal outcome, providing a contemporary context in which to view integrated movement behavior.[36] This idea provides space for the coexistence of both established linear learning paradigms and newer DST models. In other words, motor learning and performance require both for the most successful outcome, given a specific movement intention. Furthermore, the authors state, "In sport, compensatory variability can be observed in performers who are skillful at exploiting the high dimensionality offered by the many motor system DOF (degrees of freedom)."[37] This is an important statement, and one that supports the SomaLab construct, which lays the foundation for a practice that centers flexibility, as opposed to stability and habit. A SomaLab session is designed to identify numerous possibilities and encourages choice in movement outcomes. In other words, developing fluctuation in performance is a good thing, a goal even, as movers gain the ability to respond variably, and successfully, to environmental cues in a given moment. Instead of practicing a particular skill to form habit and patterned movement, *process* becomes the basis for praxis.

Smith and Thelen also reframe the idea of variability in their work regarding human development and dynamical systems, explaining, "systems can generate novelty through their own activity."[38] Often seen as a negative in behavioral research within a typical laboratory setting, they propose methodologies that track performance in similar contexts over time, and search for a more long-term kind of stability, or patterns in process and approach. Indeed, they see flexibility in responses as a "blessing" rather than a "scourge." Additionally, in accordance with Davids et al., they cite evidence for differences in variable outcomes between practiced and novice performers in laboratory settings. For example, in studying the dynamic nature of learning, Yan and Fisher presented adult subjects with the tasks of learning a new computer program.[39] They found that during initial learning, or "skill construction," performers exhibited a large degree of variation in output and final performance was dependent upon many factors, such as task complexity, previous experience, and personal affinities regarding computer skills. In addressing the complicated nature of movement behavior, Smith and Thelen state that a dynamical systems approach assumes that development itself is a source of complexity, and interactions with the environment make it even more so.[40] Furthermore, complexity does not mean chaos; indeed, a bodymind can exhibit coordinated responses sans the existence of a central processor and can organize itself in accordance with environmental provisions: "self-organization means that no single element has causal priority."[41]

This affirmation of a non-centralized executive that governs human behavior is consistent with both DST and 4E cognition, and demonstrates an overarching approach to learning and performance, as well as an interest in accommodating the holism of the bodymind. The researchers use the example of infant crawling and walking as driven by self-organization. Crawling is described as a resultant behavior of a baby's current strength and coordination, coupled with a desire to locomote. For a period, crawling is a consistent pattern of movement and reflects a baby's biological state as well as intention and environmental constraints. As the baby becomes stronger and more coordinated, walking is a more efficient means by which to meet intentional goals. So, in a dynamic systems approach, a motor program as described in information processing models (see Chapter 2) doesn't exist, rather a child's means of locomotion is dependent upon the interaction of present circumstances.

The non-linear nature of dynamic models is furthermore described by Smith and Thelen as nested timescales, where learning is not identified by serial processes, but happens simultaneously, with other embedded occurrences.[42] Thus, neural change and development does not progress as a single entity, but in concert with other events such as biological growth or emotional maturity. It is difficult, then, to parse out single events by expanding individual and environmental constraints (controlled laboratory research); the totality of the changing and adaptable dynamic system must be considered.

In a study more specifically addressing dance and rhythmic movement, Miura et al. offer a review of literature that focuses on interpretation of results through common theoretical frameworks, and prioritizes movements that require synchronization with music, or movers to coordinate bodily movements with other movers.[43] They point out the complexity and importance of dance and motor control research, as in this kind of synchronization, the human organism negotiates a tremendous number of degrees of freedom, including all the different ways the human body can move as well as environmental input. Like Smith and Thelen, they conclude that change from novice to skilled behavior is not so much a result of continued invariable practice, but of the individual's reorganization of their own systems as their needs and experience change over time; even small shifts in behavior can reorient an entire system. Thus, artistic development, within a DST framework, results from an individual's ability to work independently of affinity patterns and expand movement responses to a complex array of possibilities. Other researchers' views may support this perspective, for example, Bernstein proposed early on that the ability to produce spontaneous solutions to movement problems is critical to ingenuity in human beings.[44] It does stand to reason that while adequate access to knowledge, memory, and experience is important, the ability to incorporate and produce in the moment is what deepens expertise. In essence, this is what drives humanity forward—the ability to utilize what's at hand, coupled with new perspectives of what is possible.

Delving more experientially into DST and dance-making, Hansen, Kaeja & Henderson apply system principles to the creation of a self-generating choreographic structure, via dramaturgical frameworks, to a live performance work, *Crave*.[45] In this case study, they describe their approach as allowing for variability within a set of constraints, realized through performance tasks and rules, and constructing an environment where both stability and volatility are possible. In their words:

> In a system many of the variables and parameters are accounted for and the system's boundaries are known, and yet it is open towards new choices and at times even new sources. While it initially attracts certain self-organizing patterns of interaction, over time this openness can thrust such patterns into turbulent transitions and produce unpredictable changes in behaviour.[46]

Their methodology equates performance tasks and rules as constraints, while situational variables are attributed to the individual lived experiences, affinities, and/or current states of the performers. For example, a new lived experience that occurs between performance "A" and performance "B" shifts the environment by introducing an additional source of interaction that influences outcome. Thus, the performer reorganizes their performance behavior in accordance with new input (information). In short, they experience something different, and the audience sees/hears/feels something different too.

We could apply this line of thinking to all live performance, as there is always some element of unpredictability; a baby crying in the audience, a head-cold brewing in a performer, technical elements that don't reproduce as rehearsed. Experienced performers of live art gain knowledge over time regarding how to respond to different situations and become more comfortable with different outcomes; the individual becomes "practiced" in such responses, and some even occur more than once, creating a memory/response loop. Framed within DST, each situation is a new environment with differing constraints and variables, where the individual must self-organize to respond to the circumstances at hand. This self-organization leads to growth in biological developmental, toward maturity and expertise.

Fluid performance conditions might also be viewed as contextual interference, as discussed in Chapter 2.[47] Differing settings force self-organization, leading to superior results over time, but less success during the reorganization period. And Limons and Shea showed that in laboratory tasks, providing more information to subjects hindered learning, a phenomenon they called "deficient processing."[48] Perhaps self-organization, as proposed in DST, creates situations that require sustained energy (more work), leading to growth and development. Indeed, it is the aim of this text to present differing perspectives, ideas, and theories that explain human behavior, and how they might work in concert, as

Figure 4.4. Adriane Fang, left, and Stevie Oakes navigate new environments, and cues from each other, on tour with Elizabeth Shea's *Last Good Thing* (author's collection; photograph © 2018 Yi-Chun Wu).

opposed to competing, with each other. Laboratory research, case study, and phenomenological information are all considered equal and relevant.

Creativity and Contemporary Systems

The investigation of creativity can assuredly provide fertile ground for contemplating learning, performance, and living in a way that accounts for the totality of the human experience. Colloquially, when we think about creativity, visions of extraordinary artists who make work beyond our own imaginations come to mind. More practically, we might consider "thinking outside the box" to be creative, especially in workplace situations. But we are all creative every day as we navigate an unpredictable world and devise solutions to obstacles that appear suddenly. Experience and knowledge cannot account for every action/reaction, every permutation and combination of events—so how do we do it?

The scientific literature regarding models of creativity largely consists of two camps—those that examine creative products, defined as artifacts that are novel and worthy, and creative processes, which is more engaged with the ways that individuals achieve creative thoughts and actions, although clearly there is overlap between the two approaches.[49] Indeed, scholars conclude that creativity takes on many forms, all happening simultaneously over given time periods, and are co-dependent on responses to specific contexts, producing variable outcomes. This brings us back to the idea of praxis—*how* do humans develop creative abilities? Can we become expert at producing divergent responses in the same way we become expert at, let's say, consistently hitting a golf ball—through practice?

The first part of this chapter presents a 4E approach to human expression as a contemporary theory of learning, performing, and living. To summarize, *embodied* reminds us that cognitive processes do not exist separately of the soma and *embedded* further elaborates the non-separation of perception and action systems. *Extended* expands the range of the mind past the physical body to include tools, instruments, or any learning/living aid that influences cognition. Finally, *enactive* provides a framework where human cognition is less centered on the body-mind in a vacuum, but extends to the environment, other people, with all elements informing the other. Clearly, 4E cognition and DST overlap in terms of decentering the individual as executive, and both offer important frameworks in which to view creative behavior, with 4E focusing on holistic, integrative factors such as social contexts, and DST providing an additional model for learning and information processing through continually shifting self-organization.

This overlap may provide insight into superior conditions for creativity and praxis. In fact, van der Schyff et al. suggest that further research based on a dual view of 4E cognition and DST can provide important information regarding what kind of environments best support creativity, more specifically in music performance and education.[50] Is there an optimal environment, or set of conditions, in which to "practice" being creative? And can creativity be developed, facilitated, in all individuals within a more general view of how we function in the world? These are exciting ideas in which to consider SomaLab structure and application.

Too, artists/scholars are actively pursuing these questions outside of the research laboratory. Purvis explores the idea of creativity and 4E cognition through a practice of immersive theatre, termed "in the wild," a performance situation which supports opportunities for problem-solving in the moment.[51] Working with high school students who focus their studies on art and technology, an assignment that integrates audiences into performances works to create new worlds at each iteration of the experience. This approach centers embodiment, or treating the integrated bodymind as a thinking instrument, one that responds wholly to situational change, and extends holistic thinking past the self. Introducing tasks in the dance studio or stage where success equals variable responses, and not rote repetition of codified skill, encourages embodied performance. Group collaborations in project design fulfill 4E's inclusion of embedded social structures, including the interactive audience. Finally, enacting recognizes the parallel nature of perception and action and embraces the interconnectedness of self and environment.

Creativity, in the lay world, is often referred to as "unlimited possibility." We (the authors) would like to offer in summary that, practically speaking, a balance exists between these innumerable options and a safe creative space. Too many choices can overwhelm both students and professional artists alike, causing states of inaction, or defaulting to previously learned responses. Carefully planned constraints that manage the environment are desirable at differing levels of experience; as the individual "practices" self-organization and gains confidence in their ability to act in the present moment, a sense of safety and success develops over time.

The Optimal Theory of Motor Learning

Another forward-thinking theory of movement learning that has gained popularity over the past several years among theorists and practitioners alike is the OPTIMAL (Optimizing Performance through Intrinsic

Motivation and Attention for Learning) theory of motor learning. Wulf and Lewthwaite propose that a body of evidence exists showing the importance of both internal (intrinsic) motivation and attention of the mover in successful performance, and more traditional information processing models do not account for "the social-cognitive—affective—motor nature of 'motor' behavior."[52] Discussing this model in the context of the ideas presented earlier in Part 1 and in the first part of this chapter brings us full circle, and supports the thesis that human behavior is complex, diverse, and dynamic.

A key tenet of the OPTIMAL theory is that we cannot examine various aspects of human behavior separately when constructing frameworks for learning and performance, as neuromotor and psychosocial influences are nested within each other. Here, motivation refers to a variety of internal states, influenced by social and cultural factors, mindsets, and "fundamental psychological needs." Interestingly, Wulf and Lewthwaite point out that the words "motivation" and "motor" have a common Latin root, *movere* (to move).[53] They highlight two aspects of motivation: "enhanced expectancies," or the chance of success in each situation, and "autonomy," or the idea that the individual is the key to achieving goals in a way that satisfies human psychosocial exigencies. This thesis aligns with the enaction component of 4E cognition, where autonomy is important to sense-making, necessary for human stability and viability. Furthermore, expectancies are embedded within memories and lived experiences, so predictions of what may happen are not just based on present circumstances, but past outcomes. For example, let's say you're attempting a new yoga pose, Crow Pose, which requires balancing the knees on the triceps while the arms are flexed at a 90-degree angle. Physically, this pose requires coordination, strength, and flexibility. If you have been successful most of the time when attempting new poses, you have an increased expectation of success and happily engage in the process. If you struggle with new body positions, you might be more primed for failure and expend less energy and effort with the attempt. The social context of your efforts will also affect performance; if you're practicing in a group situation, you may be more aware of the judgements of others, and if you're alone you may lack motivation to expand bodymind knowledge. And of course, expectancy combined with social context yields an exponential combination of possible results. The term "self-efficacy" is used in the sport psychology literature to refer to the degree of confidence of an individual's capabilities in performance situations.[54] Wulf and Lewthwaite report that factors that influence self-efficacy include both positive feedback (how well one is doing) and social-comparative feedback (how well one is doing in relation to others), as well as perceived task difficulty, overall ability, and overall affect.[55] The authors further propose that increased positive affect may be tied to increased dopamine production.[56] Remember from Chapter 3 that dopamine is a neurotransmitter involved in reward, motivation, attention, and learning, demonstrating the cyclical relationship between environment, bodymind, and action.

Furthermore, the OPTIMAL theory posits that when an individual experiences a sense of control over their environment (autonomy), performance becomes more successful. It's interesting to consider this aspect of the model within a context of 4E cognition theory and DST. All three frameworks emphasize the importance of the environment, in that learning and performance cannot be considered independently of circumstance outside of the bodymind, with 4E specifically tying enaction to autonomy. OPTIMAL however, emphasizes the psychosocial ramifications of such interactions and positive or negative outcomes of attempts.

Shifting now to the second main tenet of the OPTIMAL theory, recall that in Chapter 2, attention was presented as an element of study within the field of movement learning (attention is also important in Part 2 of this text). Described as "a spotlight across the visual field, and the spotlight enhances the efficiency of detection of events within its beam," attention is largely studied in the field of motor learning and control as a resource in terms of performance, and one that can be magnified or divided. Wulf and Lewthwaite summarize that external focus (attention outside of body parts, including imagery of the intended outcome) has been shown in laboratory research to have a more positive effect on movement outcome than internal focus (what a body part is doing): "An external focus of attention seems to be a precondition for optimal motor performance."[57]

Let's revisit learning Crow Pose with this attentional application. If you focus on the deformation your hands make in the mat or use the image of the torso hovering parallel to the floor, supported by breath, you have a better chance of achieving the pose than if you attend to the angle of the elbows, or the curve of the back. Or perhaps you imagine your back lined up with a beam of light from the window, as opposed to shifting your shoulders forward. This approach has tremendous implications for cueing, which is standard in many forms of movement pedagogy, and imaging, used largely in the movement arts, but perhaps less so in other performance endeavors. As the use of imagery, visualization, and mental practice plays a primary role in SomaLab tools and tasks, this support for external focus lends credence to the framework.

One investigator put theory into practice, utilizing the OPTIMAL theory as a basis for teaching classical dance techniques to second-year conservatory students.[58] Recognizing the traditional, and authoritarian approach still utilized in the instruction of many codified forms, Knapp was interested in "the need for individuated learning practices which promote and highlight individual uniqueness, dynamic collaboration within the classroom, as well as between teacher and student."[59] As a point of interest here, Chapter 7 outlines SomaLab methodology for incorporating somatic-based constructs into groups, including students learning codified forms.

Employing an action research approach, a pedagogical tool where the researcher simultaneously investigates a problem as they seek to solve it,[60] Knapp applied various treatment modalities to classroom teaching. These treatments were designed to encourage holistic learning as described in the OPTIMAL theory, for example, students were asked to perform a simple dance movement using an external focus cue or image and given autonomy when choosing a degree of difficulty (i.e., a single or double turn). Positive feedback and enhanced expectancies also played an important role in the OPTIMAL approach to learning classical dance. A variety of data collection techniques were used, including, but not limited to, observation grids, photographs and videotape of student performance, and questionnaires to gain knowledge regarding changes in student learning and states of being over time.

Data Collection Instrument	Objectives
• Logbook	• Introduction to OPTIMAL Theory (OT) through a given lesson • Development of the use of OT in teaching a given unit • Promotion of students' autonomy • Application of OT during an extracurricular context
• Photographic images/video recordings	• Definition of technical and artistic deficiencies • Promotion of quality in movement execution through an external focus • Recording of a student performance with structured observation grids
• Structured observation grids	• Determination of the current level of motivation and self-assessment of current learning progress • Promotion of students' autonomy and motivation

Figure 4.5. Knapp, using an action research model, utilized logbooks, photographic images and video recordings, and structured observation grids to record data based on specific objectives in their 2022 study (author's creation).

Following phase-based data analysis, the author concluded that utilizing the three pillars of OPTIMAL theory in classical dance training led to improvements in student performance, as demonstrated by both motor and psychological measures. Thus, dance educators should consider movement training holistically, and in the context of the developing individual; self-knowledge allows the learner to create autonomy over their own actions. Finally, Knapp notes that the OPTIMAL theory and applied teaching methodologies promote safe and healthy atmospheres for learning, where language is important in student performance outcomes (see Chapter 9 for more thoughts on teaching and language).[61]

As this discussion of Wulf and Lewthwaite's OPTIMAL theory of motor learning concludes, it's important to note that while the authors' arguments for holistic human action are broader and more inclusive of psychosocial function than established information processing models, the theory is still deeply rooted in the widely accepted principles of the motor learning and control literature, where the individual as executor is the primary focus.[62]

Conclusion

All three of the theoretical models put forth in this chapter, 4E cognition, dynamical systems theory, and the OPTIMAL theory of motor learning, have one unifying element: they all seek to contextualize human behavior as nested and inextricable from the physical body as an instrument. In other words, individual lived experiences must be considered in learning, performance, and living. Interactions with the environment also play key roles, albeit in different ways and to different degrees, in determining outcomes of human action. In recognizing that learning, performance, and living require an understanding of complex workings and innumerable environmental, social, and cultural conditions, these theories acknowledge the contemporary nature of a quickly changing world, one where new generations of movement artists value individual agency, autonomy, health, and safety. It is with an understanding of the unique mosaic of circumstances that affect how we learn and move in the world, that we segue to Part 2, and employ our theoretical knowledge regarding human movement behavior in practice via a framework for deepening efficiency in learning and expression in performance: SomaLab.

Part 2

SomaLab:
Efficiency in Learning; Expression in Performance

5

What Is SomaLab?

"When I walk into [the studio] I am alone, but I am alone with my body, ambition, ideas, passions, needs, memories, goals, prejudices, distractions, fears."—Twyla Tharp[1]

Introduction

Tharp's reflection on art making, and her deep intuition regarding the bodymind, pointedly speaks to the essence of this text: we exist in this world holistically and are the sum of our physical instruments, our environments, and our lived experiences. The art we make and how we practice it are unique to each being; how each of us moves, thinks, feels, and creates is singular in the universe.

Part 1 of this book presents a historical and theoretical framework for examining various approaches to mind/body theories by scholars from many disciplines and schools of thought, all of whom study the behavior and existence of the totality of the bodymind. Origins of and arguments for somatic practices in Part 1 are based on contemporary research in cognitive psychology and kinesiology, including motor learning paradigms, theories of embodied cognition, neural plasticity, and dynamical systems. Part 1 focuses on movement learning and performance, with the understanding that mental and physical processes are neither separate nor separable. No more credence is given to work performed by artist/scholars in controlled laboratory conditions than to artist/scholars whose work is more phenomenologically based and relies on first-person experience. Indeed, systems of human behavior and performance are complex, multiplicative—it would only stand to reason that no one theory alone could responsibly account for all human behavior. Research in the social and psychological sciences often revolves around simple laboratory tasks that have limited real-world relevance; nonetheless, this work does not require that we pit somatic and embodied approaches against more traditional motor learning theories. Perhaps each has its place in the development of learning and performance in the movement arts. For example, are there times in the learning process where declarative knowledge is useful? Most certainly. And can explicit instructions impede intrinsic learning? Also, undoubtedly so. It's useful to remember that many scientific truths began as one person's seemingly unrealistic idea that pushed against firmly held beliefs of their time (for example, Einstein's theory of relativity).

The work of artists/scholars who have invested their lives studying human behavior provides context for the practical application of work in somatics with the hope that a deeper understanding of one's own set of values regarding the bodymind instrument will emerge. When modern dance pioneer Martha Graham observed "movement never lies,"[2] she perhaps understood the fundamental truth inherent in movement, as well as the completeness of communication the bodymind can offer.

SomaLab

Today's dancers and movement artists are asked to interpret, and subsequently reproduce, a wide variety of movement styles. College curriculums are broadening, incorporating non-western dance forms alongside or replacing the traditional western canon; commercial approaches, long excluded from academic programs, are emerging; supporting movement studies such as yoga, aerial dance, and marital arts are encouraged. Screendance and the dominance of social media bring new movement ideas to viewers daily, opening the bodymind to limitless possibilities. Young artists are less concerned with the maker/company model historically associated with concert dance and are more focused on their own individual experiences and dance values. The sheer volume of genre and form may seem daunting to both emerging and experienced artists, and serial learning feels quite impossible. Likewise, expressive capabilities are muted without serious practice of the bodymind, where an individual's existence and empathy toward others' lived experiences inform their artistry. Therefore, a more holistic approach focused on developing a flexible psychomotor system seems important to explore the wide range of movement approaches available to movers in the 21st century. SomaLab is a collection of experiences that facilitates dance and movement by deepening the practitioner's bodymind connection. This approach is designed to increase the flexibility of the nervous system and promote efficiency in learning as well as expressiveness in practice and performance.

As discussed in Chapter 1, many somatic systems focus on re-patterning or replacing an unwanted or unhealthy habit with a new, more ergonomically aligned movement. SomaLab works toward "non-patterning," or the idea that habits and patterns are not the goal; rather, the result is a process where movers can become experienced and sensitive to internal and external cues. By training the system, and not specific movement patterns, movers can work toward a larger repertory of movement capabilities and an increase in expressive range. Think of it as the difference between memorizing words on a page and learning a process that allows you to read them. Or honing the bodymind by seeking practice in supporting forms outside of movement arts such as strength training or meditation. The end goal is to enable an immediate embodied understanding of a concept (conceptualization, as defined in Chapter 4) as expressed through movement. SomaLab is a supporting practice that can complement more formal study of genre, and aids artists in reaching their fullest potential as they move between and within various areas of interest.

SomaLab is not a system or codified set of activities; it is a framework for movers that allows flexibility in designing tasks that are appropriate for diverse populations and centers their own personal experiences and knowledges in the dance and movement space. There are eight tools that comprise the framework, each of which will be discussed in depth later in this chapter: breath; imagery, visualization, and mental practice; intention/attention; self-guided/intuitive movement; physical awareness (kinesthesia); embodiment in action; movement empathy; and reflection/incorporation (see Figure 5.1).

The framework is and continues to be informed by both scientific concepts and first-person experiences. Integral to this system is a dual adaptation paradigm, which employs both implicit and explicit learning mechanisms. In other words, skills are acquired both consciously (explicitly) and tacitly (implicitly). The dual adaptation paradigm implies that both information processing and dynamical systems theory are at play during learning and performance.[3]

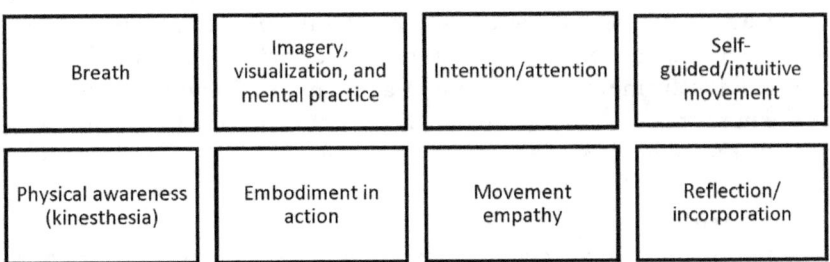

Figure 5.1. The SomaLab framework consists of eight tools that guide task choice and create an individualized practice (author's creation).

In addition to SomaLab's psychomotor applications, there are social and cultural considerations to employing systems that account for differences in movement studies and don't rely solely on specific patterns. A key tenet of this system is movement empathy, that is, understanding another person's perspective through observation of movement patterns, even if they are outside of your own habits and cultural immersion. Providing opportunities for movers to engage in experiences which blur the line between genre, and even create new, hybrid movement forms, allows practitioners to take ownership of their choices,[4] and widens the environment for a plurality of movement experiences, encouraging inclusiveness in practice and performance. The development of a first-person experience of movement praxis, either self-led or conducted by a facilitator, is invaluable to deepening the sense of self, autonomy, and individuality as a movement artist.

A Framework for Efficiency and Expression

Recall from Chapter 1 that Brodie and Lobel identify four principles of training (breath, sensing, connectivity, and initiation) that are found across most somatic systems.[5] The framework for SomaLab embraces these broad concepts while utilizing a system of tools and tasks that all work toward building the bodymind. This chapter focuses more generally on the tools that constitute the practice, while Chapter 6 presents specific tasks and practice formats for the reader (some tools are also tasks). Tools are defined as the eight broad categories that form the SomaLab framework, and from which specific actions, or tasks, can be built. Understanding how the tools work informs task choice for praxis. Tasks are defined as smaller units of specific activities created to fulfill the work of the tools. The scientific principles that inform these tools are outlined in Part 1; here, they are summarized and discussed with reference to their use in somatic work. I also introduce tools utilized in some form in codified movement practices (i.e., yoga, dance), with special regard to their place in the SomaLab system. Each framework component additionally includes first-person experiences that facilitate viewing theoretical and practical approaches through a common lens.

1. **Breath**

Breath is our lifeforce; its cyclical nature serves as a metaphor for human existence. When we inhale, we take in nourishment, and when we exhale, we send out waste and materials that are no longer useful to us. Each SomaLab session begins and ends with careful attention to breath;

5. What Is SomaLab?

indeed, the entire practice is informed by breathwork, or *pranayama* (from Sanskrit, *prana*, meaning "breath of life"; *ayama*, meaning "to stretch, extend").

Attention to conscious breathing was first introduced by Brahman priests, who discovered that controlled breathing influenced states of consciousness. *Pranayama* is integral to the ancient practice of yoga, which has four goals: regeneration or health, and the end of suffering; skillful action; integration or self-knowledge; and liberation.[6] The goals of yoga are markedly like that of many other somatic practices, forging pathways to embodiment. Indeed, consider the very embodiment of breath—we sigh when we are bored, yawn when we are tired, breathe quicker when we're excited, slower when we're at peace. This physical connection to emotion and thought is as embodied as language itself, another key system where movement influences the symbols we choose to express our states of being. And recall from Chapter 3 that the results of research studying meditative practices demonstrated structural change in the nervous system following breath praxis.

In all physical endeavors, the relationship between breath and movement initiation is key. In somatic work, it is especially so: "movement rides on the flow of breath."[7] Finding the very beginning of each movement, and traveling to the very end, can be linked with a conscious breath process. This filling and emptying drives the movement and forges symbiosis between the body's biomechanics and the laws of physics. Indeed, an entire wing of modern dance techniques, specifically the work of Doris Humphrey, pictured in Figure 5.2, and her protégé José Limón, who also inspired contemporary release techniques, have been built on this principle. Romita and Romita remind us, "breath is both autonomic and muscularly controlled."[8] Practice and attention to breath creates healthy habits by training the diaphragm and intercostal muscles, providing the functional basis for expressivity in movement.

I've witnessed the transformative power of movement-fueled breath in countless movers and performing artists. As a teacher of yoga in the community, participants new to the practice often arrive to the space unaware of the impact conscious breathwork can have on both the practice itself, and on everyday living. For centuries, western society has prioritized the work and talents of the mind over that of the body; thought takes precedence over movement, and the breath is an afterthought. First, we think, speak, or write, then we move. We've seen in Part 1 that this is a simplistic approach to human behavior, and theories of embodied and 4E cognition suggest that movement is key to language development. The very first step in uniting what nature provided, but humans pulled apart, is attention to breath; we can begin to move from thinking to feeling and prioritize the somatic experience. In essence, breath is the first gateway to holistic bodymind experiences. Conscious attention narrows mental processes, while the movement of the lungs draws attention to the soma. In *Meditations from the Mat*, Rolf Gates writes:

> Standing at the crossroads between asana and the purely contemplative aspects of the eight-limb path, *pranayama* encompasses both the physical and the contemplative. The science of yogic breathing trains the mind in one-pointed concentration while radically improving our ability to accrue, store, regulate, and use the energy we receive from the air we breathe. Utilizing physical technique, we begin our journey into the metaphysical.[9]

In the movement studio, drawing attention to the breath works very much in the same way. Many performing artists and movement practitioners spend decades honing codified technique; the attention to form can be extreme. Learning often comes through visual feedback, and kinesthesia develops based on repetition, creating finely ingrained habits. Muscles move the bones, sometimes inefficiently, requiring great physical exertion, which can result in injurious action upon joints and soft tissue. So, learning to use conscious breath can serve two functions here: first, to embrace a more somatic-informed movement practice, and second, to use the breath to take advantage of the body's natural biomechanics and response to gravity. This is especially true when a body moves through

Figure 5.2. Modern dance pioneer Doris Humphrey dances outside, in her choreographic work *New Dance*. Breath was foundational in creating her unique approach to moving (Jerome Robbins Dance Division, The New York Public Library. "Doris Humphrey [outdoors] in "New Dance," New York Public Library Digital Collections. Accessed February 14, 2025. https://digitalcollections.nypl.org/items/68273aec-b813-cf85-e040-e00a18061c89).

space, and significant physical effort is required to keep it in motion. Using breath to propel the body can aid in efficiency of movement and discourage "over-efforting."

There are artistic considerations, as well, to increased attention to the breath. When breath brings us closer to somatic experiences, the full capability of our human expression is realized. Whether sliding into a character, or stripping down to the authentic self, accessing deep and meaningful truths that are communicated through the body necessitates somatic experience and skill. Breath practice is an important tool in realizing the full manifestation of the mind/body relationship, one that is easily accessible and, like all tools in the framework, is inherent within us.

2. *Imagery, visualization, and mental practice*

As noted in Chapter 1, Mabel Todd introduced the idea of using imagery to change physical behavior in *The Thinking Body*; she conceived the practice of ideokinesis, which was later developed and codified by Dr. Lulu Sweigard.[10] Imaging techniques are a critical component of somatic experiences, as we all experience the world differently; our own unique bodies, minds, identities, and emotional tendencies play a primary role in our cognition and perception. Indeed, "meaning making,"[11] first discussed in Chapter 4, is a key tenet of SomaLab; specifically, uniting our remembered experiences while moving, and expanding our repertory through observations of other's behaviors, or even what we might imagine them to be. So, we can begin to make sense of the world by replaying our lived experiences and broadening our knowing through imagery.

It's important to clarify at the outset that visualization and mental practice are two separate cognitive endeavors. They both involve "seeing" a physical task being performed in "the mind's eye," and a person or object moving in time without an actual physical response on the part of the practitioner. Both are used extensively in SomaLab tasks. Visualization refers to a kind of imagery that may or may not exist in the physical world, for example, one's body growing roots into the ground, or floating above the earth. Movers may be asked to visualize dust being swept into a pan, slow it down, and put it under a microscope. The goal here is to broaden an individual's repertory beyond their own direct, physical experiences, and prime the nervous system for accepting novel sensory information. Mental practice on the other hand, is more focused on sequencing, seeing one discrete movement being performed after another, either for the purpose of memorizing a sequence or to encourage optimal performance. In somatic work, this is not generally some easily measured physical phenomena (i.e., leg height or speed of movement) but more of an embodied success on the part of the artist.

Visualization in SomaLab encourages movers to see themselves performing a task exactly as they want to experience it, even if they have never done it before. It even encourages visualizing movement as a non-human or non-living object, like a leaf being blown in the wind. How would that feel? What would it look like to some else?

Through my own lived experiences as a teacher/facilitator of dance I've observed how profoundly visualization tools can deepen and expand movement practice. These anecdotal observations led me to engage in a series of unpublished action research projects. For example, early in my teaching career, I was often presented with groups of movers who came from diverse backgrounds and life experiences; I became interested in developing pedagogical tools to meet students where they were, encouraging growth and development in the most efficient and meaningful way possible. Providing optimal guidance to each learner was at the forefront, regardless of their prior training, and it was clear that a "one-size-fits all" teaching style would only reach some. I began work on a method for assessing and centering individual differences based on past movement and related experiences, which can greatly affect how someone learns, particularly in the context of meaning making. The result was the Individual Movement Inventory (IMI), (Figure 5.3) a survey instrument that can be used in furthering a practitioner's understanding of how prior knowledge pertains to their learning and performance of movement arts. The tool focuses on drawing connections between previous study and new concepts, facilitating transfer between similar motor skills and experiences.

Individual Movement Inventory
Please include self-taught or self-guided experiences

A. **Movement Experiences**
   1. *All genres of dance training*
   2. *Experience with yoga, Pilates, martial arts, or other related forms*
   3. *Training or experiences with somatic practices*
   4. *Formal experiences with sports and athletics*
   5. *Recreational activities that are movement-based*

B. **Skilled Activities**
   1. *Training in music, or musical instruments*
   2. *Other specific training in motor skill activities like juggling, painting, woodworking, etc.*

C. **Related Art Forms**
   1. *Specific training in artistic genres other than dance*

D. **Personal preferences**
  1. *Hobbies or recreational activities that play a large part in your daily life*
  2. *Any other information that is pertinent to assembling an individual movement inventory*

Figure 5.3. The Individual Movement Inventory allows leaders to gain deeper insights into learners' repertory of lived experiences, and facilitates their own deepening of self-knowledge, affinities, and cognitive approaches (author's creation).

Hypothetically, let's say a movement learner reported in the IMI that they were on the diving team in high school. A leader might have observed their ease with moving into vertical space, as well as their struggle in broadening the body and discovering core-distal connection. The learner may also feel challenged with moving fully into their kinesphere. Visualization can, in this case, be used to expand the repertory of movement possibilities prior to physical praxis. The leader might suggest a process uniting prior knowledge with new goals, like imagining their body is sideways as they propel themselves forward, then seeing mental images of their bodymind performing a novel movement into the horizontal space. After visualizing and preparing the nervous system, the learner may feel more comfortable with new material, thereby facilitating physical practice.

I've used this tool successfully in many teaching and leading situations and have also presented the IMI methodology to colleagues at various workshops and conferences. In addition to facilitating learning and performance, this kind of individualized approach allows learners to feel seen, and their prior movement experiences valued, even if they are not dance or movement arts based. The union of mental and physical processes, as well an acknowledgment of the whole person, is fundamental to the SomaLab framework.

There is also ample empirical data to support the use of imagery-related practices to enrich movement experiences. Batson and Wilson state, "More than a third of a century of scientific evidence from imaging studies now supports the use of mental practice for neuromuscular re-education."[12] The use of these practices supports neural activation, albeit not with the same robustness as actual movement. Indeed, Sweigard presented the use of imagery through Ideokinesis to prime the neuromuscular system, not take the place of performing the task itself.[13] However, introducing imagery, visualization, and mental practice into somatic work can greatly inform the bodymind's knowledge, and contribute heavily to developing deep and meaningful movement experiences that draw artists closer to their expressive goals.

3. *Intention/attention*

In somatic work, intention precedes attention: what does the mover wish to experience today, and how will the process enrich efficiency and expression? Attention is the tool necessary to guide the practice and begins with the first conscious pairing of breath and movement.

Intention means making choices, and attention is ministering to those choices. What are you aiming to feel? What movement qualities do you want to exhibit? Every time we change our intention or thought, our bodies change in response to and/or in preparation to accomplish the action.[14] In other words, if you think about something a little differently, you will produce an observable change in performance.

As we noted in Chapter 2, attention in performance can be examined and defined in many ways and comprises several sub-categories, approaches, and theories. Attention can be regarded as conscious behavior (controlled, as opposed to automatic processing) and the amount of mental effort required to attend to such behaviors.[15] Recall that William James defined attention in 1890 as "…the taking possession by the mind, in clear and vivid form, of one out of what seem several simultaneously possible objects or trains of thought. Focalization, concentration of consciousness are of its essence. It implies withdrawal from some things to deal effectively with others."[16] Here, attention enhances the efficiency of conscious work on one task. Recall too that much of the investigation into how attention works in motor behavior has focused on attention as a resource, and what happens when it is divided or distracted. The result of this research indeed suggests that we can attend to more than one task at the same time, however, the closeness or relationship between the originating resources affects the capacity to attend to each. This "multiple resources" theory of attention postulates that differing neurological structures and spaces are designed to handle particular kinds of processing and action.[17]

We also know from Chapter 4 that attention is an integral part of the OPTIMAL theory of motor learning. Wulf and Lewthwaite cite evidence that external focus has a more positive effect on movement outcome than internal focus, concluding that the former is critical to successful performance.[18] Here, optimal motor performance is reached through focused attention outside of the body.

In the SomaLab framework, conscious attention is a necessary tool for practicing sensing and feeling. Carefully attending to sensation during movement exploration allows the artist to make discrete changes in patterns on a second-by-second basis, an ultra-fine-tuning of sorts. It encourages the practitioner to seek experiences beyond habit and what is known. For example, it may take some time to focus when first participating in a group movement experience, like a yoga class. You may find the breath sounds of others near you distracting and want to use visual information to see what your classmates are doing. After time and practice, however, you can selectively attend to your own experience and largely disregard the praxis of others.

The ideas of intention and attention are important in bodymind practices. There is a goal to the work, something practitioners are striving to achieve, and attention is a critical element of a successful somatic event. Indeed, practice is a key word here, and expanding the range of practice—staying broad as opposed to narrow, conscious as opposed to automatic—in time develops process, as opposed to singular movements or habits. While intention and attention are two different things, they are also closely intertwined, working most efficiently in concert. Attention as a tool is integral to the SomaLab practice as one works toward openness and readiness of the bodymind to respond to the environment, informed by experience and supported by imagination.

4. *Self-guided/intuitive movement*

In their seminal text exploring methods of improvisation, *The Moment of Movement*, Blom and Chaplin write:

> Artists often speak of trusting their intuition to guide them, or even more radically of becoming a channel through which the vast creative forces of the universe can speak. The creative act thus takes on a life of its own. By becoming the instrument rather than the master, we gain access to broader realms. The impulses spew and spiral at will, seemingly of their own accord.[19]

This view of self-guided, or intuitive, movement as something tacit that uncovers hidden knowledge and truths is essential for movers as they work toward a process-driven practice. Providing opportunity for the physical manifestation of a conceptual prompt, without conscious decision-making, allows the practitioner to find what feels true in their own bodyminds. Within a meaning making model, responses will be informed by lived experiences. This is not to imply that the work relies on automation; indeed, the mover is carefully observant of their free flow of movement during improvisational work in a SomaLab practice. Eventually, the mover makes choices and seeks affinities to specific movements to deepen their insight into their own knowledge base and degree of understanding. While the movement flows, the dancer attends to (both implicit and explicit processes at work here) and observes it. Later, in a group setting, practitioners may have the opportunity to observe others' implied knowledge, with the goal of expanding their own realms of experience and discovering movement empathy. Language, thought, and movement are irrevocably linked, encouraging embodiment. This process is supported by the contemporary paradigms presented in Chapter 4, where holistic and interactive approaches to moving and performance are indicative of best practices.

I would like to note as we explore this element of the framework that I am using the terms self-guided movement, intuitive movement, and improvisation interchangeably. However, improvisation can refer in some contexts to a specific way of guiding and organizing dancers, and tasks, that is particular to the post-modern movement in 20th-century American dance. In this context, I am more interested in improvisation as defined by Blom and Chaplin as a tacit mechanism, almost metaphysical in nature, and one that allows for honesty and authenticity to emerge.[20]

Many movement artists embark on a pathway of somatic explorations following years of formal training, and bring habits, style, and tradition along on the journey. These patterns are undoubtedly part of an individual's working instrument but can be softened and diffused as approaches to movement become more process-based and conceptually considered. While movement artists work to cultivate less attachment to a particular way of moving, improvisational explorations can provide a sense of physical and emotional satisfaction and foster curiosity and creativity—again, the mover seeks fulfillment in the *process* as opposed to the product.

Often, movers who have spent many years developing form and goal-oriented movement habits ask the questions "how do I begin? And how do I let go?" In Chapter 2 we discuss interference, where previous or future learning affects current skill sets. Motor learning theorists have proposed a model of retroactive interference to explain the interference of new tasks when recalling older ones. However, in this context, the phenomenon of proactive interference (previously learned material interfering with acquiring new skills) more easily explains the discomfort in moving from codified practiced forms to more process-oriented activities where the goal is broad and conceptual, as opposed to narrow and specific.

These two modes of acquiring skill and performing—form-based and process-oriented activities—are quite different, although both support human expression through movement. When practicing form-based actions in a traditional learning situation where there are clear roles of teacher and student, performing specific movements in a manner dictated by the form itself, and relayed through the instruction of the teacher, is optimal. This aids each mover in acquiring the specific skill mandated by the form; here, there is little room for individual interpretation. In contrast, when practicing self-guided or intuitive movement, the goal is very different; indeed, the development of the process itself holds great importance. This is a main tenet of SomaLab: to practice a process that expands meaning making with every session, revealing deeper levels of embodied knowledge that inform the movement arts and everyday life.

Whether approached as a companion process to more traditional movement instruction, or as a stand-alone experience, the framework provides a foundation to explore, invent, and be present.

There are pedagogical considerations here regarding the simultaneous practice of process and product. If proactive interference is responsible for slowed or impaired learning of intuitive movement processes and approaches after significant time engaged in form-based instruction, it makes sense for learners to practice both together, simultaneously. This will, by design, create an environment of contextual interference (a practice condition addressed in Chapter 2), where learning each skill may be impaired temporarily. But we also know that this kind of learning situation creates long and lasting performance capabilities, and in time, the learner will feel comfortable in multiple movement situations. Additionally, while motor learning is defined as change that is relatively permanent, acquiring physical skills also takes time. So, introducing codified movement activities alongside self-guided and intuitive movement practice earlier in artistic education, even during a developmental critical period of learning, may provide optimal opportunity for full individual expression.

Figure 5.4. Movement therapist Jordyn Kahler finds an improvisational moment (author's collection; photograph by Stefanie Nemes).

5. *Physical awareness (kinesthesia)*

The processes of sensing, noticing, and perceiving play major roles in somatic-based movement systems. Gibbs goes so far to say that people do not perceive in periods of stasis but require movement for perception, thus linking all of sensing/perceiving to kinesthesia.[21] This view also discounts the idea that perception and action are separate activities, as put forth by information processing theorists, and is more congruent with 4E cognition and dynamical system approaches. Furthermore, it is the differentiation and distinctiveness of sensory information that feeds perception, as opposed to simply noticing sensations without additional cognitive processing.[22] This idea of distinguishing has close ties to the motor learning literature, as well as aligns to sense-making, critical to 4E cognition.[23]

In Chapter 2 we learn that sensation is both exteroceptive, or coming from outside the body, and interoceptive, or sensing from within—it is interoceptive information that is most applicable to this element of the SomaLab framework. Recall that vision has proprioceptive (interoceptive) properties, and provides data regarding the body in space, informing physical tasks like balance. The inner ear also provides proprioceptive information and is critical to supporting posture and maintaining balance in the human body—the vestibular apparatus detects head position as we work with and against gravitational forces. Repetitive turning or spinning can also tax these systems, where visual focus and sensory input lag behind that of the vestibular system. Any movement artist who has practiced formal or self-guided rotations in succession can attest to the disorientation caused by turning. Spotting, or focusing on one area of the mover's environment, often allows for re-orientation in the body, and gives visual systems a chance to catch up to inner ear mechanisms.

Additional receptors and structures in the body let us know what we're doing, and where, providing cues that indicate joint position, muscle tension, and spatial orientation. For example, cutaneous receptors, located on the skin, guide our sense of touch; human fingertips contain the largest number of these receptors. Many movement practices include touch and/or two bodies working as one, such as partnering in contact improvisation, and karate. Some pedagogical methodologies in the movement arts also utilize touch, such as assists in yoga by the instructor, or the positioning of a participant's body (all with permission) by a teacher in studio dance practice. In summary, form, function, safety, efficiency, and expression are all important aspects of practice and performance in the movement arts.

Kinesthesia is often referred to as the sense that allows us to know where our bodies are and what they are doing in the surrounding environment. As we move, we sense, perceive, and act, although not necessarily in this linear configuration, but simultaneously, and all the while making fine motor adjustments as feedback loops play over and over. SomaLab utilizes several approaches that draw information from the body, such as targeted muscular engagement, which amplifies proprioception from both small and large muscle groups. Other tasks guide the mover toward

5. What Is SomaLab?   125

Figure 5.5. An artist's vision of the joy of touch through a creative and social dance experience (illustration by Abby Jones).

"subtle engagement" of the musculoskeletal system, allowing natural body mechanics to achieve movement goals without over-bracing and tensing.

Body organization is also an important concept in proprioceptive practice, such as exploring postures which enhance spatial awareness and strengthen the mover's relationship to the environment. Placing focus on the organic and anatomically sound placement of the bones using techniques inspired by Ideokinesis and yoga not only provides safety but facilitates the flow of energy throughout the body and encourages an appreciation of the role of gravitational force in all movement practices. Embodying lines and curves found in the natural world, too, helps develop a highly evolved sense of the individual that feels linked to their environment; undeniably, our bodies share much in common with both traditional and fractal geometric shapes.[24] Heightened physical awareness can inform, develop, and strengthen the practitioner's understanding of human behavior, and is an important step in sense-making and meaning making.

6. *Embodiment in action*

The "embodiment premise" as presented by Raymond W. Gibbs, Jr., in *Embodiment and Cognitive Science* describes an approach to human behavior where cognition is tied to language-body connections. In other words, "people's subjective, felt experiences of their bodies in action provide part of the fundamental grounding for language and thought," and movement is central to the mind/body relationship.[25] Embodiment also plays a major role in 4E cognition (embodied, embedded, extended, enacted) as presented in Chapter 4—here, the soma is crucial, and necessary for cognition. Indeed, all three theories discussed in the last chapter of Part 1, 4E cognition, dynamical systems theory, and the OPTIMAL theory of motor learning, highlight complex processes where the bodymind works as an integrated, not disparate, entity.

The premise that conceptual thought can result in meaningful action, and meaningful action can inform conceptual thought, constitutes much of the SomaLab framework, both theoretically and experientially. Through visualization of motion and sensing, free-flow movement improvisation, perception and kinesthetic awareness, artists can practice linking language/concept to movement output (conceptualization, as described in Chapter 4), eventually making choices concerning the truest expression for their individual bodyminds. These choices are informed mightily by the bodies themselves, one's lived experiences, cultural and social environments, and a willingness to embrace things unknown. Indeed, Albert Eisenstein, in one of his "thought" experiments, imagined he was a photon moving at the speed of light, noticing what he saw and felt. He then imagined himself a second photon, observing the first photon.[26]

Can we practice embodiment? Can this very human way of existing be developed to augment artistry and expedite movement learning? The larger body of somatic work and practices clearly demonstrate the benefits of developing the mind/body connection, but by "activating embodiment" we can isolate the relationship between language and movement, tease out nuance, and facilitate conceptually based movement output and performance. It is this practice, the quickening *and* broadening of idea (input) and subsequent movement expression (output) that is critical to SomaLab praxis.

Referencing an email communication to members in November 2023, Integrated Movement Studies, an educational organization, underlines the fact that the use of the word "embodied" has entered our everyday culture. This is particularly true for leaders and practitioners of wellness and bodymind praxis. Supporting Gibb's embodiment principle, the email's authors hypothesize that a full, dynamic living experience depends on the connection between moving bodies and cognition, emotion, and spiritualism.[27] We are, indeed, always embodied, unable to separate or silo disparate parts of our human organism.

This begs the question, are we ever not embodied? The answer is "no," but we speak of embodiment as something we can turn on or off; some people have it/use it, while others don't (although recognizing that this may be less of a choice for neurodivergent individuals). Perhaps a view of this essential bodymind connection is best approached as something that is inherent to us all, albeit in different ways. For some, it is waiting to be awakened, while for others it is a clear and insistent way of being, necessary for full human expression. When we *practice* embodiment, through any somatic experience, our plastic nervous system changes, and structure is altered; we feel different, we think differently, we *are* different. Modern life has taken us far away from the need to move as a means of survival; we order food, we live in already assembled dwellings, we often celebrate our humanity outside the realm of movement. We engage in somatic work to restore basic human function and to live in true harmony with our biological selves. Much wisdom lies within us, both ancestral and modern, and movement allows us to access our knowing.

Hanson and Mendius explore the idea of embodiment as a way of achieving presence and living in each moment in *Buddha's Brain: The Practical Neuroscience of Happiness, Love & Wisdom*.[28] The overactive cortex becomes accustomed to the unnecessary reliving of past and future events and causes avoidable suffering. Many life events are painful; that cannot be avoided. But how we respond to the actions of the universe is under our control. We can change our brain structurally through practice, and embracing our embodied nature is a clear step forward. As discussed previously in the "breath" section of the SomaLab framework, conscious breathing is often the gateway for somatic practice, and the first step to embodied living. We find ourselves empowered to feel and act with multiple sources of information at our fingertips. There is a particular sense of intention (also addressed previously in the framework) that emerges with an embodied focus—instead of the river carrying us away, we can drive the boat and exert agency over the destination. As part of the SomaLab framework, we practice the embodiment of ideas, feelings, language, knowing, allowing us to move more deeply into movement praxis. The full expressive capabilities of our instruments expand, and the experience is not only felt more deeply in our own bodies, but in the bodyminds of others, providing a perfect segue into the next element of the framework.

7. *Movement empathy*

The SomaLab framework doesn't focus on transfer of knowledge as defined in traditional motor learning principles. Conversely, it is the building of experiences that broaden the mover's palette and provide them with a way to solve movement problems when presented. Movement empathy, or kinesthetic empathy, is an important tool in building a flexible nervous system. Visual feedback need not be constrained to self-observation of movement; it is also key in discovering how others are experiencing prompts or self-exploration. This widens the performer's scope of what is possible and contributes to the pool of possibilities. Veritably, movers will tacitly be drawn to embodied information, so amassing a strong knowledge base is critical.

German philosopher Theodor Lipps (1851–1914) famously presented a theory of kinesthetic empathy, or *Einfühlung* (empathy), arguing that spectators who perceived artists in motion could themselves experience a sort of movement. John Martin, an early modern dance writer and critic, further elaborated on these ideas, defining the term "kinesthetic sympathy" where he proposed audiences could personally enact neural pathways when viewing dance.[29] Using functional magnetic resonance imaging (fMRI), contemporary neuroscientists have indeed found that action simulation (mental imaging) stimulates the parietal, premotor, and subcortical areas of the brain and is influenced by familiarity, conceptual knowledge, and physical plausibility. Furthermore, a review of the literature indicates that the motor and premotor areas classically associated with movement preparation are also active when simply observing the actions of others but are not as active as during action simulation.[30] These findings are relevant to the concept of movement empathy in that observing movement *does* stimulate movement areas of the brain. Recall the role of mirror neurons, discussed in Chapter 3, structures that activate when we move, and/or view others moving. As we practice unfamiliar movement and that movement becomes more embodied, the scope of brain function structurally widens.

One example of widespread movement empathy that occurred during the Covid-19 global pandemic was a social dance that went viral. In this instance, the #jerusalemadancechallenge involved musicians and dancers from Angola, who united an entire global community through dance during shutdown and isolation. In exploring the scientific basis for this event, Niezink and Train define empathy as having three categories: cognitive, emotional, and kinesthetic. Cognitive empathy allows us to understand another's point of view, while emotional empathy triggers like and shared feelings. Kinesthetic empathy, they write:

> …is the capacity to participate in somebody's movement, or their sensory experience of movement. It makes use of mirroring of sensations and movements of the body to enhance connection and synchronicity between people. With kinesthetic empathy, you explore, and become more aware of, how you influence each other's physical space. When we dance together or when we see others dancing to a catchy rhythm, we start to display physiological linkage. Our bodies show similarities in patterns of autonomic and nervous system activity such as heart rate and pulse activity. We physically synchronize with one another.[31]

Figure 5.6. Justin Sears, left, and Rachel Newbrough experience kinesthetic empathy as they move rhythmically together during a performance of Elizabeth Shea's *Memory Object* (author's collection; photograph by Steven Pisano).

We have previously discussed the role of empathy in dance for the concert stage, but this phenomenon, described so aptly, describes the deeper basis for the draw of social dancing. Empathy is at the heart of the how and why humans are drawn to group movement experience. In referencing mirroring, the authors are describing a situation where human subjects in laboratory settings have demonstrated mimicry of facial expressions of others, facilitated by mirror neurons, thus the term mirroring. Have you ever been in a social situation where an embodied reaction seems almost contagious, like yawning, or even crying? When you see others moving, do you experience "an itch," a want or need to move yourself? Community facilitates movement empathy, and movement empathy strengthens community.

But what happens when we find ourselves in novel, or unfamiliar movement situations? Can we practice and develop our skills as kinesthetic empathizers to expand our own resources? Remember that our nervous system is flexible, plastic, and capable of great change. The SomaLab framework encourages the development of empathetic process through various modes of praxis. When we study codified forms, we are already exercising kinesthetic empathy; we look to movement cues of teachers and/or demonstrators, we listen to verbal instruction and employ subsequent action. We strive to mimic, to copy, techniques as they are offered. By developing a process of approaching new movement situations and materials, our learning and performance becomes more efficient and expansive and ties us to a larger global experience.

This view of empathy relies heavily on embodiment; we see now how the elements of the SomaLab framework begin to work together. We attend to breath, initiating embodied processes and activating sensation and perception. The bodymind is then prepped to engage mental constructs, which in turn facilitates the human ability to empathize. This spurs our willingness, our desire to explore new movement processes through improvisational and self-guided movement, and it all leads to greater expansiveness of our movement world, diversifying our repertory and guiding our ability to express, truly and authentically.

Moving past our own affinities allows us to draw distinctions between ourselves and other movers, confirming a healthy sense of individuality as well as an appreciation of performance outside traditional learning, societal, and cultural norms. New ways of moving are introduced, and soon, they, too, become familiar.

8. *Reflection/incorporation*

As we explore the last tool of the SomaLab framework, reflection/incorporation, consider some of the great movement artists in recent dance history; clearly genre creates no boundaries. Performances from the likes of Julie Kent, Trisha Brown, Baba Chuck Davis, Gwen Verdon, and Camile A. Brown, to name a very few, all share the commonality of embodied expertise. It's important to distance ourselves from the idea that somatics is a specific way of moving, a genre. Somatic work can facilitate crossing forms and styles by focusing on the conceptual ideas behind a technique instead of the movements from the form itself. In the absence of a linear approach to motor learning, what is left is the development of the nervous system into a flexible, ever-changing mechanism. The bodymind is prepared to work to problem-solve intelligently when presented with new information that requires an immediate response. By reflecting on our experiences, and incorporating new knowledge, we become more expert at doing so, as well as at the task at hand.

Chapter 4 introduces a dynamical systems approach to human behavior as just that: a self-regulating, non-linear set of responses that are produced in real time and are inextricably informed by the mover's environment.[32] As the mover moves and the dancer dances, sensing and perception are constantly and consistently drawn into a loop of action/reaction informed by both internal human experience and the external world around us. Humans' movement decisions, then, are not preprogrammed and unalterable; rather, they're fluid and process based.

This leads us to a discussion of expertise, and how it develops. Laboratory research in expert performance clearly supports the idea of deliberate practice over an extended period in a specific area of study.[33] But perhaps this specificity is not just the acquired habit, but an overall mechanism of constant investigation and subsequent action. This theory appears supported by dynamical systems theory, where individuals become more expert as the bodymind reorganizes over time, not due to rote repetition of skill. The great performers previously discussed, and many others, while all celebrating differing types of dance forms are capable of brilliantly fine-tuned and nuanced performance in addition to exhibiting flawless technical skills. They demonstrate the constant and consistent use of

Figure 5.7. Robert F. Burden, Jr., has achieved a virtuosic level of expertise in tap dance (courtesy Robert F. Burden, Jr. Photo by Michael Pilla).

process, the persistence in seeking the purest form of expression. Somatic systems like SomaLab support this conscious, intentional approach to movement practice that draws a wide circle of performance and discovery. The intelligent bodymind is constantly at work in acting, moving, deciding, processing.

Feedback is an important part of the self-regulating process, and a diverse array of augmented feedback mechanisms, such as those presented in Chapter 2, are certainly instrumental to incorporation—especially when paired with intention and attention. Intrinsic information, accessed via proprioception, gives us one set of information about movement and the body in space. Augmented feedback comes from sources outside the body and tells the mover if their attempt was successful or not. KR (knowledge of results) specifically has been shown to be critical to successful learning and performance, although certainly as expertise develops, a movement habit becomes more consistent.[34] The challenge here is to equate habitual performance with the actual goal so that proprioception does not lead the performer away from success.

As we discuss feedback in the context of this last tool of the SomaLab framework, consider that we contextualize multiple sources of information, some of it with somatic roots and some from extrinsic sources. Here, the repertory of bodymind knowledge is expanded, and incorporation deepens movement practice—in other words, we become more expert at practicing the process. The continuous ability of a human organism to reorient and reorganize itself and respond to cues both intrinsically and from the environment is crucial to change and developing knowledge, and the ability to know. In essence, the reconstruction process is part of expertise itself. Take a moment here to reflect on your own approach as a movement expert; do you consciously attend to cues intrinsically and extrinsically? Post-reflection, are you able to incorporate specific movement situations with larger phenomenological views?

This is the final, but also constant, work of the SomaLab framework—dynamically linking mind, body, environment, memories, presence, future, goals—into one movement life. Somatic work allows us to feel more deeply, notice more fully, and know more completely our own unique selves in the context of society, culture, history, and an ever-evolving world. The deeper we dig, the more we incorporate, connecting the intrinsic and the extrinsic as we engage in holistic living. Feedback then, both internal and external, can provide a rich source of information that expands our ability to reflect, reinvent, and move forward in the development of our self-definition of expertise.

Conclusion

Many great minds have been invested in the function of the bodymind instrument, and many have codified their own ideas and ways of organizing their thoughts. With each new contribution we learn a little more, see things a little more clearly. Some ideas contradict each other. That is to be expected, as our own bodyminds, in both structure and function, as well as our lived experiences, predicate the way we see the world. But it is the critical analysis of ideas, the ability to distinguish as well as find common ground, that moves us closer to understanding, inches us closer to the how and the why. It's also important to acknowledge that embracing a broad swath of somatic systems allows a diverse group of people to practice and benefit from this important work, in accordance with their own affinities, preferences, and cultural identities. As we move into Chapter 6, the tools presented in this chapter guide more specific tasks that take the form of praxis, and we begin the journey of creating our own individual movement experiences.

6

Building a Personal Practice

> "An artist must be free to choose what he does, certainly, but he must also never be afraid to do what he might choose."
> —Langston Hughes[1]

Introduction: SomaLab, A Framework

SomaLab differs from prescriptive somatic practices in that it presents an overarching framework rather than a systematic collection of activities. While I offer examples of tasks in this chapter, the mover can design, for themselves or for others, activities that fall within the framework, yet speak to and celebrate the individual by developing a personal practice that fosters individuality, considers lived experiences, and is inclusive of cultural identity. Langston Hughes, in his 1926 writings reflecting on Black art making, urges Black artists to embrace their beauty, their cultural world, without regard to judgment. Undoubtedly, the inability to express our humanity authentically, whether due to internal or external constraints, is unsurvivable; a flexible somatic approach allows artists to cultivate their expressive capacities and center their own voices.

Thus, a framework is valuable in that it allows many kinds of practitioners to participate in a somatic experience regardless of prior training or movement encounters; what is known is juxtaposed with what is new and unknown, and creates a space where incorporating, changing, and growing can live and thrive. Whether practicing alone or with other movers, sharpening empathy, learning, and fine-tuning prosper.

In Chapter 5, we identified the elements, or tools, of the SomaLab framework:

- *Breath*
- *Imagery, visualization, and mental practice*
- *Intention/attention*

6. Building a Personal Practice

- *Self-guided/intuitive movement*
- *Physical awareness (kinesthesia)*
- *Embodiment in action*
- *Movement empathy*
- *Reflection/incorporation*

While all framework elements are included in each of the task categories and examples (true to the holistic nature of somatic work), some are more particular to certain praxis, and will be addressed during task descriptions. Again, there is great plasticity in creating and organizing a personal approach to SomaLab, and practitioners are encouraged to follow the leads of their bodyminds.

It is useful to organize the SomaLab framework into three parts, where tasks are deconstructive, reconstructive, or integrative. Each of these framework constituents serves a specific purpose, allowing for focused attention to fall on processes that are critical to holistic moving. While the framework tasks build upon each other in an additive fashion during a singular praxis, they inform each other exponentially over time. The adaptability afforded by the SomaLab framework provides opportunities for tailoring specific tasks within deconstructive, reconstructive, and integrative parts that focalize individual lived experiences and affirm cultural worldviews.

The opening of a SomaLab-designed practice begins with deconstruction, a process that disassembles linked performance elements from each other to focus on smaller parts; it is largely an attentional mechanism. This allows for a priming, or readying, of separate cognitive and physical processes that facilitate embodiment. While this may feel counterintuitive to the end goal of whole mind/body integration, the opportunity to delve deeply and extract a single idea or intention can help build essential knowledge through meaningful neural and sensory experiences. Exploring the inner workings of the mind, sans movement, and conversely concentrating on the proprioception of targeted muscular contractions, deepens embodied understanding, and builds the language of the body. By narrowing attention to individual elements, we create the opportunity to develop and strengthen neural networks.

Deconstructive tasks center breath, imagery, visualization, and mental practice, intention/attention, and physical awareness (kinesthesia) elements of the framework. Focusing on the body's breath is a prime mechanism for initiating somatic engagement, and places attention on the practice ahead, sharpening proprioception and facilitating presence and being. As previously discussed, breathwork is often the segue, the transition, the introduction to many mind/body practices and movement arts techniques. While conscious breath praxis is employed throughout a SomaLab session, initial attention to this cyclical process is fundamental to the work.

Imagery, visualization, and mental practice also contribute to deconstructive tasks by igniting neural networks that will later facilitate movement. These processes can be used to move the mind into novel and experimental situations, revisit past experiences and memories, and/or make connections between the two (meaning making). This work is also an initial investigation into sensation and feeling, where one can imagine sensation before experiencing it. Physical awareness, or kinesthesia, is the next step, engaging the bodymind in movement and completing the neural network of central to peripheral nervous system. The distancing of thought and sensation provides a sense of separation between the mind and body and might feel contrary to end goals. But frame it this way: if you walk outside in the winter without a coat, and then put one on, you understand the incompleteness of the previous situation. And, more specific to movement situations, recall the discussions of attention in Chapters 2 and 4, where a narrowed focus is shown to enhance learning and performance. For example, attention to breath starts in deconstructive tasks, but is eventually reconstructed into the large whole, and guides the entire praxis throughout.

Once the system is fine-tuned, reconstructive tasks work to bring the mind and body back to a more balanced union of motion and thought. This begins the process of "noticing" or self-observation, without attaching value or judgement. Acknowledging sensation and feeling leads to distinction, refinement, and a greater understanding of individual movement patterns and affinities later. It is simply a mental and physical recording of what is. There is also an emphasis on the body in space; how does the mover connect *to* their environment? How does the mover connect *beyond* their environment? What is the geometry of the body; what is the geometry of the space we occupy, both close by and far away? Reconstructive tasks work to unify newly awakened components of the bodymind system, preparing the mover for more fully embodied experiences that lie ahead.

Reconstructive tasks continue to center physical awareness (kinesthesia) and utilize self-guided/intuitive movement. Sensory-based improvisation takes center stage here, and the priority is attending to sensation while the body leads in movement. Responding to conceptually based prompts while feeling and perceiving supports the reconstructive process. Likewise, physical awareness plays a strong role in the relationship of body to environment; we know from Chapters 2 and 5 that proprioception provides information regarding limb position in space in addition to muscle tension and stretch. This portion of the SomaLab process begins to draw together disparate mind/body function.

Finally, integrative tasks facilitate connections between thought, movement, sensation and feeling, requiring deep work that is the heavy lifting of the SomaLab experience. There is a braiding, an intertwining of memory, knowledge, and perception, with exploration, goal-setting, and problem-solving, that leads to new paths of movement-making and mastery in expression. Language, our symbolic representation of everything around us and everything we know, takes on heightened importance as we shift mental constructs into embodied understanding. This conceptual translation (again, conceptualization, as described in Chapter 4) is the heart and soul of SomaLab—with the bodymind primed and practiced, the instrument is ready for integrated investigation. Using verbally guided concepts, participants work toward an even richer interpretation and understanding of something than even language allows. Here, embodiment in action and reflection/incorporation are key, while the practitioner also explores the beginnings of movement empathy (this framework element is also featured in Chapter 7). Self-discovery through embodied thought and action brings the bodymind to full function through the exploration of concept; the embodied principle[2] governs as thought inspires movement, and movement inspires thought. We experience movement empathy by embracing the creations of others into our own soma; the exchange enriches our own knowledge and likewise highlights the wisdom of others. We expand the work of learning how to learn and learning how to experience. And finally, it is all brought together through reflection and incorporation, as dynamic processes assemble our knowledge and memories with our present environment and explorations, creating new avenues of expertise and providing a space where future goals and bodymind research can flourish.

The following sections provide specific examples of deconstructive, reconstructive, and integrative tasks that have been successfully (as defined by anecdotal observations) used in SomaLab practices. To be clear, these examples follow a framework and can be tailored to fit individual preferences. Practitioners can also create novel tasks based on activity parameters, which are listed here as well to facilitate an individualized experience. Indeed, the very act of task self-creation works to extend the capabilities of the bodymind as an instrument. The generation of new movement ideas and problem-solving are tantamount to the practice itself and can deepen self-knowledge as well as contribute to the realm of somatic study. Thus, the practitioner is an active collaborator in the SomaLab process and contributes mightily to the evolution of the framework.

Before we commence, I'd like to note that theming is an important pedagogical tool that warrants discussion, and as such will be addressed more fully in Chapter 7. However, for the purpose of providing examples

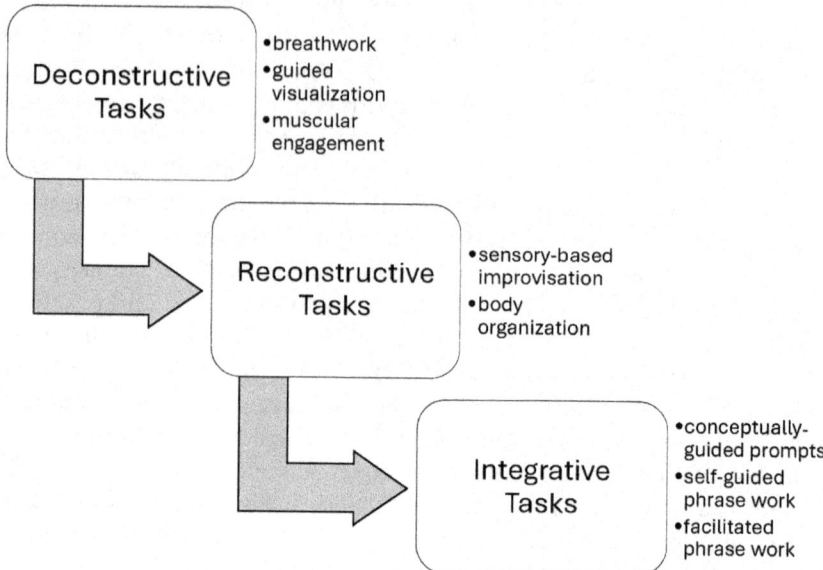

Figure 6.1. This table illustrates the organization of SomaLab tasks (author's creation).

that feel cohesive and work toward a goal that is beneficial to all movers, the "A" examples will focus on the task in and of itself, while the idea of "subtle engagement" will serve as a thread in the "B" examples, so readers can see how a theme might be applied to the framework. "Subtle engagement" refers to finding just the right amount of effort; not hanging on the bones nor over-efforting with muscular engagement that impedes freedom of movement. In yoga, this is sometimes referred to as "relaxing the grip" or "finding the middle."

Deconstructive Tasks

Breathwork

The parameters of breathwork draw from yogic, somatic, and modern dance canons, and include:

- The use of breath practice as a metaphor for the cyclical nature of life
- Attention to conscious breath, forging first-person experiences with embodiment

- Connecting inhales and exhales to gravity, and the rise and fall of the physical body

EXAMPLE A

Find a comfortable place on the floor, reclining on your back. Begin to draw conscious attention to your breath. As you inhale, feel the belly expand into the space above you, and as you exhale, notice how the belly falls softly into the spine. On your next inhale, focus on expanding the ribcage, filling the space above, to the sides, and underneath your body, and as you exhale, feel the midbody soften and close. On your third breath, deepen your inhale to include broadening through the sternum, and exhale sequentially, sternum, ribs, belly. Continue with this three-part breath, filling the belly, ribs, then sternum on your inhale, and releasing your sternum, ribs, and belly on the exhale. As you seek familiarity with this process, also notice any new sensations in the body or awakenings of the mind.

At the point where this three-part breath feels comfortable and practiced, begin to shift attention to a mental construct, or image. As you inhale fully through the torso, visualize the breath traveling beyond your lungs, into the large, proximal joints of the shoulders and hips, creating space between bone and soft tissue, and encouraging future mobility. As you exhale, feel the breath retract back to the source. Even though the expander has ceded, the space remains. On the next breath cycle, allow your image to move further away from the center, into the elbows and knees, growing the reach of the breath and its capability to open and stretch, as well as encouraging a sense of falling, sinking. Finally, see the breath move fully into the fingers and toes, bringing nourishment and sensation to every part of the body, and conversely, removing depleted air from every cell and sending it back into the environment. The breath not only acts upon the individual body but makes us all part of the larger world.

EXAMPLE B

Find a comfortable place on the floor, reclining on your back, and begin to draw conscious attention to your breath. Notice the steadiness, the reliability, the predictability of the breath cycle. Bring even more stability to your in- and out-breaths by attaching a count that is evenly distributed. For example, as you inhale, count one, two, three, and as you exhale, count one, two, three. Pair this work with a mental image that shows the practice as a loop or circle, immersing yourself in the process, and seeing your body respond to the breath, rising and falling, lifting and sinking, over and over again. Begin to feel comfortable and familiar with this work.

After a time, expand the breath-loop to encircle the entire physical body, moving under, around, and to the top of your kinesphere. As you visualize the air encompassing arms, legs, torso, head, see color begin to seep into the airstream. Throughout your inhale, the color saturates, intensifies, and when you exhale, it fades, softens, becoming opaque. Continue this breath/imaging practice, reveling in the shifting chromaticity as the body rises and falls, expands and contracts. Become entranced, enamored with the kaleidoscope of color initiated by simple breath, and begin to associate movement with this luminous transformation. Eventually, envision the superabundance of color and air lifting your body-mind off of the earth, floating and swaying, and gently releasing back down.

To resolve this practice, begin to work through the steps in reverse, subtly leaving a previous element or dynamic behind, until only the even, conscious breath remains. Revel in the memory.

Guided Visualization

Guided visualization utilizes imagery but without corresponding movement. Parameters of guided visualization include:

- Phrenic preparation involving attention and presence, bringing focus to "the mind's eye" and quieting the physical body
- Mental practice of known movements utilizing imagery that may fall outside the natural world and beyond realism
- Visualization of novel actions and images

Example A

Find a comfortable place on the ground, fully reclining and yielding to the earth. Initiate a preferred breath practice as you work toward internal focus on a singular process. Start to feel your attention draw inward as the breath calms, heals, and protects. When external stimuli feel outside of your immediate consciousness, begin to see a small, glowing white light in your mind's eye (the space between your eyes at the top of your nose). As you inhale, the light grows and intensifies, and as you exhale it shrinks and dissipates. Become accustomed to the growing and shrinking of the light. As you feel comfortable, see all your daily thoughts, tasks, and worries appear like tiny pieces of paper, floating in your mental space. Take a long inhale, and as you deliberately exhale, see a third of the papers flutter beyond your sight. The empty space is filled with luminosity, now larger and more persistent. After a few breaths, take another long in-breath, and strongly exhale, as more of the paper-thoughts float out of consciousness. Bathe in the glow, radiant and peaceful. Finally, a third breath cycle gently coaxes the remaining paper pieces away from the mind's eye. A purity of thought remains; the mind is cleansed and ready to receive.

EXAMPLE B

Find a comfortable place on the earth, reclining on any surface of the body. Draw attention to the breath, finding smooth, even, inhales and exhales. After a time, begin to slowly scan the body from top to bottom, noticing if the steady breath can release pockets of tension. Begin with the skull, move into the facial muscles, and down toward the neck. Let the shoulders drape, and drop, as heavy arm bones and hands fall into the floor. The chest and sternum are soft, but open, leaving the heart accessible. Ribs fall, and the pelvis relaxes and spreads. The belly is soft. The legs feel heavy and weighted, and the feet relax. The entire body ever so slightly rises and falls with each in-breath and out-breath. Immerse yourself in this state of full relaxation.

Slowly begin to awaken your mind's eye, and visualize yourself reclining in a beautiful, comforting environment, perhaps a sandy beach, or the soft, quiet forest. You are completely relaxed, free of any muscular tension or control. You must be moved by external forces for your body to change its shape. In time, you feel a gentle wind blowing that lifts your limbs in succession, floating for a short span before returning to the

Figure 6.2. Practitioners engage in the deconstructive task of guided visualization (author's collection; photograph by Lindsay Osten).

earth. Right arm, left arm, left leg, right leg. The wind begins to pick up slightly, rolling your body back and forth, as your limbs indirectly flail; it is a pleasant feeling, this non-control. The wind ceases, bringing you to stillness, spreading skin, muscle, and bone. In the quiet your sand settles, drawing you to the ground. It is safe and comforting and your mind drifts. Quite suddenly, a strong gale picks up and sweeps you completely off the earth. You turn, tumble, and spin, every which way, rising higher and higher, finally floating gently in the clouds. You are exactly where you want to be, and the sensation of being supported three-dimensionally is exquisite. After a time, you are carried ever so gently back to the ground, easily grazing the surface as your body is placed delicately and comfortably where you began. The memory of being moved is delicious.

Targeted Muscular Engagement

Examples of targeted muscular engagement here are based on yogic practice but can come from any codified set of actions that employs consistent application of holding the body in or moving the body through space. Parameters include:

- Drawing attention to the physical body
- Moving from thinking to feeling; increased sensory awareness
- Balancing strength and flexibility throughout the body's muscle groups

Example A

Find your way to an easy seat. Begin to bring attention to your breath, feeling steady and spacious in the body and the mind. Roll over your shins into a table-top position, knees under hips and wrists under shoulders. Press down into your hands and shins, feeling the shoulders separate, and the belly engage. The quadriceps pull up into the hips, and the low back is broad and long. The breath is like a ripple, a wave, and as you inhale, extend your right arm forward, thumb up, neck long and right ear even with right bicep. The long muscles of the core that wrap around the torso stabilize, and square hips and shoulders. This muscular action increases the space between the anterior torso and the floor. On the next in-breath, the left leg floats, heel even with the hip, extended long. Find length, radiating from flexed heel to middle finger, and as you exhale, come to sit on knees and shins. Allow the lower back to neutralize, come back to breath, and then repeat on the second side.

From the shin sit, or Hero's Pose, lean forward. Clasp your hands,

6. Building a Personal Practice   143

placing the outside of the forearms and gripped hands on the earth. Push down, steadying the shoulder girdle. Extend one leg at a time back, coming into a forearm Plank Pose. The knees can drop if it's more comfortable, if you experience unreasonable discomfort or pain, or if it simply makes sense in your body. Push into the toes, equalizing the pressure between the lower and upper body. Imagine your belly button pulling upward toward your spine and soften the distance between your low ribs and hip points, expanding the lower back. Stay easy through the neck, keeping the gaze down so the cervical spine remains long. Breath steady, stay spacious for ten breath cycles. Take one more in-breath, then drop the knees and widen, shifting the pelvis back into a Child's Pose, completely releasing the shoulders and neck as you rest your forehead on the earth.

Example B

Find your way to standing, feet planted firmly hip distance apart, shoulders wide, heart open, and arms falling long by your side in Mountain Pose; the hands are soft. The crown of the head reaches high as the toes press down, creating space through the waist and side bodies. The in-breath draws you taller, and the out-breath grounds you down. On your next in-breath, step the left foot back and a little out for stability, bending your right knee and drawing the arms high as you arrive in Crescent Lunge. Find balance in muscular engagement as the legs work just enough to hold you upright; the core engages subtly to align the pelvis, ribs, and shoulders; the arms reach but also feel supported as the shoulders move down the back. The breath is steady and spacious. On the next in-breath bend both knees, squatting down and firming the thighs, and bend at the elbows squeezing the forearms and shoulder blades toward each other; as you exhale, release the extra effort, and return to Crescent Lunge. Find repetition in this flow, noticing how you feel when you brace and squeeze, and how you feel when you release to the middle—the place that is neither too hot nor too cold. Let your body lead you into stillness, back to Mountain Pose, and allow the sand to settle, embracing the stillness. When you are ready, step back with the right leg to find the second side.

Still standing, step the feet together, toes pointing forward, and as you bend the knees deeply, sink the hips back, and draw both arms long by your ears into Chair Pose. Inhale, and energetically engaging the legs, press them together as you sit lower and stretch the arms higher. As you exhale, relax and release, bringing your seat higher and letting the joints fall (safely) out of alignment. Repeat and then find the place where you subtly engage to hold the body in a strong and stable position without over-efforting. On the next in-breath, step back with the left foot and straighten the legs, toes pointed to the left side of your space. Keep the left leg extended, and as you bend through the right knee, bring the joint into alignment over your second big toe. Stretch the arms long and away from each other as you come into Warrior 2. Inhale and straighten both legs, squeezing quadriceps, hamstrings, and biceps as the arms come over head, and return to Warrior 2 on the exhale, softening into the pose. Repeat, coordinating with breath cycles, moving between a shortening of the muscles, exerting effort from the outside, and releasing long from the center, in a relaxed but just-right state of holding the body in safety and truth as you explore space

Figure 6.3. Anya Gustafson, left, and Riley Savage find awareness in the physical body through targeted muscular engagement (author's collection; photograph by Lindsay Osten).

from the inside out. Step forward into Mountain Pose, finding a balance of strength, stability, and release. Appreciate the stillness and notice the lingering sensations in the body that result from your work. As you're ready, step the right foot back to even out the effort on the second side.

Reconstructive Tasks

Sensory-Based Improvisation

Any well-crafted score can serve as a basis for sensory-based improvisation. Parameters include:

- Centering feeling as opposed to thinking

6. Building a Personal Practice

- Bringing immediate presence to the forefront; memory, and future planning fade
- Allowing the body to lead, and trusting its intelligence

EXAMPLE A

Come to stand in a comfortable place, facing a direction that feels closed away from traditional front. Take a few moments to center the breath, feeling the parasympathetic nervous system equalize as the thinking mind relaxes. Bring the gaze internal; see life's background blur, as your body comes into focus, much like a portrait. Ever so subtly, start to move from the most central place in your body, deep inside the belly, slowly, and carefully. Take time to feel the most minuscule shifts as the soma begins to move in concert with the breath; inhales start deep within, initiating flow, and stretches the movement out toward the limbs; the exhale brings all back to center. As you breathe and move, work out of the abdominal area and into the hips and shoulders, finding both linear and circular patterns in the large joints. Notice how each feels, and take note of your affinity, without attaching value. Make the movement even larger, working into the limbs, toward the first joint, knees, and elbows, and then finally into hands and feet. Locomotion is now possible as the body moves through space and explores all levels and planes of action. The rhythm remains slow and steady. The breath continues to initiate from the core, radiating throughout, as the exhales close and soften. Immerse yourself in the process, centering sensation, and perception.

After reaching the height of this experience, begin to reverse the range of movement and depth of breath, traveling back along the paths and trails you have created, while trusting the body to find new ones. As you move, draw back close to the large joints, and finally the belly. Indulge in those final soft movements as you come to close in a comfortable resting place, standing, sitting, or reclining on the earth. Take a moment to remember how the flow of breath and movement felt as it coursed through the body. Would you like to feel that way again? In what other situations are core/distal patterns part of your movement repertoire? How can you use this pattern of sensation in more codified movement activities?

EXAMPLE B

Recline on your back, completely releasing your weight into the floor. Scan the body from head to toe and begin to see small connections from your posterior surface form to the earth, and flowing into it, much like roots. These connections are cool and comforting, and still allow for subtle movement. The breath is steady and spacious as you begin to create a pattern of rising and falling in your bodymind, gently resisting gravity on the inhales, and succumbing to it on the exhales. Stay in this place for a bit, feeling, and focusing only on the present moment.

Gradually, you become interested in stretching your roots and connections, and with the inhales you move peripheral parts away from the earth, fingers, toes, as the exhales allow them to fall back heavy. After a time, experiment with lifting the heavy head, and gently returning it to make contact; then experiment with lifting the heavy pelvis, and gently returning it as well, then head and pelvis together, using the hands and feet as support. Trust the body to take you where it wants to go, in a free-flowing investigation of weight. The roots and connections begin to loosen, allowing for a greater range of movement as you move three-dimensionally into the space around you, exploring higher and broader in all planes of the spatial matrix. Perhaps your research becomes a little stronger, as you oppose gravity, maybe faster to increase momentum, embracing the body's natural biomechanics. The release on the exhale is key and always present.

After reaching a pinnacle of weightlessness, begin to reverse the process back down to the earth. Take your time, finding nooks and crannies that were hidden before, exploring dimensional shifts as the body grows heavier. The ground beckons; it is time to return, to regrow those roots and connections. Finally, you are still. What was the experience of embracing weightlessness? What was the experience of embracing weight? Does the contrast give deeper meaning to your kinesthetic understanding of the body's capabilities? Rest here, knowing this enterprise has provided learning, wisdom.[3]

Body Organization

Experiencing movement three-dimensionally is the foundation of body organization; many codified dance techniques and somatic practices feature patterns and sequences that facilitate spatial understanding. Parameters of body organization include:

- Recognizing the body in space
- Understanding the geometry of the body, especially regarding planes of action
- Connecting the physical body to the surrounding environment

Example A

Find a comfortable vertical place, with your feet grounding into the earth and all four corners firmly planted. Stack the joints efficiently; ankles are straight and in line with the toes, knees align over the ankles, the pelvic bowl is parallel to the ground, shoulders rest easily over hips, and the crown of the head reaches tall into axial extension. The ribs are soft and flexible as your breath cycle brings you to presence and moves you to a place of perception and sensation.

Inhale, and as you release your breath, flex at the ankles, knees, and hips and take a few bounces before you inhale again to suspend and recover. Use this drop and rise to find your bodymind in the vertical space. The heavy pelvis and base of support provide stability for this action. Breathe, drop, bounce, rise; breathe, drop, bounce, rise. Use imagery to see the top of your head piercing the atmosphere, and the pelvis dropping like a basketball through a hoop.

Figure 6.4. Sensory-based improvisation helps Isabel Danton, left, and Grace Gdowik move from thinking to feeling (author's collection; photograph by Lindsay Osten).

Moving into the frontal plane, draw the right arm out from the side to overhead on an in-breath, and on your out-breath, release the arm successionally, bending at the elbow and at the waist, curving to the side. Allow the weight of the head to continue the path of the curve forward. Catch the momentum and continuing the circle of the torso to the left, lift the left arm through the wheel plane, arriving again overhead on the second side. Continue to repeat and exchange sides, moving through planes of action and noticing the bodymind's affinities.

Finishing this sequence, begin to swing one leg front to back, adding in the arms. Suspend on the inhale, and as the working foot falls to the earth, use the exhale to facilitate the fall. Notice the back-and-forth motion, and how the body responds to moving in vertical space. Balance can be challenging when standing on one leg; how does your knowledge and experience in verticality inform your stability? Move to the second leg every few swings. When a rhythm develops, add rotation at the hip, front to back, crossing the transverse plane, and increasing the dimensionality of your movement. How do you respond to this new complexity? Is this action more comfortable on one side of the body than the other?

Example B

Come to stand comfortably with your feet under your hips; knees are soft. Take a minute to find your breath, smooth and steady, as your bones stack naturally and safely, allowing your body to respond to the effects of gravity. You are only expending as much energy as is necessary to hold your body in space. Experiment with differing degrees of muscular engagement to feel secure and grounded in this stance and arrive at your own subtle engagement. As you inhale, the spine lengthens from the belly button to the crown of the head as the ribs soften, and as you exhale, the pelvis hangs heavy and the feet ground into the earth. This is the first embodied understanding of the body in vertical space. Take another in-breath, and on your out-breath begin to curl, or "roll down the spine," starting with the cervical spine, then the thoracic; as you arrive toward the lumbar spine and the pelvis, break at the hips, allowing the chest to fall on the thighs as the knees flex as much as

Figure 6.5. Lila Hodgin explores movement in the sagittal plane, experiencing body organization through spatial awareness (author's collection; photograph by Lindsay Osten).

necessary for comfort and to feel the weight of the upper body. Release the head completely, allowing the neck to gently traction, and the crown of the head to fall heavy toward the earth. Complete one or more breath cycles before returning to a standing posture. Repeat until you feel comfortable moving vertically and can kinesthetically distinguish between the body's differing responses to gravity.

As you arrive at the top of the next inhale, allow the arms to float up as you stretch even further into the vertical space, and as you exhale, completely release your weight, allowing the arms to fall heavy with no or little control, and then swing back as your upper body falls toward your thighs. Find a rhythm in this swing exercise, suspending the stretch at the top, and catching the release at the bottom to make full use of the body's natural biomechanics. Work toward the energetic middle; when do you need to employ force, and when can you harness momentum? As your arms move in the sagittal plane, can you feel a connection to the geometry of the space beside you, and beyond your immediate surroundings? Come to a rest, and after a few breaths, gently step/shift your weight side to side and front to back, appreciating and distinguishing between frontal and sagittal experiences.

Gradually drop the front to back steps/shifts and keep the feet going side to side. As you inhale, float the arms from the sides, and as you exhale, twist the torso, allowing them to fall back. Coordinate the float/drop with your side steps, focusing on moving in your "table" or transverse plane. Can you feel the arms smoothing as they travel parallel to the ground? What other actions/images does this movement conjure? Play with tempo as you experiment, searching for balance in force/release. And, as you feel comfortable, add in circular motions of the legs (focus on thighs, knees bent) in the hips, finding symbiosis of effort in the arms and legs, as body halves move in all three planes of action simultaneously.

Integrative Tasks

Conceptually-guided Prompts

We all come to dance and movement with our own set of felt experiences and unique perspectives. How does this embodied knowledge inform what we think to be real and true? How can we be open to expanding our perspectives, creating new felt experiences, and forming new truths? Parameters of conceptually-guided prompts include:

- Using visualization to recall movement knowledge and imagine new experiences

- Investigating bodymind understanding through movement improvisation
- Discovering personal truth and movement affinity

Example A

Find a place of stillness and quiet, bringing your gaze internal. Use your knowledge of breath practice to draw attention to your authentic self and reconnect to your true essence; just be. Work in the present of being as you privilege feeling and let go of thinking. Inhale, exhale, inhale, exhale.

Identify a movement concept you would like to explore and choose corresponding language that can guide your investigations (this is best done with some planning before you begin). For example, perhaps you are interested in the sensations created by moving outside of your personal kinesphere; the verbal representations of reach, rotate, and shift may be a useful place to begin. Start this process using imagery and visualization. As you remain still and breathe, see yourself doing familiar tasks that require reaching, maybe getting something off a top shelf, or stretching to close a door when you're a bit too far away. This awakens your embodied knowledge of the action. Maybe the action of reaching has a place in your artistic practice; when do you engage in reaches with any parts of the body? Is this familiar or foreign? After recalling your lived experiences, move into a realm of fantastical thinking—what would it feel like to stretch for the basket like Michael Jordan in *Space Jam*? Dip your toe way out in the middle of the ocean, while standing on shore? Extend the head high into a cloud? Even though the thinking mind is active, you are focusing on creating new perceptions and sensations, not dwelling on how a movement looks or creating an aesthetic.

When you feel you've come to the end of your imaging journey, begin to explore "reaching" through embodied action, allowing the bodymind to respond readily to the prompt freely and tacitly, much like free-flow writing or journaling; allow the body to lead. Engage, indulge. As you work, you will find some physical places do not feel right or true; let them go. Likewise, there will be sequences that perfectly represent your developing understanding of the word "reach." Hang on to these, maybe repeating the explorations again and again, and finally putting them away for later use. Bring it to a close, using stillness and breath as a sort of palate cleanser. Allow the idea of "reach" to fade away and begin to envision your work researching "rotate." Repeat the process, and then again, for as many verbal representations as is necessary to fully explore your concept.

6. Building a Personal Practice

Example B

Choose a place in your current surroundings that affords you an area where you can locomote through space. Take a moment to let the idea of release rain down on your body; as you breathe in the stillness, feel energy dripping off you toward the ground, re-configuring your relationship to gravity. Succumb to weight on your exhales and gently reestablish yourself on your inhales. Subtly engage just enough to hold your body gently in space.

Gradually transition to movement, working your way linearly across the area and back as you use the verb "drip" to guide your flow. Center kinesthesia as opposed to focusing on cleverness; an understanding of your embodied knowledge is the goal as you develop and expand your practice.

Figure 6.6. Following a period of visualization and mental imaging, Sophia Franiak explores the concept of "reach." Much like free-flow writing, the concept guides her movement, honestly and authentically (author's collection; photograph by Lindsay Osten).

As you return, take a moment to let the experience wash over you; what felt authentic and what felt forced? Leave any false ideas behind as you travel and explore once again, revisiting the authentic, and perhaps taking it to new dimensions or playing with time. As you return this second time, can you again filter uncomfortable explorations and work on your third pass to distill the flow to bare-bones, stripped-down expression. After several passes, bring your work to a close and take a moment to breathe, reveling in all you experienced and feeling confident in your growth.

Repeat the process as your time allows; suggestions for verbal prompts include fall, suspend, rebound, rush, and undulate.

Self-Guided Phrase Work

Discovery of personal truth and movement affinity can lead to a deepening of felt experiences and the growth of embodied knowledge. Allowing tacit movement choices is part of this process. Parameters of self-guided phrase work include:

- Making movement choices that directly express embodied knowledge
- Including the unique, individual bodymind as part of the basis for these choices
- Creating a movement idea from one's personal instrument

Example A

During the "conceptually-guided prompts" task of the SomaLab framework, practitioners had the opportunity to explore and deepen their embodied understanding of movement concepts through both guided imagery and movement improvisation. Here, tacit movement choices were sensed and practiced. Let's revisit the concept presented in "Example A: what would it feel like to move outside of your personal kinesphere," further defining this idea with the verbal representations of reach, rotate, and shift.

Find a comfortable place (standing, seated, or reclining) to engage in memory through imagery and mental practice. Begin by recreating a state of heightened consciousness by utilizing breath and preparing the bodymind to receive sensation. Gently let the mind drift to your earlier explorations with "reach," and the affinities and movement concepts you discovered. Begin to replay and repeat, not just remembering sequence, position, etc., but also the sensation associated with performing the movement. How did your body feel? Were there also emotive responses? Gradually move from remembering to direct experience; return to a movement practice of your best understood patterns regarding "reach." Make choices here and create a sequence you can repeat and remember. Continue to focus on kinesthesia, following movement that feels best, not moving into a creative practice that privileges some movements based on another set of circumstances. Repeat this process for "rotate" and "shift."

Once you have identified specific patterns for each verbal prompt, take some time to string them together in a way that feels right in your body; add transitions as necessary and make any other adjustments that seem to make sense. Again, strive to allow the body to lead as opposed to the critical mind (working in a space without mirrors or with mirrors that can be covered can assist in this process), especially if you have knowledge and/or practice in traditional dance-making methods. Repeat your phrase again and again, perhaps slowing things down on some rehearsals to engage more thoroughly. Can you go deeper into your felt experience with each repetition? Finish by reflecting on your growth during this self-guided process. Is there a difference between the kind of learning you experience in a self-guided experience versus one led by someone else? If so, how is the learning different?

Example B

Let's return here to the idea of "subtle engagement" and work toward a deepening of this theme in the bodymind. Once again, in organizing phrase work that is self-guided in nature, participants will work with embodiment, trusting the knowledge amassed through individual felt experiences.

Find a comfortable place to begin, and using breath, begin to center awareness and presence. Choose a verbal prompt to work with that contains at least some elements of release; "swing" would work nicely. Begin to play with swing-like movements in the body, migrating to different body parts such as arms, legs, head, hips, etc. Warm up the process by playing and exploring for a bit until you feel comfortable in the

Figure 6.7. SomaLab practitioner Megan Allman, right, and her peers create phrase work from ideas gleaned during conceptually-guided movement investigations (author's collection; photograph by Lindsay Osten).

activity. Gradually, narrow your focus to sensation, and when you encounter a movement or sequence of movements that speaks particularly to the idea of "swing," repeat it several times, clarify the movement as you investigate. After you feel confident in this embodied pattern of movement, continue your explorations, continuing to reveal actions that further your work. Repeat the process of rehearsal and refinement and add new information to previously identified actions, beginning to build a phrase that best represents your understanding of the verbal prompt "swing." When you feel this journey has come to an end, perform your phrase at different tempos, maybe moving elements around, developing a pattern that expands your understanding. Change facings or move to different parts of your space for new context. As you close, reflect on other movement experiences with "swing." How is this self-made experience similar? How is it different?

Facilitated Phrase Work

While self-guided phrase work can be a very effective tool in training the nervous system toward efficiency in learning and performance, facilitated phrase work, or movement sequences/patterns coming from a source outside the self, can also be beneficial in creating knowledge of process. Parameters of facilitated phrase work include:

- Identifying meaningful and accessible movement from an outside source
- Exploring the material through a personal lens, focusing on embodied knowledge
- Approaching and molding the material to center individual expressiveness

Example A

If you are a practicing movement artist, you may have a phrase or sequence of movements you are presently working on. Outside-sourced material can often be challenging, as it is truly lives in the bodymind of the creator. Choose to work with material that feels challenging, difficult, or even foreign in your instrument, with the goal of facilitating expressive performance and using your own embodied knowledge to enrich communication and understanding.

Locate a place where you can be comfortably still but can also easily segue into movement when it is time. Begin by mentally practicing the movement you will explore, initiating a review of sequence and body position. Once you are confident in your recall, go further with your

6. Building a Personal Practice 155

visualization—which elements do you remember feeling appropriate and satisfying, and which elements felt disagreeable and unpleasant? Begin to transition from thought to movement, letting go of the work of memory, and focusing on your felt experience. Work one element at a time, pausing to note which pieces sit well in your bodymind, and which pieces would benefit from additional efforts.

Continue practicing one bit at a time and assign a verbal label to each chunk that best aligns with your own understanding of the movement, as opposed to pulling from codified vocabulary. For example, instead of thinking "developé," think "extend" or "lift." This shifts the movement's impetus from a rote reproduction to a living, curious, always changing investigation, and one that has personal meaning. As you rehearse, indulge in the sensation of your conceptual understanding. This is best done without mirrors, deemphasizing visual results.

Take liberties now in terms of time and space. Does it make more sense to perform some pieces very slowly, and others more quickly? Where would stillness make sense to you? What kind of rhythms do you feel most comfortable with? Do lower levels feel more comfortable in your body; do you relate to weightiness? Do you prefer soft, arcing, curvilinear movement, or do you find power in spoking, linear shapes? Take time to rehearse and perform the phrase as you would have arranged it, paying particular attention to the more challenging moments.

Now, go back and revisit the phrase as it was presented to you. Do you perhaps know more; are you more readily able to infuse your own embodied knowledge into work from an outside source? Can you be rich in performance and expression? Perhaps you will have an opportunity to share your new knowledge or even show it from your own perspective.

Example B

Over-efforting is a typical response for performing artists when presented with new material. Anxious to master and quickly succeed, learning and performing can feel forced, unnatural. This unnecessary quality of attack can disrupt efficiency and expressiveness, narrowing the channels of experiences from which to draw. How can we use the full range of our embodied knowledge when presented with phrase work from outside our own realm of felt experiences?

This example can be used in real-time situations but practicing the process many times before applying the work will prepare you for a successful experience; mental practice can be a useful tool here. Start by finding a quiet place where you can bring your gaze internal and come to presence. Focus on smooth inhales and steady exhales, balancing the sympathetic and parasympathetic nervous systems. When you feel a sense of calm in your bodymind, gradually shift your attention to imagery and visualization, seeing yourself learning unfamiliar movement with confidence and ease. You can use embodied knowledge and learned processes to make associations with new material, creating a personal movement language, and relating the phrase as a whole to a concept that has value to you. This way, when new material is presented that you don't particularly have a natural affinity to, you are able to view it through a different lens and calmly work through the challenge by making the unfamiliar familiar. What is it like? What does it feel like? Are you able to keep your physical body relaxed and easy?

When you're comfortable with this visualization technique, try using it in an active learning situation. Ask a friend or colleague to share a short phrase with you or try mastering something from YouTube or social media. Stay steady in your approach—focus your attention on the task without letting past experiences or future worries interfere. Keep steady as you breathe. When you encounter movements you find difficult or you're not sure of the creator's intent, insert your own—approach the sequence as you would something that is habitual to you. For example, if you encounter an element from codified ballet vocabulary, but you are primarily an improviser, borrow from your knowledge. What impetus or quality can you assign a leg moving straight out in front of you? Maybe a giant hand lifts the limb, or a strong wind sweeps it up and carries it gently back down. Creating your own story also builds meaning making, and strengthens your embodied experiences, so next time you encounter something similar, you think "oh yes, I remember another situation that was similar, and I...."

Finish by finding stillness and reflecting on your experience. Did visualization of new learning transfer to a real-time experience? What parts of the process are best experienced physically in the bodymind?

Conclusion

The examples provided in this chapter are just a few illustrations of often-used tasks that have been successful in building efficiency and expression in learning and performance, especially when practiced regularly over time. However, remember that SomaLab is a *framework,* so any event that includes the task parameters can help develop the nervous system's capacity for flexibility and further embodied knowledge. To reiterate, building an experience is a creative act in itself, and this process can help the participant gather information concerning movement affinity even before practice begins.

Figure 6.8. Phrase work coming from an outside source can be facilitated by individual movement research, as demonstrated by Ariel Cole, left, and Maggie Derloshon (author's collection; photograph by Lindsay Osten).

You may have noted that imagery, visualization, and mental practice are often suggested tools in many SomaLab tasks and examples. As addressed in previous chapters, these activities are highly useful in forming and developing neural pathways. In Chapter 5, I referenced Hanson and Mendius who, in their text *Buddha's Brain: The Practical Neuroscience of Happiness, Love, & Wisdom*,[4] explain the science behind neuroplasticity (as does Chapter 3) and outline steps that can lead to permanent changes in one's mind states. Many of the activities proposed involve thinking about something differently and often to make changes in neural pathways and connections. These changes are *embodied*, meaning they prompt structural and functional changes in the mind *and* physical instrument.

Lastly, the prominent benefit of a framework as opposed to a codified set of activities is the capability for movers to center their individuality, especially in strengthening identities regarding culture, class, gender, sexuality, and other aspects of one's life that may not be addressed in traditional movement practice. The building of self is integral to a healthy mind/body relationship; we return once again to the words of Martha Graham, "Movement never lies. It is a barometer telling the state of the soul's weather to all who can read it."[5]

While this chapter centered the experience of the individual, Chapter

7 broadens our gaze past the self and into the movement lives of others. Our study of contemporary learning systems in Chapter 4 scaffolds this work, and reminds us that we move, and live, among a community and in a physical world.

7

Moving Together
The Somatic Community

"It doesn't hurt me.
Do you want to feel how it feels?"
From "Running Up That Hill (A Deal with God)"
—Kate Bush[1]

Introduction

The lyrics from Kate Bush's iconic 1985 hit "Running Up That Hill (A Deal with God)" serve as a perfect metaphor for how embodied communication can work. She begins with a statement that lets us know how she feels, and then asks if we want to experience sensations as she encounters them. Feeling moves us closer to knowing, and we gain knowledge from shared events. As the verse concludes, she relays that she has a plan of action, and asks if we'd like to hear it, aware we now understand. This is the process of empathetic embodiment.

Chapters 5 and 6 position SomaLab as a framework that can provide a multi-faceted and meaningful approach for individuals to build a personal practice and develop skill as an expressive and efficient mover. Tools and tasks facilitate creative choices that allow each movement artist to work in a way that affirms their unique affinities and informs process by the very act of designing an experience. As effective as these methods are for self-praxis, the SomaLab framework is made even richer through inter-personal interactions. Group work is a natural next step after the practitioner becomes comfortable with their own inner gaze and wishes to share and learn with an outward view; they are now primed to investigate and develop movement empathy, appreciation, and compassion for forms and innate tendencies outside of one's embodied self. We live together; we teach each other. Through these experiences, our world becomes both smaller and bigger at the same time.

Bringing SomaLab principles and tasks into codified learning situations also provides fertile ground for focusing on individuality and discovering nuance when the creator is outside of the practitioner. Teachers and leaders of all movement arts can utilize SomaLab to encourage learners to find their own voices within preliminary technical exercises or develop a common phrase into a qualitative performance. Again, a framework approach also has the benefit of respecting participants' identities and experiences.

This chapter explores the parameters of group design and offers examples of specific tasks that will foster creative learning in the studio and beyond. A renewed discussion of movement empathy in the context of community praxis follows, as does the role of cultural relevancy in somatic work and foundational pedagogical principles, scaffolding the conversation. Finally, experiential models of movement offerings integrated into both self-guided and codified movement situations provide the reader with specific information that are useful in collective environments.

Empathy

Looking outward, seeing, hearing, and/or feeling another person's kinesthetic energy through mindful observation can certainly enrich our own field of knowledge and understanding. Empathy occurs when we identify with the inner states or experiences of other people and can, in a sense, embody another person. We can "feel how it feels" through practice and using somatic principles in group learning situations, as our nervous systems are built for empathy. Hanson and Mendius explain that specific areas of the brain are activated when we observe another person performing movement tasks in a way that is not dissimilar to the neural activity generated when we ourselves are moving—this gives us an idea of what someone else may be feeling in their own bodies.[2] They further elaborate that this phenomenon is also present in non-movement, or emotional situations. For example, "the insula and linked circuits activate" when humans experience strong emotional responses, but they also mobilize when we witness this behavior in others, especially if they are individuals that we view with affection. And the more we develop our own perception and proprioception of our bodymind instruments, the more informed we are when making sense of the moods and actions of others. They conclude, "In effect, the limbic networks that produce your feelings also make sense of the feelings of others."[3] Recall our discussion of the limbic structures in Chapter 3, which are associated with emotional responses and learning and memory, as well as the limbic-related insula, thought to be involved in emotion and body awareness.

Indeed, the term "theory of mind" is used in psychology to explain how we understand each other, identifying with the actions, emotions, and thoughts of others. It is an important aspect of empathy, and often, we "try on" what it is like to be someone else.[4] This principle is the basis for group work in the SomaLab framework, where observation, sharing ("gifting"), and incorporation work together to foster movement empathy.

So, how do these approaches to inter-person facilitation work in concert to honor individual identities? Think of this process in developmental terms—after the self becomes defined and there is confidence in that definition, the mover feels emboldened to take the internal gaze external. We tap into a sense of communal understanding, an idea that we are all part of the same universal matrix and share certain fundamental characteristics (including non-human, and non-sentient objects). And as we become aware of this belonging, we can solidify our own unique role and contribution to the larger world within this context. We can critically analyze (often innately) what is the same and what is different, which further

Figure 7.1. Lalah Hazelwood, right, begins the process of shifting her attention outward, facilitating empathetic movement exchange during performance, as Rachel Newbrough maintains her internal gaze (author's collection; photograph by Freddie Kelvin).

defines who we are, and continue to construct an evolved sense of self. In time, we are ready to share our uniqueness with others, and we can likewise receive embodied knowledge from a moving cohort. As we learn from each other, not only are the boundaries of the individual expanded, but our empathetic connections clear the way for entire groups of people to move forward, together. The self is not separate, but part of a larger community that supports its members in growth. We can all exist, be, feel, in a way that is truly embodied, as the juvenile self is relaxed, and firm boundaries become flexible.

Cultural Relevancy in Movement Experiences

The idea of empathy through movement too has ramifications in conversations surrounding cultural awareness, cultural competency, and cultural relevancy. As a truly embodied expression, it is imperative to recognize that dance and movement integrate the bodymind, and that the body carries not only our individual identities, but cultural signifiers, too, that are inseparable from our instrument.[5] So, the question arises: can a more process-based approach in practice and performance build inclusivity? When dance artists have agency over their own movement, can they prioritize cultural signifiers and preserve them in a way that honors identity while allowing others to embody their experiences?

Often, in traditional codified group movement situations practitioners' cultural identities can be actively and/or passively erased and excluded. Stakeholders (professional performers, artistic directors, educators, et al.) in the movement arts have an opportunity to provide optimal conditions for learning and performing, and to lead in best inclusive practices. In her widely regarded text, *Dance Pedagogy for a Diverse World*, Nyama McCarthy-Brown explains:

> Culture is a lifeline for all people. Meaning is made through cultural informants and reference points. These cultural informants act as building blocks that people use to develop an understanding of the world. Thus, culture has a significant impact on the lens through which the world is seen and understood. Research findings indicate that students learn more when pedagogy practices are culturally relevant.[6]

When an artist's own culture is honored, celebrated, and respected, they too will flourish, and expressive capabilities will deepen. Perhaps self-guided work, when shared and embodied by others, can be a step in broadening knowledge beyond the self.

How We Learn

In Chapter 2, we examined principles of motor learning and control that are important in understanding how humans acquire movement knowledge. Our exploration of the nervous system in Chapter 3 facilitated our understanding of neuroplasticity, or the ability of the brain to alter its structure following changes in behavior. Chapter 4 broadened our gaze to include psychosocial and environmental influences, and nested timescales in learning and performing into our movement lives. Viewed comprehensively, we see that structural and behavioral change is at the foundation of our capability to acquire new skills and expand already existing neural pathways. These principles are relevant when considering both self-guided and group-led movement experiences, and practice is key.

The fundamental question, though, is *what* do we practice? If we repeat a movement over and over again, our brains structurally change to accommodate learning this new skill. If learning a discrete movement is the goal, then this makes sense. But if the goal is to develop a large palette of human movement that is diverse, expressive, inclusive, malleable, and able to accommodate new concepts when prompted, then this warrants a different approach. In this case, we practice *process*. Developing skill in reacting to new, changing environments, thus expanding artistic capabilities, aligns with a dynamical systems theory approach to movement behavior. You will remember that according to dynamical systems theory, many things are happening simultaneously—the individual, task at hand, and the environment all interact to create a spontaneous movement response to a specific situation. So, practicing the ability to react spontaneously in different kinds of situations might be important. Serial repetition of movement might be more akin to an information processing model, where the goal is predictable reproduction of skill in a known environment, acquired through rote repetition under similar conditions. Instead of engaging in linear, inefficient repetition of specific movements, we practice responding to new concepts, drawing on what we already know, imagining new actions, and then giving it all a try.

Let's also review here contextual interference effects, where rote but random repetition of several tasks is practiced simultaneously, thus creating a more unpredictable environment during rehearsal. In study after study, the superiority of random practice situations over serial practice conditions in extended memory holds firm. This sort of hybrid practice arrangement can also be utilized in the SomaLab framework when creating individual or group experiences. The very nature of a group event magnifies the number of factors that guide environmental influence, thus creating a more complex and fluid learning structure. If practicing new

Figure 7.2. Movement artists (from left) Jillian McCabe, Pandora Basset, and May Saito focus on procedural knowledge as they deepen their craft through journaling (courtesy Stefanie Nelson; photograph by Rachelle Saker).

processes, and responding to unpredictable cues is a *positive* thing, as proposed by dynamical systems theorists, then interactions between individuals can only expand the experience.

We also learn by exposure to different kinds of information. Procedural knowledge, or knowing what to do through a mental construct, is cognitively driven. Leaders can utilize differing cues and images to adapt to different learning styles and lived experiences, as in the IMI discussed in Chapter 5. Experiential knowledge is practice or experiencing a task physically. Through repetition, we develop kinesthetic memory and familiarity. Feedback, both internal and external, can deeply facilitate this mode of learning. Modeling is also a kind of experiential learning, where we tacitly gather knowledge from an expert, observing their actions and behaviors. We notice and imitate their performance, engaging in mirroring, and broadening our understanding of what is possible.

Learners are often eager to change and deepen their craft, and leaders can greatly facilitate their progress by understanding how movement learning occurs and drawing attention to process. Through mindfulness and attention, repetition, and feedback, movers can manifest success in discovering a full range of experiences.

Pedagogical Considerations

In creating and leading SomaLab experiences for a group, there are pedagogical considerations to address as participants build a practice that has value for all involved. I want to note here that novel forms and systems are first and foremost research in the movement arts, though they may be disseminated through pedagogy. Innovative methodologies and creative acts are indeed original investigations, and, like other research modalities, will be shared, taught, and documented over time. Thus, the aim of this section, and chapter, is not to provide a thorough examination of current best practices for movement pedagogy but to enable practitioners and leaders in their construction of a communal SomaLab experience.

It also feels appropriate here to address the inclusion of example sessions in Chapters 6, 7, and 9. These example sessions are not lesson plans in the tradition sense, but rather are blueprints for the reader to observe the process of session construction and illustrate how SomaLab principles are applied. Language, too, is important, and pertinent to the implementation of the tools. In summary, the examples provided are critical for the practitioner in creating their own SomaLab experience.

Two pedagogical considerations, however, theming and progression, have a strong presence in the safe and effective teaching of movement and are discussed here in the context of optimal presentation. These applications can provide a developmentally appropriate framework for exploring concepts as a group, while allowing for individual and phenomenological knowledge to interface with a leader's own sense of what is important.

Theming

Choosing directions, or themes, for movement sessions can start with a facilitator's own values and priorities. What ways of moving, and understanding movement, are important to you? Where has your own wisdom and experience led you as you practice embodiment? For example, you may have discovered, over time, that to achieve the best use of the body's own biomechanical properties, breath and movement initiation are linked. There is an efficiency, an ease, that follows this pairing. Perhaps you have also come to know the value of practicing floorwork to deepen a mover's understanding of gravitational forces upon the body. The mover here can discover just how much muscular engagement is necessary to move through space on all levels, and how to conserve energy when opposing forces collide.

It is equally important to consider what a group brings to an experience, and to question how you as a facilitator can benefit from the insights and ideas of others. Perhaps a group member is a devoted practitioner of meditation whose movement patterns are deeply informed by stillness, or whose dance experience includes non-western practices that are steeped in rhythmic integrations of the bodymind. Can you spotlight unique knowledges within the group, weaving new movement ideas into a practice as you lead? This requires an openness, a flexibility, in presenting thematic materials and creating opportunities that have room to expand in the moment.

These are just a few examples of how themes might show up in SomaLab group design, and answer a basic question posed by backward curriculum methodology—what do you want the cohort to know? Now you can go about the business of creating an experiential plan that allows individuals to extend existing knowledge and make new discoveries.

Progression

Progression is the process that allows skills to build upon each other, encouraging optimal learning. In movement practice, preparation of the body is especially critical to ensure safety and longevity of a practitioner's physical instrument. The SomaLab framework is innately structured to support progression of the entire bodymind system; deconstructive, reconstructive, and integrative tasks prepare the nervous system, and slowly engage muscles and joints as the mover advances from simple to complex sensations, thoughts, and movements. Flowing from individual focus to group interactions is a sort of progression as well, as the gaze moves from internal to external and movement experiences grow richer from the contributions of others. Expanding the SomaLab framework beyond the individual builds a community of somatic practitioners who learn from each other and explore embodied empathy together.

SomaLab Activities for Groups

A SomaLab group session can begin by offering elements of deconstructive, reconstructive, and integrative tasks as presented in Chapter 6, utilizing principles of theming and progression as markers for organizing material. After fully experiencing the arc of somatic practice through an individual lens, movers may be ready to engage with other participants, expanding their own bodymind knowledge.

Observation and Embodied Re-Practice

A first step for group practitioners following individual movement exploration is to broaden their personal focus and begin to see outside of their own instrument. This action initiates the process of receiving, reflecting, and incorporating a larger repertoire of movement information.

EXAMPLE

Find a place of stillness and take a moment to focus on the sensations in your bodymind. What do you perceive, right now, in this present moment? Can you reflect on changes, or new understandings that have appeared? Breathe in, breathe out, letting this information settle, sink in. After a time, gently let go, and prepare to begin a new journey that embraces happenings outside of yourself. Start with the senses, seeing, hearing, touching. With ease, notice the space around you—are there patterns on the walls, is the paint around the windowpanes cracked? How does the floor feel underneath your feet? Are there sounds of a busy world close by, cars, conversations, or indications the environment is shifting, changing? Do you hear wind, rain? Maybe a certain texture in the space is interesting to you, and you reach out to touch it—what does it feel like, what do you experience? Is it rough, or smooth, moveable, or static?

Figure 7.3. Aerin Webber, standing, broadens his movement gaze by observing fellow Soma-Lab practitioner Lucy Morrison (author's collection; photograph by Lindsay Osten).

Gradually shift your gaze to the other practitioners in the space. As you travel around the room, make eye contact, perhaps offering a greeting through facial expression, words, or touch. Let each fellow mover impact you in some way, feeling the effect of your inclusion in this somatic community. Begin to gravitate toward one or two group members, deepening your observation to include movement patterns (the leader can also assign partners at the start of the session if this feels like a good choice). As you slowly circle each other, one person begins to share a phrase, motif, or any part of repertoire gleaned from individual exploration, repeating the sequence several times. Careful, three-dimensional observation by partners allows for empathetic embodiment and new understanding. Repeat this process until everyone has had an opportunity to share and observe movement. Briefly separate and take some time on your own to revisit the work you shared. Has the opportunity to learn and empathize broadened your own understanding of how you move, what you know? Do you feel any different, or are you experiencing a new sense of fulfillment?

Embodiment, Visualized

Utilizing visualization and imagery techniques from the SomaLab framework, practitioners can take some time sans external movement to begin the experience of embodiment outside of themselves. Priming the body through the mind, much like deconstructive tasks in personal practice, can ready the soma to receive and experience another's way of moving, and being.

EXAMPLE

Find some personal space in your group environment, and become comfortable, settle—this can be standing, sitting, or reclining on the earth, wherever you feel most focused. Bring your gaze internal as you breathe deeply and evenly, preparing to engage the imagination. Recall a member of the movement community that you had an opportunity to observe, and reflect on their unique way of moving, and the choices they made. What might this feel like in your skin? Perhaps there was a pattern of percussive movements that conveyed a sense of power. What would it be like to embrace this concept in your own body, particularly if your affinities lean toward softer, successional movement? How might you grow, and change? Conversely, maybe you are a strong and powerful mover, and yearn to experience a sense of gentleness, calmness in your approach. Did you have a chance to observe a peer who exemplified this way of being? Here, maybe you can feel a sense of vulnerability and openness instead through the chest and sternum, releasing the tension in the muscles throughout the body. Whatever you have chosen to take in, allow time to capture imagined sensation, and accompanying emotional and spiritual responses. Now, visualize your bodymind merging with another's, feeling what they feel, doing what they do. Proprioception shifts, and it is wonderful, fantastical, to embody another person and work outside of your own perspective. When you have fully flexed your "imagery" muscles, slowly return to your soma with a sense of comfort and familiarity. Take a few moments to work through the imagined experience and prepare to take on the next step of physical embodiment.

Gifting

Following observation of other participant's movement choices and affinities, "gifting" provides the opportunity to try on something new in one's own body. Can we feel what someone else feels? What is it like to slip into someone else's skin, even for a moment?

EXAMPLE

Come back together in your groups after re-practice and embodied visualization. Initiate the process of observation once again, slowly circling each other with one artist moving through their repertoire at a time. As each person moves, identify a small portion of their work that you would like to emulate, and incorporate the segment into your own devised performance. Choose something from each of your associates, and ask them to share it with you, using either verbal or movement cues (or both) to foster and heighten your understanding. Where does this new material fit into your own? Reconfigure, augment, and/or expand your own work as you embrace something new. Take time to practice slowly, focusing on novel sensations and reflecting on any similarities or differences between the new material and your own proclivities. Repeat this process with each person you are working with. You will also be called upon to share your ideas with others. What it is like to give the gift of movement, of yourself; to share the knowledge and expertise of your own bodymind? There is an inherent joy in this action, and a sense that someone else can know you a little bit better and understand your experiences and perspectives. Can you, as well, receive with gratitude, welcoming new material without judgement, even if it doesn't feel quite right just yet in your own instrument? After everyone has shared and received, once again take time for three-dimensional observation of each newly incorporated phrase. Can you see growth, and a deepening of each person's somatic experience? Can you feel it in yourself?

Gifting, Expanded

Receiving a piece of a collaborator's devised movement, born of a concept, is akin to having a conversation and embracing an alternative point of view. While your lived experiences may focus your ideas very differently, deep, empathetic listening can expand your way of thinking. So, too, can different ways of moving, or moving from another perspective; your repertoire broadens, and you practice the *process* of differentiation and subsequent incorporation. There is satisfaction as well in the act of giving, of amplifying another's direct experience, that connects you in a very real way to the greater matrix of existence. So, the natural next step is to share more, to give more.

EXAMPLE

After "gifting" a small portion of your devised somatic repertory, offer the entirety of what you have made to your gifting partner, and conversely, they will offer you their creative work. Instead of employing traditional pedagogical methodology, where language is used to dictate sequence, verbal cueing, effort, quality, etc., consider a unified movement praxis of repetition bereft of words as a means of communication. Slowly,

Figure 7.4. "Gifting" is the process of sharing a piece of self-created repertory with a peer. Payton McCollam, left, and Baylee McAllister expand their knowledge through movement exchange (author's collection; photograph by Lindsay Osten).

deliberately, move through each other's phrases, alternating back and forth. Both movers are simultaneously observing each other, learning, and investigating while also tuning in to individual sensation. How does it feel when you encounter movement you had previously gifted? Is there a flash of recognition, feeling at home in the body, or do you crave the exhilaration of the unknown? Continue this process until each partner can move through the other's material comfortably and knowledgeably. Separate to continue practice, creating the opportunity to bring the gaze inward once again and sink into the sensation of moving. As you flow, notice which elements you have embraced and understood, and which are still unknown. Why the discrepancies? Reflect on these missing pieces as you bring this session to a close.

Duetting (Repertory Informed)

Duetting, or making a dance with another person, follows the experience of "gifting," and can further the empathetic experience. Moving alongside another individual, feeling their breath on your body, sensing their innate rhythm, entering their kinesphere, and making decisions in real time deepens somatic understanding as learning and exchange occur tacitly when bodies interact.

EXAMPLE

Identify (or a leader can assign) a fellow participant as a partner. Ideally, this is someone you've collaborated with during "gifting," as there is already a history of shared movement and space, but any pairing can provide a successful experience. Locate a perimeter within your practice environment that is clear and safe for the work of two bodies. Very slowly, in proximity (if it is comfortable—please choose a spatial arrangement that is agreeable to all), both partners begin to move through the most recent iteration of somatic repertory discovered during SomaLab practice. As you experience each element, slowly, mindfully, how can your partner's choices and performance inform your own?

Approach this unfolding improvisationally, allowing for changes in your own work as you stay open to new information and different ways of sensing and moving. Stillness and silence can be taken as needed. As you work, begin to let go of devised movement and sequence, and gradually shift into a self-guided approach to partner interaction; release any repertory and allow the body to lead. How does your body fit into another's, and what does this tell you about your own affinities and predispositions? Perhaps you notice that you are most comfortable responding as opposed to leading, but your partner is bold in their initiation. Can you embody their mindset, and begin to feel what they feel? When something is felt a little differently in your own bodymind it looks different, too—changing the function, and ultimately the structure. Moving into another person's mindset also shifts your movement, and the emboldening you now experience is inspired by a shared kinesthesia. Alternatively, you may often find you are leading, but responding seems unnatural or difficult. Can you soften and release, and allow yourself to be led by another's bodymind, as opposed to your own? What is this experience like? Now, see if you can toggle back and forth between approaches, blurring the lines between where your learned experiences begin and your new investigations end. This research allows you to stretch your repertory of initiation and response, both through giving and taking. The exchange broadens your view of movement, as it does for all participants, and builds appreciation and understanding across genre, culture, and individuals.

You can repeat this process many times, playing with the speed, rhythm, spatial arrangements, and the movement quality of your work. Note the shifts in your bodymind as your sensory awareness and empathy expands. Also note your own responses as you moved from a devised fitting of your movement with another's to a more authentic exchange of information. It's important here not to attach value to your observations, but simply to register occurrences. After fully exploring and embracing this interaction, bring it to a close, reflecting on your growth, and incorporating new knowledge into your repertory.

Duetting (Action/Reaction)

In repertory informed duetting, practitioners work to embody different approaches to moving and reflect on how another's bodymind can affect their own. This first step focuses on identifying similarities and differences between individuals. A next step, duetting action/reaction, can go beyond previous duetting experiences, focusing now on the work of two bodyminds merging as one. Can we release comparisons and learned habits, embracing new movement as our own? In this exploration, contact between two bodies is an option; individuals should discuss and agree on the role of touch before they begin, and only pursue this avenue of movement research if both are completely comfortable. Please note the experience can be just as rich without touch or contact.

EXAMPLE

Recall the impetus, or concept, for your made work, i.e., perhaps the original prompt was the word "sweep." Now, start anew, letting go of previous repertory—you may find yourself with a richer pool of movement after prior interactions. One partner begins by offering an action as a means of genesis, and the other reacts spontaneously, authentically, through movement, to this offering. Already, a new stream of investigation stemming from the interaction of two bodies is born. Repeat this process of one partner performing an action, and the other reacting through movement. While a mindful approach is useful to start things off, after a period the soul of the work takes over. Initiations and subsequent responses can come from either individual, creating a seamless flow of movement between the two partners. Specific prompts can serve as an important point of inception, but they need not limit the explorations of each pairing. As the process continues, and partners experience each other's understanding of concepts, they can create something new through a collaborative investigation that is singular to these two bodies, in this time and place. Information is offered, shared, experienced anew, and grows exponentially when absorbed into existing frameworks.

If you have engaged with physical contact with your partner's bodymind, there is opportunity to add kinesthesia from an outside source into this encounter. Skin receptors augment visual and auditory information, and proprioception ignites as you take and release the weight of another body, muscle tension increasing and decreasing. Bracing and counterbalance are also present, and the work expands to encompass shared force between partners. There is the knowledge that one mover cannot exactly recreate this intimate experience, although the remembered sensation will add to your palette of movement and lived experiences.

If you and your partner chose not to engage in physical contact, the opportunity is ripe for increased observation and sensation, particularly through visual and auditory means. Can you focus on curves and angles of limbs, the ebb and flow of the breath cycle? Can you visualize an exchange of energy and information, skin to skin, without actual touch? Can you imagine the effects on your own body, and on your partner's, if you were to touch? A non-contact event yields the benefits of two-person interaction as does one with contact; they are different, but one is not better than the other. Consider that all movement occurrences are valuable, regardless of their nature. And our plastic nervous system is made to adapt—in the absence of one thing, it will turn to another to provide the organism with the most optimal experience possible, one that will ensure health and success. This adaptability is the very heart of SomaLab—we develop the system for change, not for statis.

Practitioners will sense when the cycle of exchange is ready to end and can bring it to close, taking time to reflect on the experience through movement, discussion, and rest. After a period, as an individual, revisit the repertory you initially brought to your pairing. How can you bring

Figure 7.5. Somatic investigations into shared body weight can be part of "dueting," a SomaLab activity for groups, demonstrated by Chloe Albin, front (courtesy Julia Dicenza; photograph by Julia Dicenza).

new knowledge and the embodiment of others' values and experiences into your own? Has your collection expanded? Move carefully and slowly as you sense change and growth.

Summary

As we reflect on the collaborative experience and all it has to offer, consider the words of Jawole Willa Jo Zollar, iconic dance-maker and founder of the legendary dance company Urban Bush Women:

> …when you're collaborating with someone who thinks differently than you, who solves differently than you, I think you both end up going to a growing place where you're both pushed. I know the ways that I can solve things just on my own, but when I've got somebody whose brilliant, creative mind solves it very differently than how I solve it, and they watch me solve things very differently, then I think we grow together. What I see is that collaboration is not a compromise. That's collaboration, I think, at its worst. Collaboration is about trust and learning together, where you create an environment where you can both learn from one another and then grow to create this thing that is a dynamic entity based on this new relationship with one another.[7]

SomaLab Framework and Codified Movement Practice

Many traditional approaches to teaching movement forms focus on the external, the physical, with the goal of achieving certain places in the body and ways to get there—for example, consider a high leg extended to the side, achieved through stretching sequences, abdominal strength work, and efforts to externally rotate the leg over many months, even years, of training. Specificity of practice is an important principle that has been validated in the scientific community, and useful when performance of a singular form is the goal. However, as discussed early in Chapter 5, today's dance environment asks movement artists to be versatile, fluid, and able to move between forms, processes, and approaches. Is it possible to incorporate the SomaLab framework into learning situations where a specific form is the goal? And under what conditions might this be desirable? Recall that Knapp, as described in Chapter 4, employed the OPTIMAL theory of motor learning to the teaching of classical western dance techniques, and using an action research paradigm, saw significant and successful results.

Indeed, somatic work can be woven into the study of codified techniques, supporting a rich understanding of one's own bodymind instrument and allowing the practitioner to dig deeper into the genesis of form. Employing this kind of movement integration can be critical when learners from different modes of genre and style come together, as they do in many higher education programs. By evening out the playing field, movers can find common ground. Studio environments that include students with disabilities at all levels of learning can also benefit from a somatic approach to leading form-based movement techniques. Likewise, experienced artists can expand their repertory, not replacing what they already know, but enriching their movement base, in an exponential, rather than additive, manner.

Integrating the SomaLab framework into a more linear-based movement practice can also highlight the process of "learning how to learn." Often in early training there is an emphasis on reproduction of shape and flexibility, strength, endurance, and less focus on embodying thoughts and ideas to build an expressive body. Consider the concept of "non-patterning," as movers release unsafe or constricting habits in moving their praxis forward. At the heart of this knowledge of process is awareness, mindfulness, and presence while moving, as artists apply attention to and monitor the body via perception and sensation for kinesthetic change. Movers who embrace process over product will experience an extraordinary amount of growth, and fast, in any movement learning environment. The following section offers examples of expanding the teaching of codified technique and form to incorporate a somatic framework.

Warm-Up

The role of a warm-up in group presentation is to ready the bodymind for learning. This means addressing all aspects of the instrument—the physical body as well as the energy body, assembling the community to work together, and helping movers become present and deliberate in their approach. This first example (Example A) allows group participants not only to prepare to move, but to forge the beginnings of groupthink and empathetic behaviors in learning. A leader can also encourage this process in a way that individualizes bodymind preparation and allows the participant to make choices informed by their lived experiences, present state of being, and goals for praxis (Example B). Offering a framework that "checks-in" with various bodily systems can be an effective means achieving readiness.

EXAMPLE A

Identify a partner or two. Introduce yourselves and start moving the body as you begin a verbal conversation. Perhaps if you know the person or people well, the discussion can take on a deeper tone; if you've just met and are getting acquainted, you can focus more on sharing information. When you arrive at an area of common interest, stay there for a while. As the conversation narrows and you find common experiences, bring the verbal portion of the conversation to a close, but keep the physical conversation moving along, starting to align breath, and movement quality, but without words.

As this general warm-up runs its course, begin to focus on more specific areas of the body and its movements. One partner can take the lead, suggesting a body part (i.e., "shoulders") or, a movement (i.e., "circle ankles"). Take turns offering general warm-up areas/movements. As this process naturally draws to a close, allow participants some personal time to finish preparing for moving and learning.

EXAMPLE B

Find a comfortable place lying on your back, engaging in full, even breaths. Scan your instrument from head to toe, taking time to notice tension, soreness, or other areas of discomfort. Visualize the breath moving into these places, warming, softening, and opening. As you begin to release and slow down, turn your attention to the mind, noting here distractions, worries, planning. Over three focused breath cycles, move errant thoughts from your mind's eye, coming to rest in the present moment.

Begin to work with circular movement in the joints, targeting areas that you previously identified as needing attention. Maybe ankles are stiff, or hips feel tight. Explore actions that slowly and easily manipulate insertions and surrounding soft tissue. Move through the body, indulging in sensation and noticing change. When the joints are sufficiently prepped, turn your attention to muscular states, engaging in dynamic stretch and self-touch/massage. As you're ready, pursue contracted states to further engage muscles, i.e., variations of plank for the core, back, and shoulders, lifts against gravity for the legs and hips. Focus on areas that require readiness and may be employed during the upcoming group practice.

Lastly, join breath and movement through gentle shape-flow, extending from the core to distal body parts as you inhale, and shrinking and closing as you exhale. Maybe you visit familiar shapes, or perhaps you're more interested in investigating new places. This is an opportunity to unite the mind and body in a way that best supports your goals and intentions for praxis.

Figure 7.6. Raegan Shapiro, left, and Kylie Furlong use conversation and movement to warm the bodymind as they prepare for a codified movement experience (author's collection; photograph by Lindsay Osten).

Center Work (Free-Form)

In scripted dance techniques, center work normally consists of specific movement sequences meant to provide a foundation for the form's underlying intent and values. These exercises are part of a progression that prepares the bodymind for more complex, and/or rigorous, approaches later in the session. In non-dance movement art practices, this portion focuses on the same type of development, as the bodymind is made ready for a "peak" or final experience. The key to incorporating a somatic path into progressive work is to identify underlying ideals in the form, and work from there.

Example

Begin by identifying a key concept, or value, of the form you are studying, for example, "release" in contemporary dance practice. Use improvisation to explore this idea in your bodymind, free of codified constraints. Perhaps you come across a particular cue, or specific movement, that assists you in your research and understanding of this concept. As you explore, notice sequences that feel authentic and honest in your own instrument, and repeat them several times to develop a sequence of your own; in other words, create your own series of progressive work that makes the most sense to you, individualizing to both complement and challenge your movement studies. A leader may ask you to use a particular rhythm, or use a pre-determined set or counts, or create within a defined amount of time. This allows for everyone in the community to dance together, sharing a common, and defined, temporal constraint, while meeting the desire of movers to work as individuals. After sufficient repetition, share your devised work with other community members, with leaders allowing time for practice. This process can be repeated in accordance with session goals.

Center Work (Structured)

A free-form approach for center work allows for an investigation of concept within a loose framework. Somatic approaches can also be explored within a more structured setting, where specific exercises are offered to support skills necessary for a particular technique. For example, let's consider the "plié," a dance exercise used in ballet and some contemporary dance forms that increases and decreases angles of the ankles, knees, and hips through flexion and extension. There is an aesthetic component to this movement that supports technical forms, but the very act of bending and straightening the legs is found in many other dance styles and practices, as well as in sports and recreational activities. If we remove the aesthetic, we are left with the action itself, one that is worth investigating.

Example

When engaging in center work, provide learners an opportunity to follow a prescribed series of movements, or remove aesthetic components and investigate the core actions of a particular offering. Consider "pliés": the flexing and extending of knees, ankles, and hips. How can the action itself benefit your movement goals? Flexion and extension provide important information regarding joint position and muscle tension and focusing attention on the activity while engaging in movement heightens the experience. Take some time to experience concurrent movement through the ankles, knees, and hips without considering form—the only rule is safe alignment, which is achieved by stacking the joints. The legs can fall at any position regarding internal and external rotation and the spine can sit anywhere in relation to the legs that doesn't cause discomfort or pain. As you focus attention, what do you experience? How are sensations of straightening limbs different from bending and creating shorter angles? Perhaps you feel a sense of sinking, or falling, when the legs bend, drawing you closer to the ground and amplifying your relationship to the

Figure 7.7. Practitioners create their own center work to explore the concept of weight, as prompted by a SomaLab leader (author's collection; photograph by Lindsay Osten).

earth. Conversely, when the legs straighten you might experience a sense of lengthening through the spine, coaxing a relationship with the space above you. Both experiences are important and can enrich your somatic repertory. Investigations can be performed without temporal structure or can adhere to rhythms offered for more prescribed actions.

Phrase Work

Phrase work, or longer movement sequences, may be introduced during a codified community experience to bring conceptual approaches into a practice that is more akin to an actual performance of the technique; it is often the end phase of the progression that has been in place throughout the entire period of study. Phrase work is often leader-directed, but can also be learner-augmented, and/or learner-generated, or hybrid, and reflects the values and form of the genre in a more complex, and often physically vigorous, way. Like warm-up and center work, phrase work can be approached somatically by focusing on approach and intention and centering the individual.

EXAMPLE A (leader-directed)

The leader offers a phrase to the group, taking time to identify core principles that are integral to performance. As the phrase is given, take time to ask yourself the following:

What is the sequence?
Where is the body in space?
What is the timing/rhythm?
What movement qualities/energies are featured?
What are the cues?
What do I value?
What do I know?
What can I learn?

Actively participating in the learning process provides a much richer experience, and promotes critical analysis of information, as opposed to rote repetition and reproduction of material. In a sense, you work harder, focusing on process and understanding.

EXAMPLE B (learner-augmented)

After a leader-directed phrase is offered, the leader provides practitioners flexibility in performing, giving time for self-exploration and personal expression. As a mover, it is possible to individualize the work while honoring the conceptual origins of the form. Perhaps particular movements are better expressed at slower or faster tempos, or there is a rhythmic structure you practice that is meaningful to you. Maybe you are more comfortable on the floor or need grounding; perhaps you are working on a less proscenium-based orientation. Can differing energies be used to better express the intersection of the technique and your own movement values? Would changing the sequence or movements support a safer practice in your body? In what ways can you further express your own values within the context of new learning?

Example C (learner-generated)

Here, the leader encourages learners to create their own phrases, basing their movement choices on a form's featured elements, for example, syncopation in tap dance. As an active community participant, you can begin by improvising/exploring these ideas through movement, as well as imaging, remembering, reflecting, and making choices that feel honest and true, much like in a personal SomaLab practice. As you identify authentic motifs that best express what you know and what you want to know, use space, time, and energy to sequence and challenge your body-mind to develop new patterns, supporting an individualized investigation of a form's conceptual framework.

Example D (hybrid)

Any of the formerly presented phrase work approaches can be practiced in a hybrid manner, or at different times in a longer course of study. You may find you prefer one method over another, and you can decide if it's best at this time in your development to rest in a comfortable situation, building confidence and refining what you value as a movement artist. Alternatively, you may feel a challenge would push you toward expanded boundaries, and you may choose a method that feels less affiliated with the familiar.

Reflection (Memory Map)

Reflection is critical to learning and growing, and it can take many forms. We tacitly reflect as we go through our days and nights, occasionally turning our attention to memorable events that are interesting or even confounding to us; indeed, thoughts and questions pervade our sleep as we strive to make sense of our world. Reflection can also be intentional, where we dedicate specific energies to ponder inquiries and perhaps identify a way forward. This thoughtful incorporation can manifest as meditation, journaling, or can be approached through movement; it is through these activities that we encourage meaning making of lived experiences.

EXAMPLE

Find a place of stillness following group practice and let the events of the session run through your mind, from beginning to end. As you are still, what draws your attention to a specific memory? Was it an investigation of circles of the hip joint early on, as the sensation of rotation was pleasing or informative? Perhaps you encountered a particularly meaningful way of investigating a core concept during center work or found leader-directed phrase work to challenge you in a novel way. After your memories of recent experiences lead you to points of reflection, begin to travel throughout your practice space slowly and easily, investigating places of meaning. Does standing mid-space right connect with the sensation of journeying across the floor, and does this trigger sensations of strength, or imbalance? Perhaps you explored the psoas moving the leg up and down, and you recall a powerful somatic connection. Allow yourself time to wander, remember, revisit, and assimilate practice experiences into your repertory of movement, dancing recalled movements partially or fully to enhance the process. You are creating a kind of memory map of the practice, one that is informed by physical time, space, and energy, as well as intentional thought. The "map" forms associations of events to bodymind knowledge; neural networks, and the capacity for new explorations, are expanded.

Figure 7.8. Garlynn Gillespie uses a framework inspired by codified techniques to delve deeper into the movement potential of phrase elements (author's collection; photograph by Lindsay Osten).

Community Conversations

All SomaLab activities for groups presented in this chapter are best manifested through sharing and witnessing. The capacity for empathetic growth and learning increases substantially through observation and reflection. One way to facilitate an in-depth and multi-dimensional community participation is through "circling." This happening can be used in any SomaLab group activity, where a collective is led by one or more individuals and showing personal approaches and decisions feels important to community learning. This exchange of information benefits all participants in their roles as both mover and observer. As a mover, having others witness your personal story is compelling and affirming, which is an integral component in any movement art practice. As an observer, the cycle of being seen and witnessing is complete, and, as discussed earlier in this chapter, the empathetic networks of the brain activate when we experience the kinetic actions of others. Too, recall Martha Eddy's words that speak to the origins of the circle in dance from Chapter 1: "The whole system perspective is embedded in Afrocentric models, as reflected in the unification of mind-body and spirit, but more importantly the omnipresence of 'the circle,' the dance and communication formation that supports the communication in community."[8]

EXAMPLE

After all community members have had sufficient opportunity to explore individual approaches in single or multiple activities, ask participants to begin to form a large circle, and begin to walk. The walking, or circling, should be performed very slowly, and stepping sideways, so the anterior body faces the inside of the circle, protecting the cervical spine and surrounding muscles from overuse. Change directions often, as to encourage three-dimensional viewing and listening. As the group observes, one or more practitioners come into the center of the space, sharing any part of recent movement practice.

Conclusion

Utilizing the SomaLab framework in group situations can be a powerful tool in centering conceptual approaches to learning and fostering kinesthetic perception. In the movement arts, it is often not what we do, but how we do it that leads to efficiency, safety, and optimal expression of the human bodymind instrument. One movement can be approached, cued, and contextualized in a thousand different ways, leading to nuanced changes in performance each time. Theming, and re-theming, codified techniques likewise produce a plethora of different, and valid, individual expressions of a maker's generalized technical scaffolding. Stripping away rote repetition and focusing on the heart of a form's core values makes true articulation possible.

This discussion of individual expression and performance in structured settings provides a timely segue to Chapter 8, where approaches to dance-making from a somatic perspective ensue. We continue to move the SomaLab framework into broader applications as we progress in Part 2, uniting all facets of our movement, artistic, and personal lives. In the next chapter, I diverge from the path taken thus far in presenting ideas, information, and associations to feature a case study from my own lived experiences as a scholar, dancer, maker, and daughter.

8

Somatic Dance-Making

A Case Study

"*I think a lot of times when people hear the word dance, they think 'oh, that's something that I can't do.' But dance really lives in our bodies and the thing that I've come to learn, embrace, and lift up is that we have history in our bodies that's living and breathing. We have our own individual history, but we also have our heritage. Each one of us has our movement language and it's about tapping into that and pulling that out. That's the thing that I try to encourage everybody because it's not about dance, it's about the movement and the gesture and how we honor it.*"—Camille A. Brown[1]

Introduction

Creative artists constantly remind us that they, too, are scientists and humanists, seeking truth, discovery, and ultimately, a greater understanding of the human condition. Abstraction in contemporary art is like putting a small piece of reality under a microscope and teasing out a novel and non-linear way of knowing. A movement-maker speaks to audiences through thinking bodies, engaging participants' senses with information translated by the performers through their own embodied cognition. There is a distinct privilege of immediacy in this work, with each unique translational relationship between creator and receiver contributing to the field overall. Problem solving is paramount, and forward thinking expands the field. In other words, all creatives seek answers and truth (although defining "truth" may take many forms across fields of inquiry). As we investigate, our respective fields grow, intersect, redefine, reframe, and something new is born.

A dance-maker is not only a creator, but an interpreter as well, both making and then leading performers into the world of their unique vision. They most often start from scratch, offering a personal interpretation of their worldview, and sometimes, a re-visioning of someone else's approach. Choreographers also cannot create without the very performers they are making dances for, and this specialized relationship mandates a symbiosis, enaction if you will, between all parties present. Thus, even the re-staging of a dance on a different cast of bodies becomes a brand-new event, open to re-learning and interpretation. In this chapter, I seek to illustrate how long-term SomaLab practice can develop bodyminds where knowing manifests itself tacitly, and dynamic environments inform creative choices.

Personal Approach and Process

In my own work, I am very much a storyteller, a narrator, a chorus. An abstractionist, I constantly seek novel approaches to telling human stories. I am continually drawn to the psychology and sociology of human behavior, my choreographies investigating and commenting on relationships and communities. My work is highly informed by the dancers themselves, the physical energy they create and their interactions with each other. Sculpting space through kinetic energy and creating highly visual images that can disappear and reform in a moment are indicative of the transient nature of our world and the power of community. The effect of one body upon another, the interactions resulting in multitudes of possibilities holds great intrigue and is ripe for investigation. Texture and quality, momentum and release, help create a specialized movement vocabulary often guided by bodies' natural rhythms but can fit into the phrasing of compositions and sound scores. New media can extend a work and provide added insights for both audience and performer, but only if it feels necessary, important.

Like all good research, my process begins with a question. Movement investigation is the next step and certainly constitutes the bulk of the choreographic process. In contemporary art, it is not so much important to answer questions, but to provide alternative perspectives and new ways of examining and seeing. Crafting the work using both traditional and experimental devices comes next, and I lean toward non-linear narrative to shape movement situations. Trusting my own somatic instincts as well as those of the dancers is paramount; I look for places that the body wants to go, and the visual trails created by momentum and the natural phrasing of human action. When working collaboratively with artists in other specialties, their unique insights and contributions inform decisions throughout the choreographic investigation. Editing also occurs throughout creation and is an important component of the research process as I seek clarity and focus in building a movement statement.

Developing and coaching performers is also part of this work, and this is where the maker becomes the director/conductor, acting as interpreter of their own vision with the bodies in each time and place. Each new community of movers brings additional information to the dance and the work itself is forever altered by a dancer's very humanity and their own unique bodymind. This makes each reiteration of a choreography deeply personal as a performer shares their embodied understanding of the world with the audience. The success of a work, indeed, depends upon this cyclical relationship involving creator, performer, and receiver, all of whom can find added depth of thinking and feeling through the art of dance. When successful, the field is expanded and enriched, the world more enlightened, and art has done its job.

For me, this approach is deeply informed by my own firm commitment to the bodymind; the wholeness of our conscious and unconscious self, and the connection that runs through the entirety of our physical being. I see the body as intelligent, inseparable from knowledge and mental processes; memories residing in living tissue, and the brilliance to create present in our bones, muscles, nerves, fascia, soft tissue, and organs. I place a great deal of trust in somatic processes, and in the body leading—can we have faith in movement that flows from our being, knowing indeed it is shaped by every moment we've ever experienced, and that it is uniquely and personally original? Can we also trust and know that even codified movements can have multiple meanings when performed by different individuals, or even by the same people in another time or place? What makes a movement expressive? Is it the movement itself or how it is carefully, mindfully, shared?

And ... what makes a dance? Is it the language that's chosen, or how a community of movers embraces a shared, almost sacred experience? I have seen highly technical work both thrill an audience and leave them stone cold, and conversely, I've seen the simplest, most authentic movement deeply move individuals, and also leave viewers confused, annoyed. One thing I believe is true: a dance has a soul, a mind of its own, and if you trust, it will take you, the maker, and you, and community of performers, and you, the viewers, where you need to go. Now we are back to the matter of trust, and the wisdom of the soma. Embracing our lived experiences, and manifesting them through movement is a joyful experience, one all humans were meant to have.

In this case study, I will navigate my personal process of dance-making from a somatic point of view. *Rhythm Runs Through It*, a recent work that grew out of the shared communal trauma of the Covid-19 global pandemic, was a work that demanded to be made—it wasn't even a choice, but a necessity of circumstance. Two seasoned performers, Kate Vermillion Lyons, and Rachel Newbrough shared their own lived experiences in the making, and together, we found our own embodied truth. I also explore the origins of a related work, *ode to a woman, lost*; this screendance speaks to collective experiences and validates our lives as survivors.

Figure 8.1. Corey Boatner, left, and Justin Sears find symbiosis in performance (author's collection; photograph by Freddie Kelvin).

A Case Study

Origins and Context

We began work on *Rhythm Runs Through It* (RRTI) in the summer of 2019. Kate and Rachel had recently been movement collaborators on a large project I directed, a site-specific work that celebrated the Sidney and Lois Eskenazi Museum of Art's grand re-opening after a two-year closure for renovations. Designed by I.M. Pei, the museum is a gorgeous, open space with a slanted staircase; beautifully welcoming, the lobby lent itself well to eleven dancers breathing, falling, leaning, and flowing north to south, east to west. Over 1,000 people visited the museum and viewed the work over six performances, and the intersection of movement, music, visual art, and community was fulfilling to us all. We missed each other and wanted to create again. So back to studio we went, with no real specific goals in mind other than a playful approach to movement making.

I had also recently moved my parents from the east coast, where they had lived all their adult lives, close to my home so I could better care for them. They were in their early nineties, and it was time. I knew I'd be shepherding them to and through death, and it was bittersweet to spend so much time with them after living far from each other for almost 40 years. So, they were part of my conscious state, past, present, and future, and my bodymind was processing all that had been and what was to come. My father's health was in decline as we began work on RRTI, and he was especially on my mind—a second-generation immigrant, a World War II veteran, and long-time employee of the Bethlehem Steel, the idea of work was deeply embedded in our family's DNA. My father was also an artist and woodworker, creating original works, and restoring all kinds of antique items that needed tender loving care. Wherever he lived, he was not without a workbench—first, a large shop in the cellar of the old farmhouse where I grew up, then something smaller (but just as well-kept and organized) in the attached garage of their senior-living townhome, and finally an old folding table in his last apartment.

So often in dance-making, we don't know why we've made something until the process is finished; our own tacit knowledge guides us to create movement solutions that seem to literally seep out of our pores. The great choreographer Anna Sokolow shared, "I never told stories in dance, although I have always been strongly dramatic. I never plan a dance. I do it, look at it, and then say: 'Yes, I see what I am trying to do.'"[2] So, we are not only feeling and sensing movement in our bodyminds, but we are also consigning our intellectual will to our instruments. This sense of trust in the body, in the process, the ability to release control and go along for the ride is, to me, the heart of somatic dance-making. And yes, our lived experiences allow our ideas to marinate until they are ready to be born and make their own way into an artistic creation. As Camille A. Brown explains, we have both an individual history and shared heritage, which interweave to create a unique movement language. The context I presented regarding my own lived experiences around the time work began on RRTI is essential to understanding the process and the evolution of practice. The making of a work is a narrative in itself and serves as a physical archive for not only an individual's phenomenology, but of the process.

Beginnings

As we began the process of movement research, the concept of labor, and the natural pulse that is a by-product of effort, was flowing through my mind and body. My collaborators listened, watched, explored, and understood with their own soma, and in the context of their own lived experiences. Rhythmic patterns were insistent and strong, and first investigations were simple walking and traveling patterns, peppered with stops, starts, and some formed movement. An early phrase ensued, and that first splat of paint on canvas was now part of the dance's world. At this primary stage, metered rhythm was the driving factor and where it felt right to invest our energies. There was a lightness, a playfulness in our time together, and working with devised timing felt good after a long project which relied heavily on unstructured and natural rhythms.

We were also creating gestures and hand patterns curated from lived experiences with tools and crafting; any kind of work that centered the hands as makers. Sometimes these motions were staged as lingering memories, forming trails in the air, but often they found their way to surfaces, like walls and floors, to be realized as definitive and easily recognized actions. I encouraged my collaborators not to "think too hard" when making movement decisions, and to let the body lead with its wisdom and knowledge. This resulted in very different and distinct sets of gestural movement, as pictured in Figure 8.2, which spoke to everyone's bodymind histories.

In a collaborative environment, movement making is not just centering your own instrument, but facilitating intuition and the release of tacit knowledge in others. How do you guide someone to trust their own intelligence, and be seen authentically? I recall a series of workshops as a young artist with post-modern great Deborah Hay, who introduced me to her process of "inviting being seen." For me, this practice means peeling back the layers of consciousness and identity and laying bare the true essence of one's being. There is a real vulnerability here, whether you're on the stage, in a studio, or moving around your living room. The very first person you need to invite being seen is yourself.

Two Bodies as One

Working with the effect of one body upon the other, watching and feeling, in real-time, an action followed by a from-the-gut honest reaction, weight-sharing, lead-sharing, and two bodies moving as one through breath, sensation, intuition—this is a particular fascination of mine when bringing ideas into the world through movement. Having danced

8. Somatic Dance-Making 191

Figure 8.2. Preliminary investigations of gesture laid the groundwork for individual expression and storytelling. Kate Vermillion Lyons, left, and Rachel Newbrough in performance of *Rhythm Runs Through It* at Dixon Place, New York, New York (author's collection; photograph by Steven Pisano).

together for over a decade, Kate and Rachel are particularly adept at this moment-to-moment way of experiencing each other, really digging into the closed-loop processes described in Chapter 2, while embracing the dynamic and enactive states proposed in Chapter 4. There is a methodology of awareness, experience, understanding, reflection, and finally effort, that is visible in these two performers. I won't call it partnering or contact improvisation because it's neither—the latter and the former both require formal study and have their own aesthetic—it's simply a deep understanding of each other's bodymind that is facilitated by somatic approaches to movement.

So, our next area of exploration involved segueing from individual histories to shared experiences, from a dual approach to a single mindset. As we added touch and momentum into our repertoire of movement investigations, several patterns emerged. First, we saw the creation of "mini machines," with one body acting on another, resulting in more structured rhythms and even locomotion through space. Conversely, periods of succumbing to gravity facilitated bodies tumbling, rolling, often on the floor, and provided a sharp contrast to the "mini machines." Inertia led to a natural conclusion and breath sounds and pulses moved the dancers through their torsos, not their limbs. These periods of unstructured flow felt like an undercurrent, a river running under a snowbank, a basso ostinato (thus, *Rhythm Runs Through It*).

A third manifestation saw one mover propelling the other through space, shifting the lead with so much ease and seemingly so little effort, that it was reminiscent of vernacular dance styles. This purity and

Figure 8.3. Two bodyminds work seamlessly as one. Rachel Newbrough, left, and Kate Vermillion Lyons in performance of *Rhythm Runs Through It* at Dixon Place, New York, New York (author's collection; photograph by Steven Pisano).

truthfulness of two bodies moving as one permeated other areas of movement research, and the dance took on an informality that suited our investigations. The ability to flow and transfer energy back and forth, shifting the lead wordlessly through eye contact and experiencing empathy through movement become a hallmark of the piece. Sensation and lived experiences were centered in the process from the beginning.

Tables, Part I

From the beginning I had a nagging idea I wanted to experiment with folding tables. At this juncture, I wasn't sure why—it was just a thought that wouldn't go away. The impractical nature of hauling heavy tables to the various spaces where we were rehearsing was a deterrent. And what about touring with the work? More adversity. Could we find tables that would support the weight of two adult bodies as an integral part of the choreography? I tried to talk myself out of the idea, but the tables were insistent as the work began to take shape. This is one of those moments as a maker where you either go with the current or swim against it—do you follow the logical mind or trust your intuition? The body holds so much knowledge, and the direct connection between experience and action that bypasses conscious cognition and language is a deep, deep truth. Learning to let the bodymind lead is indeed the nature of somatic-based making; decisions are wholly, or in-part, removed from style and training, and emerge from a path of authenticity and humanness.

The Covid-19 Global Pandemic

News regarding a highly contagious respiratory virus making its appearance in the eastern part of the globe started to trickle in sometime near the end of 2019. By early 2020, the disease was identified as a coronavirus, and as transmittable from one human to another. In mid–January, the first deaths were reported, and cases were identified globally; two weeks later, the Center for Disease Control confirmed cases on U.S. soil. The unknown virus was named Covid-19 in February, and on March 11, 2020, the World Health Organization declared a global pandemic. And then the world shut down.

The simple task of writing this synopsis instantly triggers trauma; the fear, the not-knowing, the dread, the loss. Every single person alive was impacted, and lives forever changed as the virus tore through families, communities, nations. Life as we knew it stopped, and living in quarantine became the new normal. Those of us whose work relies on collaboration and communities found ourselves in an abyss of aloneness. The work on *Rhythm Runs Through It* swiftly halted, as each member of the creative team focused on keeping ourselves, and those we loved, alive.

During the early months of 2020, it became clear my father's health was failing. He spent some time in nursing care following a short hospital stay and needed supplemental oxygen and a walker to navigate his days. Neither my mother nor father felt strong enough to leave their apartment for trips to the store or for a dinner out and were requiring more in-home care. Anyone who attended to elder adults during that time understands the devastation the quarantine brought, and the loss of control and feelings of utter failure experienced by caregivers. I purchased a Facebook Portal which was installed by the heroic employees at their senior facility, and guided by voice command, it became a crucial communication tool. Each evening, I could see and speak to my parents on a screen, and they could also call me anytime there was an emergency, or when they felt alone, or frightened.

In early May 2020, a nightly "Portal" visit saw tragedy. I had made my parents a lasagna earlier in the day and delivered it to their door. When I called them after dinner, my mother answered, and relayed that Dad wasn't doing well, and couldn't get out of his chair. I heard him say, "I'm going down," which sent my fingers flying as I dialed 911. I watched in real-time as the paramedics came and took Dad to the ER; Mom was left there alone. I could neither go to her, nor follow Dad to the hospital. This was the painful and heartbreaking reality of the Covid-19 pandemic.

My father died a week later. I was fortunate enough to secure an end-of-life visit in the hospital, where he made the decision to enter hospice. I was allowed to see my mom in person to deliver the news when he was transported, but not when he passed away. There was not much time to mourn, as the legalities of death and finances loomed. There were no immediate plans for a funeral or memorial service, as gatherings were still strictly forbidden. And then of course there was the work of getting Mom set up on her own after a 70-plus-year marriage; she would live alone for the first time in her life. I was allowed two days in the senior facility—one to pack up the two-bedroom apartment they shared, and one to move her into a one-bedroom studio. By July 2020 our lives had once again shifted, and I was deep in preparation for welcoming students back to a much-altered learning environment for the upcoming fall semester.

Kate and Rachel and I kept in touch—we met via zoom and caught up on life's events. Rachel suffered her own great loss—her grandmother was diagnosed with pancreatic cancer in the spring and passed away in June

2020 after a long and valiant battle. The family had cared for her themselves, in their home, acting as hospice caregivers, and Rachel was intimately involved. Kate shared that she had suffered a miscarriage right before the pandemic hit but was now pregnant and expecting a child in March 2021—a bittersweet joy amidst all the sorrow. We tossed around the idea of attempting rehearsals over Zoom but quickly dismissed the thought. The somatic nature of our work and how we built a dance was deeply embedded in live, embodied interactions. We didn't want to create a choreography just for the sake of doing so; the process was at the forefront and drove the dance-making.

The fall came, and like the rest of the world, we were living day-to-day, hour-to-hour, attempting to continue to teach dance and make art while taking all safety precautions to avoid the coronavirus. Our lives were a parade of masks, Clorox wipes and sprays, floor and wall tape to keep movers socially distanced, in accordance with CDC guidelines and protocols. We taught in-person, on Zoom, in-person and on Zoom at the same time; our students were traumatized, fearful, often sick, and isolated from long periods of time in quarantine. Performances were cancelled, and we filmed our works, with both students and faculty becoming newly agile in sound and video technologies. Kate needed to be especially vigilant, as the effects of Covid-19 on pregnant women and newborns were unknown. We continued to live our lives and kept our dance-making together on hold.

Sometime in the fall, my mother's senior facility began to allow short in-person visits of 30 minutes, up to two times a week. Temperature checks and symptom lists were diligently administered prior to each appointment, and after six months I could finally lay eyes on her with some kind of consistency. I could see the toll my father's death and forced solitude had taken on her; she seemed physically weak, and I sensed depression. Nevertheless, she was miraculously surviving under extraordinary circumstances (she was 94 years old). Video calls were still our main mode of communication, and I relied heavily on these precious evening interactions to continue and monitor her well-being.

In the early spring of 2021, Covid-19 vaccines became available for older and elder adults, and those with special health circumstances. Mom was vaccinated, and by late spring the preventative treatment was available in the United States to most adults. Kate's baby was born, with mother and child in good health, and it seemed like we might soon be able to continue our work together, masked for sure, and perhaps socially distanced too.

On a Wednesday in mid–May, Mom asked me to come over; she couldn't get out of bed. When I entered the apartment, the freezer door was wide open, and a few days' meals were scattered around the small kitchen. Something was amiss; this kind of disarray was not typical of my mother's housekeeping habits. I found her in the bedroom, and we called 911. I noticed a slight change in her speech, although she seemed able to process information and converse clearly and rationally. A quick examination at the emergency room yielded no explanation for the sudden loss of motor control in her legs—the best guess was an episode of gout, as tests showed elevated levels of uric acid. A two-week stay in a nursing/rehabilitation facility was recommended, and she was quickly transferred. She seemed to be making progress, but after a week I received another phone call—Mom wanted to know why she was at the fire station. And that was the beginning of the end.

Medicare will provide up to four weeks of treatment at a nursing home or rehabilitation facility. The physical and occupational therapists worked hard with Mom but didn't seem able to make much progress. Her cognition and short-term memory too began to decline; days and nights became reversed, and I needed to leave post-it notes all over the room, on the clock, by the phone, near the table, to help her navigate this new world. She was beginning to develop bedsores, and I became unhappy with her care. As the end of the Medicare-supported cycle loomed, it became clear that she could not return to even assisted living and was evaluated as qualifying for hospice. I cleared furniture out, moved a hospital bed and other equipment in, and Mom spent the last two months of her life in my home, under my care.

Nothing could have prepared me for this experience—under our current healthcare system, a hospice nurse and home health aide come once a week only. The rest of the time, family hospice caregivers are on duty 24/7. I learned how to change bedding and diapers with Mom still in the bed (it's all about the rolling), flush a catheter, clean and dress wounds, administer medications, and perform countless other medical and care tasks. I observed her movement language, trying to read the origins of pain in her body when words failed. We still laughed and sometimes cried, watched television until she could no longer follow plotlines and sequences of events. We celebrated her 95th birthday on August 23, 2021, with flowers, seafood from Red Lobster, cake, and virtual visits from family and friends. Mom passed away five days later.

Dance-making students often ask me how to "get people to do what you want." Translated, this means how do you guide movement collaborators to embody your ideas, your intentions, and embrace a specific vocabulary that may not be familiar to them. My answer is always the same—"Bank goodwill. If you invest in them, they will invest in you, honestly and authentically." I cannot think of a clearer example of this concept than the eight weeks I took care of my mother leading up to her death. She had banked enough goodwill with me to last a thousand times over, and I would care for her again and again if necessary. We often think in terms of a separate set of rules for creatives—but I think our best work is done when we remember how to live the life we want as people, and intertwine our artmaking into lived experiences, instead of the other way around. How do we want to be?

This provides a perfect segue; let's go back. After Kate and Rachel and I were vaccinated, in early June 2021, we resumed rehearsals, masked but not socially distanced. We were diligent about testing prior to our rehearsals, as we all had vulnerable people we cared for and needed to be extremely cautious. I recall how amazing it felt to reunite after such a long period of time apart, and the work we had done previously was right there on the surface, like it had been lying in wait all along. The intelligence of our bodies was palpable, and we trusted the recollection of nerves, muscle, fascia, and bones to guide us back to a place of symbiosis. But while the memory was there, we were forever changed, and everything was different.

Tables, Part II

We had begun this dance playfully, luxuriously, with no deadline in sight, and the sheer gratitude of moving together driving our work. Coming together again after a year of shared and individual trauma changed all that. We now had a strong sense of purpose, a determination to move forward after facing so many obstacles and coming out intact, but altered, on the other side. We had endured.

The timeline had also shifted—a premiere in New York City loomed, and decisions had to made. Now, I finally understood why the idea of folding tables floated through my being—Dad was on my mind, and following his death, his legacy was ever present. The simplicity of his final workbench lied achingly in my heart. The tables were in.

Having to haul heavy folding tables around a studio space not only invigorated our creative curiosity but also proved to be therapeutic. There was something about the manual labor of pushing, pulling, and lifting and the loud bangs and booms reverberating through the space that restored our sense of power and control. After spending so many months forcibly separated from the very behaviors that define our humanity, having agency over even an inanimate object felt good. Of course, the tables didn't always cooperate. Sometimes they refused to open or close; we broke several finding the perfect specimen of strength and weight that would serve our purposes. They got lost in baggage for a bit on our way

Figure 8.4. "The tables" not only provided the collaborators context for the work but added another constraint to the creative process. Rachel Newbrough, left, and Kate Vermillion Lyons in performance of *Rhythm Runs Through It* at Dixon Place, New York, New York (author's collection; photograph by Steven Pisano).

to the premiere of *Rhythm Runs Through It*, and during another performance, one of the tables buckled in the middle—the expert improvisational skills of Rachel and Kate reminded us that live performance is a fragile, precious gift.

The work opens with Kate carrying a folding table onstage and opening it—quite loudly. Small interactions follow, where blueprints are drawn, nails are hammered, and spaces are measured. The table is moved and forgotten for a while, but it works like a magnet, always drawing the performers back. Then comes a small jump onto the surface (the fateful buckle) with more weight-bearing and reclining. Beautiful duetting, on the floor, and in the air, intersperses the object/human interactions. Suddenly, a second table appears—a chance to explore again, one body manipulating another, then rhythm, unison—the dancers fall to the floor, and engage in a testament to the earth.

Now comes the fun—rearranging the props to sculpt the space, supported handstands, rolling, and turning, and at one point, Rachel stands on a table in an act of triumph—then quickly scoots down, because enjoying the moment is not quite yet back in our worldview. As the piece winds down and the energy begins to cool, both dancers join the tables and running and pushing, bodies slide in unison forward. Movement slows, and a sleepy decent to the floor signifies a valley in the dynamic of the work. The dancers slowly climb back up, gaining a bit of a second wind, and bang the tables together haphazardly, until each has their own space. The tables are packed up, Rachel's with a bit of aggression, and Kate's more matter-of-factly. Rachel slides off hers, there's no energy left, and Kate carries hers offstage, finishing the cycle, the metaphor, for our lived experiences.

A Case Study, Addendum

The months waned on, the development for *Rhythm Runs Through It* ended, and Covid-19 moved from pandemic to endemic status. Masks came off, in-person functions resumed, and the dominance the virus had over our lives slowly began to diminish. After two-plus years of day-to-day survival, it seemed there was a bit of room to breathe, allowing for some reflection about everything that had happened. So many had lost so much, yet there was little time and space to grieve. Just in the United States, well

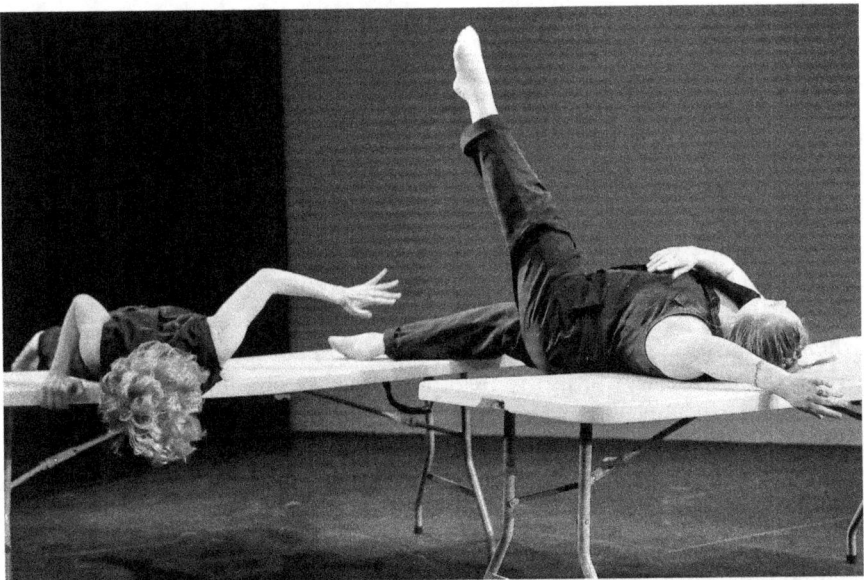

Figure 8.5. The dance artists navigate two tables, the space, and each other as the work finds natural conclusion. Rachel Newbrough, left, and Kate Vermillion Lyons in performance of *Rhythm Runs Through It* at Dixon Place, New York, New York (author's collection; photograph by Steven Pisano).

over 1,000,000 deaths are attributed to Covid-19. People had died alone, separated from family, friends, and survivors were left with unresolved feelings of guilt and loss. In addition, many experienced the passing of family and friends from non–Covid related illnesses or accidents but could not complete the grieving process due to isolating and social distancing restrictions. The rituals that are so important to culture when people transition in many cases could not be observed. Were their loved ones at rest or did they roam through space and time, unable to resolve the unfathomable sequence of events? Can we as survivors process our losses, and gradually make sense of the pandemic? The word "lost" kept reoccurring and floating through my mind. But who was it that was lost?

ode to a woman, lost

A new project, an accompanying piece to *Rhythm Runs Through It* began to take form. While the work for live performance was highly personal, and focused on the specific experiences of the collaborators, this work stemmed from a place of collective grief, a societal phenomenon we all shared. As such, a dance for film felt most appropriate; accessibility was important. Once again, this piece insisted upon its birth, another necessary artifact of the pandemic. Maybe work that reflected shared experiences could spur conversations and create support, facilitating a kind of group healing. In developing this artistic work, the lives of those lost can be recognized and honored and leave those present with the agency to process past events and move forward.

In contrast to *Rhythm Runs Through It*, this new work was a direct reaction to the pandemic; it was not an interrupted idea that germinated in another time and place. Again, my own lived experiences intruded, as I felt pulled toward the woods and hiking trails of nearby Lake Monroe, where I had spent so much time during periods of isolation. An idea of a solo female-identifying figure began to emerge; she floats through time and space, lost. But who is she? Is she someone who's departed, struggling to find rest and resolution, or someone who still walks the Earth, alone, fraught, depleted, and confused. Is she both? Can I provide viewers with the agency to align with either point of view? Regardless, does she find resolution, or does she continue her search? The urge to create this narrative from a female-identifying perspective is strong; women are still overwhelmingly, and globally, the major caregivers in their personal and professional lives.

Once again, I relied on the somatic wisdom of dance artist Rachel Newbrough. We had both experienced the loss of important women in our lives during the pandemic and had each served as non-medical hospice caretakers. We shared an understanding of itinerant emotions and the cost of unanswered ritual. Preliminary research began outside, in the woods, as we explored the idea of a largely unseen entity, catching short glimpses of motion as she meanders through trees and brush. She interacts with her environment, and kinesthesia allows me to feel her awe and respect as she moves gracefully among the elements. I film test shots on my iPhone repeatedly, seeking multiple and undiscovered perspectives, sometimes slowing time, and allowing us to be present in the moment.

As we worked somatically, instinctively, it felt like this figure needed to reveal herself over time. Eventually our investigations took us to the sandy beaches of Lake Monroe, where we finally see this being, fully, albeit from a posterior position. But how did she get there? The process of storyboarding for film allows for lapses in time, and the narrative loosens. We experiment with walking, running, lunging, all, or none of which may make their way into final film edits.

There is now stillness where before there was motion, perhaps a few moments of thought, reflection, or contemplation before a way forward is determined. The thought process is further manifested through large crashing movements, in and around the sand, extending, falling, floating, as indirectness appears as indecision. Rachel experiments with a translucent cape, which enhances the movement research, and gives the appearance of an ethereal being. Sunlight filters through the fabric, adding a pinkish glow, the hue of sunrise, or maybe sunset.

Up to this point, the dance for film has a voyeuristic feel, but now there is a transition, and I experience a first-person point of view.

I'm also interested in moving among the particles of sand, sifting the fingers and toes through fine granules, rolling, and sitting and sweeping. The cape gives the illusion of a sand-snow angel and serves as cover during periods of rest and stillness. Now I see my tacit instinct to incorporate fabric into this research is grounded in the idea of sheltering. Is there an event that leads to escape, or does it happen in the natural order of things? Or not at all?

We now experiment with water-play; Rachel falls, repeatedly, each time differently, creating varying patterns of splash droplets that also catch the sun's rays. We also test the cape's capacity to float and move when wet, taking test shots from above the water line that are beautiful and otherworldly. This separation of cape from body seems to mean something, a kind of movement in the journey, an undressing or revealing of character and intention. Rachel investigates self-guided underwater movement, with a similar score to the work on the beach, but gentler and more repetitive, as cupping and swirling motions of the arms and legs are necessary to stay afloat.

We continue to research the properties of water; Rachel stands in the lake mid-thigh and uses her arms and torso to propel the water upward. More test shots reveal geometric patterns set against the landscape. She crawls out of the lake belly first in wet, dense sand, both with and without the cape, army-crawl style. She walks along the sand, dragging soaked fabric, heavy and weighted in her hands, leaving footprints in the earth.

Something has happened in the water, some kind of transformation. We are not sure exactly what, but this part of the journey has concluded and it's time to leave the sand, the lake, as our research moves toward resolution. The woods beckon once again, but the shift necessitates a new location. We explore the shores, the forests, deep and shadowy and sparse and translucent. Precipices are appealing, and we intrinsically understand that this translates to creating around a point of departure. We land on a beautiful, elevated point that juts out over the water, and provides stunning views of the horizon. This is the place where we work, still seeking our own answers to the question of conclusion. The movement is minimal, authentic, contemplative, and finally still. The very last image we see is the figure falling out of screen, slowly, head launched back in a silent scream, seemingly floating outside of space and time. Why is still not clear, and open to multiple avenues of interpretation. Is she leaving this place, grieving for those left behind? Is she staying, trapped, in a relentless cycle of aloneness? Is it her decision, or that of other forces at work?

My hope is that those who experience this screendance will

Figure 8.6. Rachel Newbrough in a still taken during the filming of *ode to a woman, lost* (author's collection).

find something in it that they can identify with, and the work can serve as a point of reckoning, of healing. We have repeatedly validated the intelligence, the knowing, of the body throughout this text, and the great capacity of the soma to relay and understand concepts beyond the capabilities of language. Words are, after all, symbols for thoughts, and largely incomplete as the wholeness of ideas are lost in translation. In contrast, the body expresses directly, genuinely, honestly.

Somatics and Dance for Film

ode to a woman, lost provides an opportunity to open a discussion into somatics and dance for film, or screendance, as well as other forms of new media for movement. Much of this chapter presents dance-making through the lens of live performance, but how does holism in the bodymind affect work in the digital space? Over the past several decades, the integration of technology into the realm of all dance genres has made a clear and insistent appearance in the choreographic works of masters and novices alike. The abstract nature of contemporary forms continually seeks new and innovative methods for creating art through human movement. Current trends have given rise to new genres of dance-based works created specifically for video and film. Over the past three years especially, beginning with the onset of the Covid-19 global pandemic, avenues for watching film and video beyond the traditional cinema have mushroomed. Sites like YouTube and Vimeo provide 24-hour access to dance across the globe, as well as encourage sharing of these viewings with like-minded artists and associates. Dance film festivals, both online and live in-person viewings, have sprung up in major cities internationally and continue to drive the field forward. In the academy, choreography, and direction for dance on film is often an important part of cases for tenure and promotion in the dance arts.

To be clear, dance in film is much more than archival footage of live performance or rehearsal. It has become truly a unique art form of its own. According to the Dance Film Association, "Both historically and at present, dance has been an integral part of the film canon. Creating opportunities to share these films with broader audiences through public programming and partnerships elevates the work and encourages filmmakers to continue making innovative work, especially at this time of rapidly evolving technology and cinematic tools."[3] The use of film in capturing dance and movement allows for the consideration of multiple views and angles and provides the opportunity for temporal stretching and abstracting. Time, space, and energy can shift and evolve in a way that is impossible in live performance; film can move a dancer's form into a novel environment, quickly or slowly, in color or greyscale, with every detail evident, or blurred and opaque.

It stands to reason that these multiple points of view provide the diverse lens through which improvised and devised works can be experienced. Movement empathy is part of the SomaLab framework; indeed, task examples involve observation while moving, and from different angles—film can preserve these various perspectives, albeit in a two-dimensional form. I recently had the opportunity to view *Threshold*, a 360-dance film by filmmakers Malia Bruker and Ilana Goldman for VR (virtual reality), and it was an extraordinary experience.[4] I felt the performers in my own three-dimensional space as though they were right there with me; kinesthesia was strong. I am excited for the future of this form of screendance, and what it can bring not only to the field, but the possibilities for somatic engagement for all interested in moving, in any form.

Trauma and the Bodymind

Creating these works during a time of heightened global trauma greatly impacted both process and product. When creating from a somatic perspective, it is impossible, and undesirable, to separate the person from the making. Your soul is laid bare and becomes the canvas for a different kind of expression, one where movement is not a symbol, but is the message itself. Somatic-based dance-making does not rely solely on tools and craft, but lets the body speak truthfully, and is at the forefront of creative investigation.

What happens to us when presented with trauma? In his seminal work *The Body Keeps the Score*, Bessel van der Kolk observes:

> We have learned that trauma is not just an event that took place sometime in the past; it is also the imprint left by that experience on mind, brain, and body. This imprint has ongoing consequences for how the human organism manages to survive in the present. Trauma results in a fundamental reorganization of the way mind and brain manage perceptions. It changes not only how we think and what we think about, but also our very capacity to think.[5]

As movement artists, we know that practice brings desired growth and development. Chapter 3 shows us how with rehearsal, neurological structure shifts, resulting in a change in function. When we are continually exposed to trauma, the same thing happens—as we "practice" trauma, our very neural structures are altered. Part of this new state is a sympathetic nervous system that is always on call to initiate the "fight or flight" response. This is what keeps us avoiding people when they walk too close, excessively cleaning and washing our hands, and often expecting the worst.

Does this mean we can only make dances or other works of art that revolve around themes of Covid-19? Are we doomed to reinvestigate the virus perpetually? Of course not. But recognizing and understanding the context of thought and movement can help us honor our current life situations, how they influence our process, and propel us forward authentically and honestly. It is a kind of resilience, where difficulty is acknowledged without judgement. Working and creating in environments that don't honor real people, and with the expectation of "business as usual" is exhausting. Embracing all that is part of the story of our lives produces work that is truthful and encourages strong communities of artists.

It was important to document my personal journey, and that of my collaborators, as well as our societal grief during the making of *Rhythm Runs Through It,* and *ode to a woman, lost.* The development of these projects was deeply impacted by the events that occurred in and around our lives as we dove deep into the embodied research that underwrote the work. This telling, a case study, exemplifies a somatic approach to movement creation and provides further testament to somatic practice in the movement arts.

Dance-Making as a Physical Archive

In some traditions, choreography is considered a means to an end, a system by which an outcome is produced. Even process-based approaches can focus on methodologies used in creation as research, or as ways to engage with invention and originality. Somatic-based dancing emphasizes that making is so much more than this intellectual exercise; it serves as an embodied archive of specific times and places, reflective of thoughts, feelings, and perspectives of the maker and movement collaborators. This approach brings the process closer to the personal stories of individuals, making the work more meaningful and arguably essential in the lives of performers and witnesses alike.

If we embrace this view of dance-making as inseparable from life experiences, then conversely the dance itself serves as a personal archive for all parties—makers, collaborators, and viewers. Both process and product can, indeed, serve as an embodied journal, with all actions and actors having the potential to profoundly record, and subsequently impact, the histories of societies and their people. Examining a choreographic work in terms of how process creates individual narrative speaks specifically to the essential nature of artmaking during especially calamitous events in global history.

In presenting the case study of *Rhythm Runs Through It,* and its accompanying piece *ode to a woman, lost,* each section, each part, each movement can be traced to a specific constraint or set of circumstances

Figure 8.7. Kate's infant son Harvey was a frequent visitor to our rehearsals, and we often "borrowed" moments from his developing movement repertory. These moments reference specific days and events, serving as an archive for our dance-making experience (author's collection).

affecting the group. It's interesting to consider how this idea might evolve if artists looked forward rather than back—can individual transcripts of rehearsal experiences provide professional and personal insights to those involved in a dance-making experience? Can this idea transfer to a more general population of amateur and recreational movers to enhance quality of life? Can we use similar processes in future times of difficulty and trauma?

Recognizing dance as a physical archive additionally provides important new opportunities for considering inclusion and belonging in dance and dance-making. Novel avenues for creation, necessitated by social distancing during the Covid-19 global pandemic, offer broader access to all bodies and discourage ableism in the field. When movement contributions come from a wide range of sources, such as working in public spaces, or contributing from a virtual place, the traditional in-studio creation process becomes less centered. Documenting and tying personal life events to dance-making can assist those experiencing trauma toward healing by providing a scaffolding of events for witnesses to affirm.

Additionally, the very idea of recognizing a choreographic work as an archival reflection of individual stories, as opposed to a product that stems only from the bodymind of the creator, highlights the role of all participants, and can create a more welcoming atmosphere for all movers.

Conclusion

Andrea Olsen writes, "Dance is both universal and highly personal."[6] This is the heart of somatic dance-making: while the act of dancing and creating is integral to all humans, each person's unique phenomenology guides their embodied cognition, and determines perceptions of truth through experience. Style is not the constant here, and authentic creation can take many, many forms. Working somatically is a way forward that honors all individuals as opposed to centering only specific techniques. Somatic approaches to movement creation can be a vehicle for real and lasting change that advance movement arts. In Chapter 9, the final chapter of this text, we see how the SomaLab framework can support specialized populations and communities in creating this major shift in global thought and action. From start to finish, we have truly moved through the tripartite of investigation, education, and dissemination of somatic worlds.

9

The Evolving Process
SomaLab in Action

"Dance, dance, otherwise we are lost."—Pina Bausch[1]

"Body movement is not a symbol for expression; it is the expression."—Irmgard Bartenieff[2]

Introduction

Renowned choreographer Pina Bausch passionately summarizes the human need to move in one six-word sentence: we were built to experience our world, our lives, through the totality of our bodymind instrument, or else we feel *less than*. Likewise, Bartenieff affirms that our compulsion to express our innermost values and beliefs through movement stems from the purity of body expression itself. Indeed, for others to know us through what we do and make is fundamental to a shared humanity. How we choose to do this can take many forms: a lifelong commitment to dance, a weekly qigong practice, or the occasional walk in the woods can all work to satisfy our commitment to holism of the mind and body. More simply put, a somatic approach or philosophy is central to the health of all human beings, beyond those who engage in professional movement practice. Accessibility is integral to the idea of optimal wellness for persons seeking balance in their bodymind.

This chapter examines how the principles of SomaLab can be introduced to different populations and learning communities through long-established movement practices, as well as novel approaches to deepening somatic awareness. All our discussions and examinations of theory (Part 1) and practice (Part 2) thus far have led us here; we can envision and facilitate somatic activities for communities that can benefit from the work.

Yoga and Learning Communities

Yoga Revisited/Why Yoga?

Chapter 1 contextualized the historical origins of yoga as part of the larger body of somatic practice emerging from South Asia. To summarize, yogic influences can be easily identified in contemporary somatic systems; indeed, the word yoga means "yoke" and represents a joining of mind and body. The yogic discipline employs both active exertion and passive equanimity simultaneously,[3] allowing the practitioner to register life events without judgement and develop a skillful approach toward living.

The ancient practice of yoga originated in Northern India, perhaps as early as 5,000 BCE, with early teachings deeply influenced by Hinduism. However, it is Patanjali's *Yoga-Sûtras*, written sometime in the 2nd century, that outlines methods commonly found in today's modern yoga, although the physical practice did not fully emerge until the late 19th–early 20th century. One element of yoga that has greatly influenced somatic systems, as well as multiple disciplines in the performing arts, is the deliberate use of breath (*pranayama*). Conscious control of breathing is often an entry point to a healthy mind/body relationship and can facilitate the ability to attend to sensation while also promoting efficiency in movement. It's important to reiterate that while contemporary somatic praxis, especially in the west, utilizes many yogic components, these contributions often go unrecognized and uncredited.

And now, why yoga? How can this movement form encourage broader access to the benefits of somatic systems like SomaLab and promote wellness in communities across differing populations? The answer lies in the underlying philosophy of yogic systems where values and beliefs are manifested through practice in various forms, thus allowing the physical form to look and feel different for everyone. There are many approaches to contemporary yoga, and like the SomaLab framework, they value flexibility, accessibility, and individuality in both theory and practice. Although there are some branches of yoga that prioritize physical form over the "yoking" of body and mind, there is a positive, forward trend in the yoga community that recognize the benefits of yogic practice for the whole human being and encourage equanimity in the bodymind instrument.[4] In my own approach to leading and teaching yoga, the only rule is safety—making sure the body moves through places that support joint, bone, and muscle health. The real experience lies in breath, sensation, steadiness, and knowing, and in serving the needs of the bodymind in the given moment.

Let's take a moment to revisit SomaLab tools, focusing on how this methodology can support the more formal practice of yoga and bring the benefits of both to many:

- *Breath*: The practice of conscious breathing has clear origins in yogic practice, dating as far back to the 5th and 6th centuries BCE.[5] This methodology can serve as a gateway to the mind/body relationship and help us move gently from thinking to feeling during physical practice. Many somatic methods, including SomaLab, employ breath control as a foundational element of movement sessions, often beginning a practice with breathwork and continuing conscious attention to breathing throughout. To be clear, the use of breath to guide movement experiences is a principle of SomaLab and other movement systems informed by yoga, not vice versa.
- *Imagery, visualization, and mental practice*: Recall that Mabel Todd introduced the idea of using imagery to change physical behavior in her book *The Thinking Body*, a work that had a profound effect on the field of dance and other movement forms.[6] The use of these mental constructs in leading and practicing yoga can have powerful effects on the yogic experience, fostering a sense of individuality by focusing on the practitioner's specific bodymind needs. For example, someone seeking length and space in their body can be aided by supportive imagery, and mental practice of verbal cues may aid participants seeking precision in their approach to postures and poses.
- *Intention/attention*: In Part 1 of this text, we learned that attention, or consciously tending to the task at hand, is an important tool in mastering new skills, as well as fine-tuning previously acquired competencies. Focusing the mind on one's current state of being is often practiced in the yoga studio, although not necessarily with the goal of furthering or perfecting specific skills. The idea of narrowing thought, especially the act of noticing without judgement, is a life skill valued in yogic and Buddhist teachings that can ease human suffering.[7] Likewise, intention is a goal setting mechanism that can guide decisions during movement sessions that prioritize certain outcomes of practice. Both attention and intention give individuals agency in their approaches to movement experiences and allow for active personal choice in pursuing results. Providing an environment where artists choose movement values particular to their own individual goals, influenced by lived experiences, is a key tenet of SomaLab, and an important component of yogic philosophy.

- *Self-guided/intuitive movement*: The idea of the bodymind as the sole originator of movement, rather than as a conduit for another's vision, is an essential idea in the SomaLab framework and honors both the individual and their personal choices. Often in traditional movement practice, form is prioritized over agency; this custom is particularly present in western-based concert dance. While improvisation in the classic sense is not a staple of yoga offerings, the idea of self-guided movement manifests itself in the freedom to follow the lead of one's own body and deviate from an instructor-led sequence. This approach is highly valued in many yoga environments; minimizing a "right way" and a "wrong way" is a supportive mechanism for practitioners, and one that can be led and influenced by improvisational practices.
- *Physical awareness (kinesthesia)*: Prioritizing sensation and perception based in the body provides information about where we are and what we are doing in our immediate environments. Promoting physical awareness is an important component in somatic-based systems, and yoga can deepen kinesthetic experiences by creating spaces that encourage proprioception. How can we move from focusing on "how it looks" to "how it feels," and why is this important? When we focus on visual feedback, a person's own values and affinities are often minimized, with a standard form governing outcome and intention. By focusing on sensation, we can attend more closely and be present, a goal of both yoga and SomaLab that moves us away from mind-clutter and closer to more skillful states.
- *Embodiment in action*: The "embodiment premise" presents a case for the importance of movement as a basis for language and thought, not vise-versa as in more traditional information processing models.[8] For example, the action of learning to kayak and spending a day on the lake might be essential to developing a complex conceptual understanding of the properties of water, leading to broader language capabilities. SomaLab utilizes the language of memory, imagery, and action to inform movement exploration, and subsequently to develop a broader range of expression in both word and deed. Likewise, yogic practice is highly interactive with language and movement—teachers and leaders can use precise cuing and/or fantastical imagery to guide students to new dimensions of sensation and perception. Consequently, yoga practitioners have new experiences that inform language expansion, encouraging novel ways of communicating. As a bodymind practice, yoga is an excellent

vehicle for investigating the action/language, or conceptualized, relationship.

- *Movement empathy*: Referring to the act of kinesthetically engaging when in the presence of other moving bodies, movement empathy is an empirically validated phenomenon in group settings. Recall from Chapter 5 that motor and premotor areas of the brain activate when both observing others moving and simulating movement via mental imagery.[9] In SomaLab group situations, observing and embodying the movement of others is key in developing neural flexibility; visual information stimulates neural networks. In the yoga community experience, a group sense of movement empathy is accomplished, although not solely through visual cuing. A traditional yoga practice utilizes mats, so each practitioner moves in a closed space, and is encouraged to listen rather than watch—visual feedback is utilized more for balance, often by identifying a "Drishti," or a particular spot to align focus and attention. Thus, it is through audition and kinesthesia that empathy is supported. Hearing the breath of others, influenced by various tempos, rhythms, and techniques, and feeling the experience of bodyminds through proximal movement can expand each yogi's personal vocabulary.
- *Reflection/incorporation*: We process our thoughts and actions all day long, acquiring information for problem solving or simply expanding our view of the world. In teaching dance-making to college-age students, I like to introduce the idea of "rummaging around," or letting an idea germinate in your bodymind for a long time; eventually, tacit knowledge takes over and a decision emerges. This kind of processing—this constant fine-tuning of our movement practices, and our lives, through thought, social interactions, our immediate environments, and other lived experiences—is essential to developing the kind of neural flexibility elemental to mature artistry. Through a looping of sorts that integrates memory, present experiences, and future imaginings, we are constantly working, consciously and unconsciously, to make sense of the world around us. The SomaLab framework embraces our totality as complete human beings, encouraging all facets of life to be present in movement practice. Yoga, too, prioritizes observation and "noticing" during movement as a vehicle to gather information, not to form judgements or opinions. By practicing this assemblance of data and allowing ourselves time to make sense of it all, we can embrace a richness of experiences in our moving lives.

Some years ago, I had the pleasure of meeting Nora Reynolds, who was setting her mother Bella Lewitzky's *Suite Satie* on a group of dancers. I immediately observed similarities in some parts of the choreography with that of yogic postures. I asked her if Bella was a practitioner of yoga, and she replied no—but her mother always said, "some things just make sense."

SomaLab + Yogic Practices for Dancers: A Two-Week Daily Curriculum

When considering the benefits of yoga, heavily informed by the SomaLab framework, for specialized populations, it's important first to identify the needs of the community. I often offer such a curriculum for pre-professional and professional dancers, grounded in deepening individual artistic practice as well as holistic health for the bodymind instrument. My approach to yoga for dancers does not focus exclusively on developing physical capabilities that support dance techniques, such as flexibility or upper body strength; indeed, quite the opposite. I'm interested in offering knowledge and processes that work to broaden bodymind knowledge and support the very difficult work of artists. Special considerations for dancers include:

- Linking breath and movement, a staple of many dance practice approaches.
- Body safety, focusing on the alignment of joints.
- Balancing the physical practice in a way that does not privilege one way of being over another, i.e., external versus internal rotation.
- Centering sensation and perception, an important tool in artistic development and practice.
- Working steadily and with equanimity, through challenging poses and with differing energies.
- Re-focusing feedback loops beyond visual information and turning attention to kinesthetic proprioception.
- Avoiding over-cueing, which can reinforce unhealthy patterns and placements of the body, i.e., over-tucking in the pelvis.
- Encouraging evenness in energetic approaches, particularly noticing tendencies to over-effort, while at the same time honoring "brightness" or peaks in the practice, and rest/stillness.
- Carefully tuning in to individual needs and the developmental journey of each movement artist.

In summary, the goal of my personal approach to yogic practices for dancers is to prioritize physical safety and sensation, as well as wellness and mental health in movement, thus preserving the longevity, productivity,

Figure 9.1. Maya Orchin practices yoga to find safety in the body and encourage presence and focus in preparing for a day of teaching and creating (courtesy Stefanie Nelson; photograph by Rachelle Saker).

and satisfaction of careers in dance. A two-week (10 session) daily program of SomaLab + Yogic Practices for Dancers follows, with a sample session articulated for Day One. Specific postures are not referenced in detail but are offered to sculpt a vision of the practice for the reader. Each "focus" narrows a physical as well as mind/wellness construct that work together, forging bodymind unity and developing healthful skills for living. To be clear, each session is a balanced practice that approaches human movement holistically and focuses on aspects of mind and body engagement to promote learning through experiencing.

Day One

Focus: untangle the body, create space in joints, muscles, fascia; experience simple equanimity in breath.

Sample Session

Find a comfortable place on your back. We'll begin with intuitive movement, including those rituals that feel necessary in your body right now; take stock of any tightness, soreness, or discomfort. After you feel satisfied with this beginning exploration, move into stillness, feeling the body settle with weight on your mat. Now, draw attention to your breath. Even out the inhales and exhales, engaging in this simple, but full, approach to breathing. Each breath cycle brings you closer to a unified state of being in your bodymind.

Gently pull both knees into the chest, finding compression in the thighs and length in the low back. Imagine the sit bones (ischial tuberosity) moving toward the front of your mat, and the crown of your head moving toward the back. Extend one leg long, finding space where the hip and pelvis meet as you pull the flexed leg closer to your armpit. Slowly extend the flexed leg long with an in-breath, and re-flex with an out-breath, two or three times on each side. Visualize the hamstring muscles lengthening and shortening as you work.

Now, as you inhale, stretch the body fully, from fingertips to toes, noticing all the places that lengthen and expand in the process; as you exhale, release, and soften. Internally rotate the legs and flex the feet, while bringing the palms to the back of the head, elbows wide. Feel the low belly firm and contract on your in-breath and mindfully lift the shoulders from the mat on your out-breath, moving in this sequence for approximately 30 seconds, becoming aware of the core's muscular engagement as you work. Conclude with a second full body stretch and find your way to Tabletop Pose (weight on hands and knees, joints stacked).

Find supple, long, full, movements of the spine, linking breath and movement. Traditional Cow (extension) and Cat (flexion) is available or follow the body's lead into self-guided flexion and extension of the spine, inviting in the pelvis, shoulders, head, and neck. Maintaining internal rotation, stretch one leg back, lifting the heel to sit bone height, and stretch the opposing arm forward like you're shaking someone's hand. Create space in the joints as you lengthen on the inhale, and on the exhale, elbow and knee come together under the body. Flow this sequence on both sides with ease and equanimity as the breath moves you back and forth, in and out. Finish the cycle by flexing the long leg at the knee and swimming the extended arm around to capture the foot. As you press the foot into the hand, rotate the spine toward the extended arm, brightly working into an energetic expression. Finish in Child's Pose, big toes together, arms extended, forehead resting on the mat. Feel the natural conclusion of a warming series as the body rests, the breath staying even and full.

As you feel ready, move into Downward-Facing Dog, focusing on equal pressure into the mat from all four limbs: the tailbone lifts, creating distance between the hips and shoulders. As you inhale, slowly unwind into Plank Pose, and as you exhale, lower to the floor with care, elbows touching the ribs, and dropping to the knees if you choose. Untucking the toes and firming the belly, stretch into Cobra Pose; chest lifts, hands press into the mat. Repeat this version of a yoga push-up with your own breath tempo, adding or subtracting elements to fit your bodymind's temporary or permanent state.

Float the right leg on the in-breath and stack the right hip on top of the left as you exhale. Press firmly into the opposing hand, squaring the shoulders and creating length and awareness in this contralateral movement. Realign the hips with the shoulders, and mindfully carry the limb through into Low Lunge. The back knee becomes heavy as it drops to the earth, and the crown of head is light, moving into Proposal Pose (standing on one knee, hands on opposite thigh). Inhale for length, and slowly shift forward, maintaining safe pelvic alignment and engaging the core as the hip flexors open. Breathe steadily and deeply, imagining nutrients flowing into the muscles, softening, and expanding the tissue. As you're ready, with knees remaining on the ground, shift your weight onto the back leg, and extend the front leg, finding a similar opening of the hamstring. The breath soothes the muscles and drives the movement. Shift forward again and work the hands toward the side of the mat, bending the back leg deeply into a Side Lunge, with or without support from the hands. Sink the pelvis heavily for a few breath cycles, and then crawl the hands into a Wide-Legged Forward Fold, still facing the side of the mat. Bend the knees generously, bringing the chest close to thighs; the crown of the head reaches toward the earth. Opposite arm finds opposite elbow, creating a frame of the head, and using the weight of the structure, consciously release the head, neck, and upper back, leaning into axial extension. The breath is steady, and smooth. Find your way back to the front of your space into Low Lunge, and move into Downward-Facing Dog, or flow through a push-up variation, then repeat on the second side.

Bring the feet to the hands at the front of the mat, and rise into Mountain Pose, arms moving high overhead. As you exhale, the arms fall to the sides, palms open, receiving. Take time here to experience the feet rooting into the earth as the belly engages, and the head floats lightly above the shoulders. As you breathe, feel into the space, into this moment. Stillness is powerful, and allows for noticing and reflection, without judgement. Leaning into sensation moves us from thinking to feeling, and focuses a state of being, rather than doing. As you're ready, find your way to Downward-Facing Dog.

The bodymind is warmed and focused as we move into a standing series performed on both sides, designed to bring kinesthetic awareness through strength, and further create space in soft tissue. Inhale, lifting the right or left leg so it is even with the hip, toes pointed straight down for internal rotation, and smoothly step through into Low Lunge as you exhale. Spin the back foot to 45 degrees and separate the feet slightly so there is no overlap of the heels. Pressing down into the earth, rise into

Warrior 1, a pose where one leg is internally rotated and the other engages in slight external rotation, but the hips are square, and the arms are high over the head. Gently encourage the front hip bone back, and the back hip bone forward. Slip into the experience as you maintain a slow, deep, and steady breath. Brighten into the space, and turn the hips to the side, pressing into Warrior 2. Here, the front toes point directly to the front of the space, and the back toes to the side. The arms are long from the shoulders, and the hips are open. The gaze is traditionally over the front fingers but can be arranged as is comfortable or productive. The energy of this posture is strong, alive, and wonderful in the sensation it creates. Keep the legs right where they are and stretch the front fingers toward the back of your space, back fingers grazing the back leg, for Reverse Warrior. The body then tips forward, front ribs aligning with the forward leg for Side Angle Pose; the front hand can reach toward the mat or a prop, or the forearm can press down into the thigh. Please honor your body in this moment, finding what best supports your daily intention, and prepares you best for a day of moving. As you inhale, move into Star Pose, opening the entire body to the side, and lifting the heart toward the space above. Arms stretch long and gloriously overhead; the shape feels much like a standing "giant X," except for a lift through the chest. This posture may unveil emotional and mental states such as joy, vulnerability, curiosity, and wonder. Notice what arises.

Exhaling, sink deeply into Horse Pose; the knees flex and the pelvis moves straight down, like a descending elevator. Revel in the weight of the lower body, the strength of the large muscles of the legs. Inhale briefly through Star, and exhale into Warrior 2. Inhale into Reverse Triangle, a posture similar to Reverse Warrior, except both legs are straight. The extended front leg allows equal work through the feet, and subsequently encourages lengthening through the waist. Maintaining the stretch through the legs and torso, reach with the front arm toward the front of your space, imaging the ribs could move past your hip and knee, into Triangle Pose. The back arm reaches to the sky. Broaden the body, sensing energy moving in all directions within your own kinesphere as you breathe in and breathe out. Shift your focus to the earth, flexing and sinking into the front knee as the hips turn and the hands find the mat for Low Lunge. Step into Downward-Facing Dog or flow through a push-up variation. Engage in several deep breaths as you consider the state of your bodymind.

Drop the knees, fall to one hip, and move into a "Z" seat—the front shin is parallel to the front of the mat and the back thigh perpendicular to the front thigh; both legs are flexed at the knee. Shift the weight toward the front sit bone and finding a gentle Spinal Twist as you inhale, then shift toward the back hip, exhaling and working internal rotation as you twist in the other direction. Experience rotation working back and forth and sense the opening of the hips. As you're ready, fold over the front leg in a variation of Pigeon Pose, resting the front body on the earth, softening through the shoulders and neck, and allowing the weight of the body to further press the hips down. Take several breath cycles and move to the second side.

Move into Boat Pose, sitting on both sit bones, feet resting on the floor or hovering, knees flexed or straight, arms stretched to the side. The core works as we finish the practice, and we are reminded of the body's strength. Sip in a bit more air, and exhale fully onto the back, finding a full body stretch from head to toe. Indulge here in self-guided or intuitive movement, following the body's lead and trusting holistic intelligence—it is all right there, within you. When the movement runs its course, sink into Corpse Pose, releasing conscious breathwork and falling into the ground. The end of the practice is the beginning of something new; the bodymind rests and transitions.

Day Two

Focus: initiate supple movements of the spine; create fullness of breath throughout the body.

Day Three

Focus: engage external rotation; indulge in feeling, sensing.

Day Four

Focus: center internal rotation; privilege proprioception.

Day Five

Focus: extend the back and open the chest; notice sensation without judgement.

Day Six

Focus: strengthen the core to build support and awareness; remain steady through active energy.

Day Seven

Focus: open the fascia of the body's superficial back line; allow the body to lead into form and choose states of being.

Day Eight

Focus: develop and appreciate strength in the shoulders, back, and arms; breathe then flow, breathe then flow.

9. The Evolving Process

DAY NINE

Focus: investigate balance through both standing and falling; find gratitude for process and let go of product.

DAY TEN

Focus: experience stillness, and observe lower energy states; revel in rest, and care for all beings.

Summary

As previously stated, this approach to offering yoga to the dance community directs attention to the whole individual, incorporating tools for skillful living while pursuing a challenging profession. Certain poses can, indeed, provide strength and flexibility for the physical body, and this too is recognized in the sessions. Many practitioners anecdotally report an increased sense of well-being, and readiness to engage in their daily dance practice.

SomaLab + Yoga and Community Practice

I've been fortunate not only to lead specialized programming for dancers, but to offer somatic-based yogic practice in communities where I

Figure 9.2. Pre-professional dancers engage in SomaLab + Yogic Practices at Dance Italia, in Lucca, Italy (courtesy Stefanie Nelson; photograph by Rachelle Saker).

live and travel. Community practice necessitates very different considerations then that of more homogeneous populations (like dancers). Classes are often drop-in, so participant attendance varies from week to week. Each individual's knowledge of yoga, movement, and mind/body practice can vary greatly, and classes are often populated with people of various ages, genders, bodies, backgrounds, interests, and lived experiences. Everyone has a life separate from the yoga space and arrives to practice with daily events fresh on their mind. Community yoga leaders become skilled in reading the room, sensing group energy, and develop an ability to shift approaches quickly as the situation necessitates.

As I write this chapter, I am reminded how critical language is in yoga offerings, and particularly in community settings, where creating and maintaining an atmosphere of welcomeness and belonging is important. To feel othered completely works against the basic tenets of yoga; how can we join together if we feel pulled apart? How can we become vulnerable in our bodies if we do not feel safe? Indeed, recall from Chapter 4 that Knapp found language to be an important factor in supporting successful student performance outcomes when the OPTIMAL theory is applied to teaching methodologies, promoting a safe and healthy atmosphere for learning.[10]

What we say, and the way we say it then becomes especially consequential in community teaching as we strive to offer a practice that serves everyone, and in a way that does not elevate one way of being over another. For example, using the term "variation" instead of "modification" suggests that dropping the knee in Crescent Pose is not better, but different. The word "just" can also sneak into our teaching, as we strive to offer accessibility, i.e., saying you can "just" remain in Plank Pose as opposed to simply stating "remaining in Plank Pose is an option." Language that celebrates an individual's agency, such as "let the body lead" and "honor what you need in this moment" may support this concept, as opposed to "you can drop to Child's Pose if you're tired," which may inspire feelings of guilt for not coming to practice with full energy. We're all trying to do better in creating inclusive environments, and our words can go a long way in achieving this goal.

Clearly, there are different considerations for community yoga practice than that of specialized populations, although there is certainly overlap, as yogic philosophy remains constant. Considerations for SomaLab + Yoga in Community Practice include:

- Creating a welcoming, and safe environment, where all can practice without fear of judgement.
- Prioritizing physical safety in the yoga experience, offering many variations of poses that are accessible to all bodies.

9. The Evolving Process

- Teaching without assumption; community yoga leaders may have a little or a lot of information about their students.
- Facilitating a communal experience through breath, as it's the one common denominator practitioners can experience together.
- Approaching movement sequences holistically, involving multiple functions of the skeletomuscular system, i.e., flexion, extension, rotation of the spine, as well as strength, balance, and flexibility.
- Guiding class in such a way that allows practice in skillful living and encourages participants to relax the mind.
- Prioritizing embodiment and working toward non-separation of the bodymind instrument.
- Considering each student's individual needs and honoring where they are in the moment.
- Practicing steadiness and equanimity in breathing and working; "how we do one thing is how we do everything."

When designing a SomaLab + Yoga in Community Practice session, I take a broader approach than with specialized populations, focusing themes on tools for skillful living through the connection of breath and movement. Postures here provide a gentle but steady working of the body and supports philosophical practice. The following is a sample session that can be offered to a community who come together to move, breathe, and feel.

Figure 9.3. Retired architect Kris Floyd finds strength and ease in Crow Pose (courtesy Samantha Eibling; photograph by Chelsea Sanders).

Weekly Community Offering

Focus: find equanimity in movement and thought, remaining steady through differing energies and breath.

Sample Session

Come to a reclined place of comfort on the earth. If you are resting on your back, consider bringing the soles of the feet wide, toward the edges of the mat, and allow your flexed knees to fall together. The pelvis rests naturally against the floor without any adjustment of tilting or tucking, and the arms are wide in a cactus shape: elbows even with shoulders, flexed, fingers pointing to the back of the space. Scan the body for places of tightness, noticing where you hold tension in the body. As you move into a conscious breath pattern, even out and deepen the inhales and the exhales. Drawing your attention to the "mind's eye," that mental space just above the bridge of nose, imagine the day's tasks, duties, and happenings floating around like small pieces of paper. On an in-breath, they stir-up and on the out-breath, papers close to the edges of the mind space are pushed beyond sight. Breathe in again, pieces moving about, and breathe out, as more paper hides from the mind's eye. Finally, on the last breath cycle, the mind becomes clear of clutter, and you can focus on a soft, bright light, glowing and comforting. Find five more breath cycles right here, resting in ease, and being.

Gently begin to "windshield wiper" the legs back and forth, dropping one knee to the floor and then the other. The next time the legs fall, pause, finding easy spinal rotation. After a few breaths, move to the other side. Draw the knees toward the armpits, compressing the thighs; perhaps you stay, or choose to move into Happy Baby Pose, holding the outsides of the feet or the backs of the knees, enjoying stillness, or rocking side to side. As you're ready, roll to one side into a fetal position, and then make your way up to Tabletop Pose. Move through traditional Cow/Cat, linking breath to movement, and awakening the spine. Take a few breath cycles to engage in any other spinal actions that would serve to warm the body.

Pressing both shins into the earth, and grounding into one hand, lift the opposite fingertips high toward the ceiling, opening through the sternum and lifted shoulder as you inhale. Take an extra sip of air while you circle the wrist, then as you exhale, thread the lifted fingers under the supporting arm and rest the side of the body and head on the earth. Steadily breathe in and out; the top arm can stay flexed or stretch forward and then wrap around to the low back. Find the place that best supports your energy, your bodymind, in this moment. Repeat on the other side, and meet the group in Child's Pose, knees wide, big toes touching. The chest falls heavy to the mat, and the pelvis rests heavy on the heels; shoulders are soft. Return to rest, stillness, after this opening flow.

9. The Evolving Process 223

Keeping the hands long, start to pull forward on an inhale into a variation of Upward-Facing Dog; the elbows move toward straight, the chest lifts, toes are tucked, and the knees remain grounded and soft. Exhale back into Child's Pose. This time, swim the arms around back to the heels, and pressing into the hands, extend through the spine into a variation of Bridge Pose; the belly presses toward the ceiling as the heart opens. Flow several times through, moving to the rhythm of the breath, and sinking deep into sensation. We begin to rest the mind as we become finely tuned to the moment, prioritizing feeling and being. Continue to indulge in sensation as you tuck the toes and press into Downward-Facing Dog. Inhale, exhale, inhale, exhale.

Walk the feet to the hands at the front of your mat into Forward Fold, bending the knees generously so the chest rests on the thighs. The arms can dangle, or hands can cradle the elbows; both variations add weight to the upper body, opening space in the cervical spine and fascia. Enjoy the heaviness of the shoulder girdle as your upper body falls toward the earth. The breath moves into the big joints, creating space and facilitating movement. On your next inhale, move the hands to the shins and lengthen out the back in a Half Lift, then exhaling, move to Forward Fold once more. As you inhale, rise into Mountain Pose, knees soft on the journey, as the spine unravels, and the hands reach high. As you arrive in Mountain, the shoulders release, sending heaviness into the feet. Encircle a wrist with the thumb and forefinger of the opposite hand, and rising up and out of the waist, stretch to one side and then the other, changing your grip. Inhale into a slight backbend, and fold as you exhale. Half Lift once again, and exhale into Plank Pose. Lengthen on the in-breath, and either drop the knees or stay, honoring, respecting, and trusting your body as it leads you through the flow. You can choose to remain in your Plank variation, or lower to the floor, exhaling steadily, elbows pointing back as the forearms brush the ribs. If you have lowered, press down gently into the hands, and lift the chest for Cobra Pose on the in-breath, taking care not to stress or strain the neck, and then lower the chest back down on the out-breath. Wherever you are, press into Downward-Facing Dog. If Downward-Facing Dog is not the best choice for you, variations include Tabletop Pose or Child's Pose. Breathe easy and full after engaging the large muscles of the body. We'll work this hour to remain steady in our practice through the hills and valleys of physical effort.

Inhale and float the right or left leg into Three-Limbed Dog and smoothly step through into Low Lunge on the exhale. Grounding the feet into the earth, and firming through the core, rise into Crescent Pose on the in-breath, front leg flexed, and back leg extended, both internally rotated, and arms reaching high overhead. Take a moment to feel into this pose, perhaps rolling the shoulders down the back and finding ease in the neck and head. Gently press the back hip forward, and the front hip back. Taking an extra sip of air, rotate the torso toward the front leg, opposite arm stretching forward, and the other arm reaching back. Imagine the origin of the arms is in the sternum, with energy moving proximally to distally, going even beyond the fingertips. Squeeze the outer hips and engage the inner thighs as you breathe to support the upper body and drop into the experience of upper and lower body halves working together, but differently. Return to Crescent as you inhale, and exhale back into Low Lunge, hands framing the front foot. Gently stretch through the front knee into Pyramid Pose, a little or a lot, squaring and evening out the hips. Release through the head and neck, the arms taking weight, supporting the upper body. With each breath cycle, notice sensation, comfort, or discomfort, taking in information the soma provides, and making any adjustments in the pose accordingly. How do you want to be, what do you want to feel in this moment? Exhale, flexing the front leg into Low Lunge, and inhale into Plank Pose. Move to Downward-Facing Dog on the out-breath, or flow, lowering to the belly, the body in a straight line or knees dropping to the ground, then opening the heart to Cobra Pose on the inhale, and transition to Downward-Facing Dog on the exhale. I'll cue this transition as "Downward-Facing Dog or flow through." Experience the second side, and then move through the sequence once more, engaging in a pattern of one breath, one movement. Breath guides the body, beautifully, efficiently; breathe in, then move, breathe out, move again.

From Downward-Facing Dog, exhale into Forward Fold at the top of your mat, gently stepping or gliding. As you inhale, bend the knees generously, and lift the biceps next to your ears for Chair Pose, legs internally rotated, with both knees centered over the second toes. Find the spinal alignment that best supports this posture and your approach today; sit lower, firmly engaging the core and spinning the triceps in for a more "hugged-in" sensation, or rise a little higher, slightly opening the heart for a more outward, open feeling. Engage for several breath cycles, and work back to Downward-Facing Dog, or flow through.

Move into Three-Limbed Dog on the in-breath and take a smooth step into Low Lunge on the out-breath. Spin the back foot so the toes face the side of your space and use a full breath cycle to arrive in Warrior 2, swimming the same arm as back leg around and backward on the inhale, settling, and stretching the same arm as front leg forward on the exhale. Indulge in the feeling of being in this place, evening out hips and shoulders, then gently turn the gaze over the front fingers. Our body here is a metaphor for time, honoring the past, living in the present, and stretching toward the future. As you inhale, move into Reverse Warrior, front fingertips moving overhead to the back of the space, and back arm resting gently on the back leg, fingertips dancing lightly. Exhale into Side Angle Pose, front forearm pressing down firmly into the front thigh, back arm now extending high to the ceiling, and ribs, chest, and shoulders rotating open, with the front side body positioned over the forward leg. Continue to contract isometrically as you breathe, spin, expand. Reverse Triangle Pose on the inhale is next, and is similar in every way to Reverse Warrior, except the front leg extends and the range of motion may be different. Exhale into Low Lunge, moving the hips from external rotation back to internal rotation, mindfully and slowly, noticing the transition. Step back to High Plank as you inhale, and exhale into Downward-Facing Dog, or flow through. Breathe in, breathe out; breathe in, breathe out. Experience this flow on the second side, and then repeat the entire sequence, employing one breath, one movement.

Drop the knees to the earth and find Child's Pose, big toes to touch and knees any distance apart, arms reaching forward. Let the shoulders fall and drape to rest or stretch through the arms and press into the fingertips for a more active experience. As you rest in stillness, your bodymind processes and incorporates the experience, building knowledge, wisdom, and knowing. The breath remains steady and calm through the peaks and valleys of practice. Find your way back into Downward-Facing Dog.

Float one leg up, extending from the hip, and pull the knee into the chest, stepping into Low Lunge. Inhale into Crescent Pose and stretch the arms long as you exhale into Revolved Crescent Pose, spine rotating toward the forward leg. Stay, or begin to reach long through the front arm, tucking the elbow and pressing both hands together into a deeper twist. Lengthen as you inhale, rotate as you exhale. The next in-breath takes you back into Crescent Pose, and the out-breath into Pyramid Pose. Draw the same hand as your front leg to the low back and stretch the other forward about six inches. Once again, rotate toward the front leg, perhaps extending the fingertips on the low back into the air, finding Revolved Triangle Pose. The feet press down as the torso spins up, side ribs lifting and shoulder opening. Inhale a bit deeper and unwind back into Pyramid and then drop into Low Lunge. Steady the breath, reorientate the hips. On the next breath cycle, arrive in Warrior 2, the palms facing down; the front knee is safely aligned and presses toward the little toe. Inhale into Reverse Warrior, and exhale into Side Angle Pose. To further open the shoulder, turn the extended palm to the back of the space, and flexing the elbow, move the back of the hand to the low back. The breath is smooth and steady, the mind is at rest. Release this half-bind as you exhale, and inhale into Reverse Triangle Pose. Exhale again into Triangle Pose, imagining the side ribs moving beyond the knee as the waist and side bodies lengthen.

The front arm finds a place, any place, on the forward leg to rest, as the back arm stretches high. This posture has a broad, flat feeling, allowing for expansiveness into the space all around you. Breathe and widen, finding symbiosis with your environment and others with whom you share the space, sinking into sensation. Brighten into this last posture of the series, and exhale into Low Lunge. Step back into Downward-Facing Dog or flow through.

After several breaths, easily move the feet toward the hands as you fold forward. The knees are soft, and the tailbone rises. Inhale into Mountain Pose, arms rising, then palms meeting near the sternum. Firm the feet into the earth and float the crown of the head, establishing a steadiness as you stand. Gently shift the weight into one foot and lift the other leg into Tree Pose. The sole of the foot connects with the ankle, calf, or thigh; the knee presses open, externally rotating the working leg. Arms can remain at heart's center or stretch out to the side and long overhead. Energy radiates out from the core, establishing strength, balance. Expand on the inhale and release the posture on the exhale. Find some organic movements of the body here, perhaps swinging the arms or shaking out the feet. Experience Tree Pose on the other side and move into Downward-Facing Dog or flow through. Inhale into Plank Pose and slowly lower to the belly, becoming heavy in the body and resting the forehead on the hands. Allow yourself to rest as you fall into the earth, transitioning to a lower state of energy and recovery.

As you're ready, gently roll onto your back and take a full body stretch, arms and legs long, moving away from the belly button. Gather the shins, and pull the knees toward the armpits, compressing the thighs into the torso. Gently move the hands to the outer edges of the feet, or anywhere on the lower leg that suits, into Happy Baby Pose. Consider rocking side to side, or extending the legs, playfully engaging in the moment. Drawing the flexed legs into the chest once again, drop to one side for a reclined twist, arms long, but soft. The front ribs fall into the back ribs, and the back ribs rest heavily on the mat. Spend several breath cycles immersed in this imagery, then move to the other side. When you are ready, trusting your body to lead, conclude your practice with Corpse Pose, spreading out on your back. Rest easy, rest well.

Summary

My goal for community practice is always to try and lead students toward an experience that unites mind and body and establishes a foundation for skillful living. Prior to completing my 200-hour and 500-hour yoga certifications, I was a community practitioner myself (I still am). I realized during many hours of teacher training, these experiences had

Figure 9.4. Certified yoga instructor Ruthie Cohen offers health and wellness to practitioners (from left) Emily Brinegar, Rebecca Myers, and Samantha Eibling, as she gently guides them to presence (courtesy Samantha Eibling; photograph by Chelsea Sanders).

altered my very being, slowly, but surely, the plastic nervous system indeed at work. By offering knowledge with patience, and persistence, my yoga mentors had made indelible changes in my life, the way I think, the way I feel, the way I act. I am grateful for this care, as well as the opportunity to offer the same to others.

SomaLab for Hospice Caregivers

In this chapter thus far, we have juxtaposed the SomaLab framework with the ancient practice of yoga, contemporizing offerings in a way that complements the goals and ambitions of two distinct cohorts. Re-framing an already conceived movement system using SomaLab tools and tasks can be very successful and expand bodymind knowledge and perspectives. However, the framework can also be used in novel situations to achieve a specific goal, or to support individuals in challenging situations. One such need can be found in households where family members, who are non-medical personnel, are responsible for end-of-life care.

Consider the World Health Organization reports that each year, over 56.8 million people globally need palliative and hospice care; most of these patients come from low and middle-income countries.[11] Here in the United States, these services are provided by Medicare and Medicaid free of charge, and include medications to manage pain, rental of hospital equipment, and supplies for wound care and incontinence. In-home health visits from certified personnel, such as hospice nurses, who provide medical care, and home health aides, who assist with tasks of daily living, are often relegated to once weekly. Access to beds in hospice hospitals, where in-patient care is received, are few and far between. This often leaves family members, who cannot afford daily private or institutional care, with the lion's share of the work of caregiving, both during the day and across nighttime hours.

One of the difficulties of layman care in end-of-life circumstances is navigating situations where patients have compromised communication skills due to dementia, severe illness, or other circumstances. Already at a disadvantage in terms of medical training, family members or friends can struggle to read cues from patients and provide adequate levels of comfort. Im et al. report "effective communication is integral to the delivery of goal-concordant care for older adults and their family caregivers, and yet, it is uncommon in people with serious illness."[12] Additionally, their qualitative study that collected interviews analyzed through thematic analysis concluded, "alternative approaches to communication are needed to elicit the challenges that patients and caregivers experience throughout the progression of illness to improve care for people nearing the end of life."[13] Indeed, learning to discern patient body language could be one of these alternative approaches, and greatly aid care from non-medical caregivers.

Somatic study and practice may be a tool for developing observational and sensory skills in caregivers. As individuals develop the ability to notice, by experiencing and practicing movement while observing their own bodymind sensations, they also develop the ability to take these skills outward and read such actions in others. As discussed extensively in Chapters 5 and 7, kinesthetic empathy is a dominant by-product of somatic study, and by deepening our own ability to feel, we develop the capacity to know what others experience.

Closely aligned with the idea of movement training for caregivers is the relatively new field of narrative medicine. This practice utilizes art and literature to expand medical workers' listening and observation skills and allows for a holistic approach to treating individuals. For example, after listening to a patient's history, or a simple story about a past or current event, workers may write about that experience and begin to develop a larger understanding of their patient. Writings can include stories, poems, plays, journal entries, or any medium that documents observations. As in somatic study, narrative medicine cultivates empathy and allows for a broader and deeper understanding of individuals; it centers the individual as opposed to the disease. Even more practically, deeper knowledge of an individual's history and life circumstances can facilitate difficult diagnoses. Narrative medicine can also aid medical and non-medical workers alike in addressing bias and judgement in their care.

Given the close relationship of somatics/health/narrative medicine, I'm currently developing an approach to somatic training for non-medical hospice caregivers, expanding the idea of narrative medicine to include movement. Although training in the medical humanities is available for medical students, the introduction of movement study and exploration for the lay caregiver in hospice situations is less considered. Documented somatic and movement-based interventions focus primarily on the health and wellness of the caregiver, an important aspect of this work, and one that is veritably an outcome of any course of somatic study. Indeed, I have a personal investment in this endeavor—as relayed in Chapter 8, I served as my mother's hospice caregiver during the last two months of her life.

As I revisit this experience, the lack of preparedness I felt still lives in my bodymind. What did I know about end-of-life care? My mother's nurse

Figure 9.5. The author's mother, Margaret English Limons, on her 95th birthday, in home hospice care (author's collection).

who visited once or twice weekly commented how successfully I understood Mom's needs, even though she was often unable to clearly communicate what she was feeling. A conversation ensued regarding body language, empathy, and alternative ways of determining the needs of patients with dementia and other compromised mental and physical states. After my mother's death, I began to reflect on my caretaking experience; could I design a SomaLab-based program for non-medical hospice caregivers that would deepen their own ability to sense in their own bodies, and subsequently those of loved ones?

The current outline I'm developing uses SomaLab tools and tasks in a way that is safe and comfortable for non-professional—and, most likely, older—populations of movers. Participants can be seated in chairs and stand at times or even work with more physical fullness using the floor or mats, if it would support their experience. Below is a structure that utilizes somatic applications for non-medical hospice caregivers:

1. Tool: Breath
Task: Breath (deconstructive)

- *Bring attention to the breath, equal parts in-breath and out-breath.*
- *"Follow the leader" to unite breath and movement.*

2. Tool: Imagery, visualization, and mental practice
Task: Guided visualization (deconstructive)

- *Can you recall how your loved one appeared when they were well? How did they move? How did they sound? Let this memory wash over your own body; can you imagine how it might feel?*

3. Tool: Intention/attention
Task: Guided visualization (deconstructive)

- *Bring attention to a glowing circle of light in your mind's eye and let the warmth and goodness of the breath spread throughout your body.*

4. Tool: Physical awareness (kinesthesia)
Task: Targeted muscular engagement (deconstructive)

- *Stretch your left arm overhead, and feel longer on the left, and then stretching the right arm, feel longer on the right.*
- *Raise both arms together, imagining you are pushing heavy air aside.*
- *Find gentle circles of the torso, linking movement to breath.*
- *Gently lift the thigh and extend one leg at a time out toward the center of the circle, feeling the muscles contract.*
- *Practice "toe-touches" if physical capability allows.*

9. The Evolving Process 231

5. Tool: Self-guided/intuitive movement
Task: Sensory-based improvisation (reconstructive)

- *Begin to gently massage your shoulders, arms, forearms, hands, hips, and thighs; move in any way that facilitates this process.*

6. Tool: Physical awareness
Task: Body organization (reconstructive)

- *Bring both arms overhead, feeling vertical like a pencil in the space.*
- *Open your arms to the side, like the letter "T" and feel horizontal, like a table, in space; imagine your arms begin from your chest.*

7. Tool: Embodiment in action
Task: conceptually-guided prompts (integrative)

- *Take a few moments to imagine an object or your body floating in space; what would it feel like?*
- *Then, experience your arms floating in space in front of and alongside you; can your legs float in the same manner? How does it feel?*

8. Tool: Movement empathy
Task: Self-guided phrase work (integrative)

- *Recall a favorite story about your loved one, or a meaningful experience; use accessible movement to strengthen the memory.*
- *Share your story/movement with the group, if it would support you today.*

9. Tool: Movement empathy
Task: Facilitated phrase work (integrative)

- *With the leader or another participant, engage in a mirroring exercise, where one person initiates movement and the other follows. Practice both leading and following.*

10. Tool: Reflection/incorporation

- *What did you experience today, what did you feel?*
- *Can you offer yourself compassion, understanding what you do is difficult?*
- *Can you share that compassion with someone else?*

I've had the opportunity to offer this work-in-process to community cohorts and am always surprised at the impact of the experience, not just for the group, but also for myself as a caregiver. The simple act of people in challenging situations assembling is powerful, but when coupled with breath and movement, the effect is magnified. In accordance with what we know about embodiment, movement spurs conversation, and conversation spurs movement. I am also reminded of the importance of first-person application when designing a methodology where theory provides the framework. We can follow a hypothesis to begin the process, but the engagement of people, with all their uniqueness and humanity, is critical in honing a successful and healthful experience. It is this constant dialogue of theory and practice that leads us forward.

I share this work as an example of how the SomaLab framework can be applied to an infinite number of life situations and practiced by individuals who are outside of professional realms of movement. I invite all who read this text and find the work invigorating to explore applications that will benefit both their own lived experiences, as well as those in shared communities. Movement is an essential part of our lives, and for those who are experts, offering knowledge and experience is truly a gift.

Conclusion

The potential for somatic practice already exists inside every one of us; each human person has the innate capacity to feel, and to think, equally, harmoniously. The body carries enormous intelligence, and our systems of behavior are inextricably linked. As we move, our language is enhanced; our wisdom and knowledge expand.

This last chapter applying SomaLab methodologies to community cohorts and situations fully bridges scientific inquiry (in all its forms) and practical application. We can see how a way to integrate what we know into what we do has limitless possibilities for both expert movers and those seeking to enrich their lives and ease the challenges of daily living. The ability to feel deeply, somatically, is a shared commonality, and becomes manifest as we embrace the wholeness of our humanity.

Concluding Remarks

Researching and writing this book has been very much like archiving a choreography—with no perfect system in place to arrive at complete documentation, we use all the tools at our disposal to understand and present the sincerest form of what we believe and what we know. This material is informed by my own personal history and perspectives; indeed, someone else might frame the work differently, and arrive at divergent, even conflicting conclusions.

We begin this journey in Part 1 by gathering information from many trusted and reliable resources and start to construct a multi-dimensional rendering of holistic human learning and living. Fortified with strong theoretical scaffolding, I present a self-developed methodology for somatic practice in Part 2. Over the course of nine chapters, the progression of theory to practice, initiated in the opening pages of this book, is complete.

This is indeed "the story of us": how we learn to move, behave, and live by understanding the structure and function we all share, while also honoring social and environmental influences that shape us as unique, and important, people. In formulating a framework, as opposed to a specific methodology that is governed by set movements and exercises, I hope to make this work accessible in a way that can enrich the lives of many and encourage dance and movement as a way of celebrating our humanness.

There are two more points I'd like to address in these concluding remarks. First, I hope this text contributes to normalizing the integration of the lives we lead in the workplace with our lives in the homeplace. I have freely shared my own background with the intention of demonstrating that our movement behavior is holistic, and non-separable from all aspects of our living and being. The very definition of somatics describes, even demands, this intertwining, and by embracing the very nature of our human instrument, where the need to move is fundamental, we set ourselves on the path to health and wellness.

Finally, as I close, I hope this book also serves as a model for anyone who is interested in developing their own abilities to research and create. I encourage you to assemble as much information as possible, incorporating knowledge into your world, thoughtfully and purposefully, and form your own ideas and methodologies, based on what is known, as well as your own somatic experiences and instincts. Research, investigate, try, fail, try again, succeed, and grow. Learn from others and incorporate new ways of knowing and being into your own repertory of movement and somatic inquiry. Yes, this book delves deeply into why somatic practice is effective, essential, but it is also an example of *process*. It is not just a presentation of SomaLab, or any somatic methodology, but an examination of system development and application, informed by a broad approach that includes empirical research, lived experiences, situational constraints, and how they all dynamically interact.

A somatic approach to moving and living does not belong to anyone one person, or school of thought, because it belongs to all of us. The holism of the bodymind is as old as humanity itself. And whether you forge your own path, or follow that of another, move forward in motion, in thought, and with heart.

Chapter Notes

Acknowledgments

1. Emily Saliers, "Closer to Fine," Elektra Records, 1995.

Preface

1. Chip Hartranft, *The Yoga-Sutra of Patanjali: A New Translation with Commentary* (Boulder: Shambhala, 2003). Hartranft uses the term *bodymind* in this text to describe the inseparable nature of the mind/body relationship. It reminds us that the body is not an afterthought, existing solely to do the work of the mind; rather, it is an equal partner in responsive behavior.

Chapter 1

1. Martha Eddy, "Somatic Practices and Dance: Global Influences," *Dance Research Journal* 34, no. 2 (Winter 2002): 47.
2. IADMS and Glenna Batson, "Somatic Studies and Dance," 2009, www.iadms.com.
3. Eddy, "Somatic Practices and Dance," 59.
4. For a full rendering of the development of somatic practice in art and education, please see Martha Eddy, *Mindful Movement: The Evolution of the Somatic Arts and Conscious Action* (Bristol, UK: Intellect Press, 2016).
5. Martha Eddy, *Mindful Movement: The Evolution of the Somatic Arts and Conscious Action* (Bristol, UK: Intellect Press, 2016).
6. J. Kaminski, "First Nations Pedagogy," 2013, https://firstnationspedagogy.com/FN_Pedagogy.html.
7. *Ibid.*
8. Nicole Montiero and Diana Wall, "African Dance as Healing Modality throughout the Diaspora: The Use of Ritual and Movement to Work through Trauma," *The Journal of Pan-African Studies* 4, no. 6 (September 2011).
9. Eddy, *Mindful Movement.*
10. *Ibid.*
11. Olatunji Oyeshile, "The African World-View, Science and the Quest for Development," *International Journal of African Culture and Ideas* 4 (2004).
12. Beatrice Capote, email to author, February 21, 2024.
13. Richard Rosen, *The Yoga of Breath* (Boulder: Shambhala, 2002), 15.
14. G.Y. Yang, J. Hunter, F.L. Bu, W.L. Hao, H. Zhang, P.M. Wayne, and J.P. Liu, "Determining the Safety and Effectiveness of Tai Chi: A Critical Overview of 210 Systematic Reviews of Controlled Clinical Trials," *Systematic Reviews* 11, no. 1 (2022).
15. Pasi Pölönen, Otto Lappi, and Mari Tervaniemi, "Effect of Meditative Movement on Affect and Flow in Quigong Practitioners," *Frontiers in Psychology* 10 (2019).
16. *Ibid.*
17. S.L. Keng, M.J. Smoski, and C.J. Robins, "Effects of Mindfulness on Psychological Health: A Review of Empirical Studies," *Clinical Psychology Review* 31, no. 6 (2011).
18. David Lukoff and Richard Strozzi-Heckler, "Aikido: A Martial Art with Mindfulness, Somatic, Relational, and Spiritual Benefits for Veterans," *Spirituality in Clinical Practice* 4, no. 2 (2017).
19. *Ibid.*
20. Terence McPartland, "Moshe

Feldenkrais and Modern Judo: The Strange Forgotten Tale of a Physicist Who Learned Judo," 2012, http://dcjudo.com/feldenkrais-and-judo.

21. Moshe Feldenkrais and Elizabeth Beringer, *Higher Judo: Groundwork* (San Diego: Somatic Resources, 2010), 12.

22. Anders Ottosson, "The First Historical Movements of Kinesiology: Scientification in the Borderline Between Physical Culture and Medicine Around 1850," *The International Journal of the History of Sport* 27, no. 11 (2010).

23. Ibid.

24. Ibid.

25. Robin Veder, "The Expressive Efficiencies of American Delsarte and Mensendieck Body Culture," *Modernism/Modernity* 17, no. 4 (2010).

26. Ibid.

27. Karin Greenhead and John Habron, "The Touch of Sound: Dalcroze Eurhythmics as a Somatic Practice," *Journal of Dance & Somatic Practices* 7, no. 1 (2015).

28. Kelly Jean Mullan, "Somatics Herstories: Tracing Elsa Gindler's Educational Antecedents Hade Kallmeyer and Genevieve Stebbins," *Journal of Dance & Somatic Practices* 9, no. 2 (2017).

29. Ibid.

30. Patricia Vertinsky, "Transatlantic Traffic in Expressive Movement: From Delsarte and Dalcroze to Margaret H'Doubler and Rudolf Laban," *The International Journal of the History of Sport* (2009).

31. Susan Manning, "Modern Dance in the Third Reich, Redux," in *The Oxford Handbook of Dance and Politics* (Oxford: Oxford University Press, 2017), 395.

32. Martha Eddy, "A Brief History of Somatic Practices and Dance Historical Development of the Field of Somatic Education and Its Relationship to Dance," *Journal of Dance and Somatic Practices* 1, no. 1 (2009).

33. Julie Brodie and Elin Lobel, *Dance and Somatics: Mind-Body Principles of Teaching and Performance* (Jefferson: McFarland, 2012).

34. Chloë Stallibrass, Peta Sissons, and Colin Chalmers, "Randomized Controlled Trial of the Alexander Technique for Idiopathic Parkinson's Disease," *Clinical Rehabilitation* 16, no. 7 (2002).

35. Patricia Buchanan and Beverly Ulrich, "The Feldenkrais Method®: A Dynamic Approach to Changing Motor Behavior," *Research Quarterly for Exercise and Sport* 72, no. 4 (2001).

36. James Stephens and Susan Hillier, "Evidence for the Effectiveness of the Feldenkrais Method," *Human Kinetics* 9, no. 3 (2020).

37. Paula Stall and Manoel Jacobsen Teixeira, "Fibromyalgia Syndrome Treated with the Structural Integration Rolfing® Method," *Revista Dor* 15 (2014).

38. Peggy Hackney, *Making Connections: Total Body Integration Through Bartenieff Fundamentals* (New York: Taylor & Francis Group, 1998).

39. Jack Blackburn, "Tragers Psychological Integration—An Overview," *Journal of Bodywork and Movement Therapies* 7, no. 4 (2003).

40. Ibid.

41. Kimberley A. Foster et al., "The Trager Approach in the Treatment of Chronic Headache: A Pilot Study," *Alternative Therapies in Health and Medicine* 10, no. 5 (2004).

42. Janice Ross, *Anna Halprin: Experience as Dance* (Berkeley: University of California Press, 2007).

43. Judith Wasserman, "A World in Motion: The Creative Synergy of Lawrence and Anna Halprin," *Landscape Journal* 31, no. 1–2 (2012).

44. Ross, *Anna Halprin: Experience As Dance*.

45. Susan Harper, "Emily Conrad's Continuum," accessed January 10, 2024, www.continuumteachers.com/about/emilie-conrad-continuum.

46. Emilie Conrad, "Continuum Movement," in *New Dimensions in Body Psychotherapy*, ed. Nick Totton (Maidenhead, Berkshire, UK: Open University Press, 2005).

47. Bonnie Gintis, "Experiencing Osteopathy Through Continuum Movement," Cranial Academy Annual Conference, 2001, http://osteopathichistory.com/pdfs/Experiencing.pdf.

48. Skinner Releasing Network, "About Joan Skinner," accessed January 16, 2024, https://skinnerreleasingnetwork.org/-welcome-to-srn/about-joan-skinner/#:~:text=Joan%20Skinner%20had%20a%20lifetime,The%20Thinking%20Body"%20in%201937.

49. Joan Skinner, Bridget Davis, Robert Davidson, Kris Wheeler, and Sally Metcalf, "Skinner Releasing Technique: Imagery and Its Application to Movement Training," accessed May 7, 2021, https://skinnerreleasingnetwork.org/wp-content/uploads/2020/11/Imagery-and-its-Application.pdf.

50. Joan Skinner, Bridget Davis, Robert Davidson, Kris Wheeler, and Sally Metcalf, "Skinner Releasing Technique," *Contact Quarterly* 5 (1979).

51. M. Emslie, "Skinner Releasing Technique: Dancing from Within," *Journal of Dance and Somatic Practices* 1, no. 2 (2009).

52. Susan Kozel, Ruth Gibson, and Bruno Martelli, "The Weird Giggle: Attending to Affect in Virtual Reality," *Transformations* 31, no. 31 (2018).

53. Thomas Hanna, "Clinical Somatic Education," *Somatics* (Autumn-Winter 1990).

54. Ibid.

55. Bonnie Bainbridge Cohen, *Basic Neurocellular Patterns: Exploring Developmental Movement* (El Sobrante, CA: Burchfield Rose, 2018).

56. Ibid.

57. Margherita De Giorgi, "Shaping the Living Body: Paradigms of Soma and Authority in Thomas Hanna's Writings," *Revista Brasileira de Estudos da Presença* 5 (2015).

58. Isabelle Ginot, Allegra Barlow, and Mark Franko, "From Shusterman's Somaesthetics to a Radical Epistemology of Somatics," *Dance Research Journal* 42, no. 1 (2010): 18.

Chapter 2

1. Morris Kline, *Mathematical Thought from Ancient to Modern Times* (Oxford: Oxford University Press, 1972).

2. Richard Schmidt, Tim Lee, Carolee Winstein, Gabriele Wulf, and Howard Zelaznik, *Motor Control and Learning* (Champaign: Human Kinetics, 2019).

3. R.A. Magill, "Modeling and Verbal Feedback Influences on Skill Learning," *International Journal of Sport Psychology* 24, no. 4 (1993).

4. Schmidt, et al., *Motor Control and Learning*.

5. W.E. Hick, "On the Rate of Gain of Information," *Quarterly Journal of Experimental Psychology* 4, no. 1 (1952): 11–26.

6. K. Ng and S. Latorre, "How to Tie Your Shoes," wikiHow, accessed July 28, 2023, https://www.wikihow.com/Tie-Your-Shoes.

7. William James, *Principles of Psychology* (New York: Henry Holt, 1890), 403.

8. M.I. Posner, "Orienting of Attention," *Quarterly Journal of Experimental Psychology* 32, no. 1 (1980); M.I. Posner and S.E. Petersen, "The Attention System of the Human Brain," *Annual Review of Neuroscience* 13, no. 1 (1990).

9. C.D. Wickens, "The Effects of Divided Attention on Information Processing in Manual Tracking," *Journal of Experimental Psychology: Human Perception and Performance* 2, no. 1 (1976); C.D. Wickens and J.G. Hollands, *Engineering Psychology and Human Performance* (Upper Saddle River, NJ: Prentice Hall, 2000).

10. C.D. Wickens, "The Structure of Attentional Resources," in *Attention and Performance*, ed. R.S. Nickerson (Hillsdale, NJ: Erlbaum, 1980).

11. W. Schneider and R.M. Shiffrin, "Controlled and Automatic Human Information Processing: I. Detection, Search, and Attention," *Psychological Review* 84, no.1 (1977).

12. W. Schneider, S.T. Dumais, and R.M. Shiffrin, "Automatic Processing and Attention," in *Varieties of Attention*, ed. R. Parasuraman and R. Davis (New York: Academic Press, 1984).

13. J. Driver, "A Selective Review of Selective Attention Research from the Past Century," *British Journal of Psychology* 92 (2001).

14. Schmidt et al., *Motor Control and Learning*.

15. D.N. Lee and E. Aronson, "Visual Proprioceptive Control of Standing in Human Infants," *Perception & Psychophysics* 15 (1974).

16. Schmidt et al., *Motor Control and Learning*.

17. A. Cicchella, T. Popotti, and J.B. Shea, "Effect of Different Spotting Heights on Ballet Pirouette Performance," *Acta Kinesiologiae Universitatis Tartuensis* 21 (2015).

18. A. Polit and E. Bizzi, "Characteristics

of Motor Programs Underlying Arm Movements in Monkeys," *Journal of Neurophysiology* 42 (1979); A. Polit and E. Bizzi, "Processes Controlling Arm Movements in Monkeys," *Science* 201 (1978).

19. A.G. Feldman, "Functional Tuning of the Nervous System with Control of Movement or Maintenance of a Steady Posture—II. Controllable Parameters of the Muscles," *Biophysica* (1966); A.G. Feldman, "Functional Tuning of the Nervous System with Control of Movement or Maintenance of a Steady Posture—III. Mechanographic Analysis of the Execution by Man of the Simplest Motor Tasks," *Biophysics* 11 (1966).

20. Schmidt et al., *Motor Control and Learning*.

21. R.A. Schmidt, "A Schema Theory of Discrete Motor Skill Learning," *Psychological Review* 82, no. 4 (1975).

22. Schmidt et al., *Motor Control and Learning*.

23. Schmidt, "A Schema Theory."

24. P.M. Fitts, "The Information Capacity of the Human Motor System in Controlling the Amplitude of Movement," *Journal of Experimental Psychology* 47, no. 6 (1954).

25. B.C. Hatfield, W.R. Wyatt, and J.B. Shea, "Effects of Auditory Feedback on Movement Time in Fitts Task," *Journal of Motor Behavior* 42, no. 5 (2010): 289–93.

26. J.A. Adams and B. Reynolds, "Effect of Shift in Distribution of Practice Conditions Following Interpolated Rest," *Journal of Experimental Psychology* 47, no. 1 (1954).

27. Schmidt, "A Schema Theory."

28. Timothy Lee and Heather Carnahan, "Motor Learning: Reflections on the Past 40 Years of Research," *Kinesiology Review* 10, no. 3 (2021).

29. John B. Shea and Robin Morgan, "Contextual Interference Effects on the Acquisition, Retention, and Transfer of a Motor Skill," *Journal of Experimental Psychology: Human Learning and Memory* 5, no. 2 (1979).

30. T.D. Lee and R.A. Magill, "Can Forgetting Facilitate Skill Acquisition," *Advances in Psychology* 27 (Amsterdam: North-Holland, 1985).

31. John B. Shea and Susan T. Zimny, "Context Effects in Memory and Learning Movement Information," *Advances in Psychology* 12 (1983).

32. P. Del Rey, E. Wughalter, and M. Whitehurst, "The Effects of Contextual Interference on Females with Varied Experience in Open Sport Skills," *Research Quarterly for Exercise and Sport* 53, no. 2 (1982).

33. Edward A. Bilodeau, Ina McD Bilodeau, and Donald A. Schumsky, "Some Effects of Introducing and Withdrawing Knowledge of Results Early and Late in Practice," *Journal of Experimental Psychology* 58, no. 2 (1959): 142.

34. J.A. Adams, "A Closed-Loop Theory of Motor Learning," *Journal of Motor Behavior* 3, no. 2 (1971).

35. Adams, "A Closed-Loop Theory."

36. Briana K. Chen, Nathen J. Murawski, Christine Cincotta, Olivia McKissick, Abby Finkelstein, Anahita B. Hamidi, Emily Merfeld, Emily Doucette, Stephanie Grella, Monika Shpokayte, Yosif Zaki, Amanda Fortin, and Steve Ramirez Chen, "Artificially Enhancing and Suppressing Hippocampus-Mediated Memories," *Current Biology* 29, no. 11 (June 3, 2019).

37. F.I.M. Craik and R.S. Lockhart, "Levels of Processing: A Framework for Memory Research," *Journal of Verbal Learning and Verbal Behavior* 11, no. 6 (1972): 671.

Chapter 3

1. Jill Bolte Taylor, email message to author, January 8, 2025.

2. Rick Hanson and Richard Mendius, *Buddha's Brain: The Practical Neuroscience of Happiness, Love, and Wisdom* (Oakland: New Harbinger, 2009), 6.

3. Suzana Herculano-Houzel, "The Remarkable, Yet Not Extraordinary, Human Brain as a Scaled-up Primate Brain and Its Associated Cost," *Proceedings of the National Academy of Sciences* 109, no. supplement_1 (2012).

4. Scott T. Brady, George J. Siegel, R. Wayne Albers, and Donald L. Price, *Basic Neurochemistry: Molecular, Cellular and Medical Aspects* (Amsterdam: Academic Press, 2006), 532.

5. Hanna Hayat, Amit Marmelshtein, Aarom K. Krom, Yaniv Sela, Ariel Tankus, Ido Strauss, Firas Fahoum, Itzak Fried, and Yuval Nir, "Reduced Neural Feedback

Notes—Chapter 3

Signaling Despite Robust Neuron and Gamma Auditory Responses During Human Sleep," *Nature Neuroscience* 25, no. 7 (2022).

6. Marc D. Lewis and Rebecca M. Todd, "The Self-Regulating Brain: Cortical-Subcortical Feedback and the Development of Intelligent Action," *Cognitive Development* 22, no. 4 (2007): 406–30.

7. William R. Uttal, *Mind and Brain: A Critical Appraisal of Cognitive Neuroscience* (Cambridge: MIT Press, 2011).

8. D.O. Hebb, *The Organization of Behavior: A Neuropsychological Theory* (Mahwah, NJ: Psychology Press, 2002).

9. Eleanor A. Maguire, David G. Gadian, Ingrid S. Johnsrude, Catriona D. Good, John Ashburner, Richard S.J. Frackowiak, and Christopher D. Frith, "Navigation-Related Structural Change in the Hippocampi of Taxi Drivers," *Proceedings of the National Academy of Sciences* 97, no. 8 (2000).

10. Sandra E. Hockenbury, Susan A. Nolan, and Don H. Hockenbury, *Psychology* (New York: Worth, 2015).

11. Moheb Costandi, *Neuroplasticity* (Cambridge: MIT Press, 2016).

12. Brady, Siegel, Albers, and Price, *Basic Neurochemistry*.

13. Hockenbury, Nolan and Hockenbury, *Psychology*.

14. Edalmarys Santos and Chad A. Noggle, "Synaptic Pruning," in *Encyclopedia of Child Behavior and Development*, ed. Sam Goldstein and Jack A. Naglieri (Boston: Springer, 2011).

15. *Ibid.*

16. E.H. Lenneberg, *Biological Foundations of Language* (New York: Wiley, 1967).

17. Bruce Crosson, Anna Bacon Moore, Kaundinya Gopinath, Keith D. White, Wieranga E. Christina, Megan E. Gaiefsky, and Katherine S. Fabrizio, "Role of the Right and Left Hemispheres in Recovery of Function during Treatment of Intention in Aphasia," *Journal of Cognitive Neuroscience* 17, no. 3 (2005).

18. Fred H. Gage, "Neorogenesis in the Adult Brain," *The Journal of Neuroscience* 22, no. 3 (2002).

19. B.L. Jacobs, H. van Praag, and F.H. Gage, "Adult Brain Neurogenesis and Psychiatry: A Novel Theory of Depression," *Molecular Psychiatry* 5, no. 3 (2000).

20. "Brain Basics: Know Your Brain," National Institute of Neurological Disorders and Stroke, accessed September 26, 2022, https://www.ninds.nih.gov/health-information/public-education/brain-basics/brain-basics-know-your-brain#:~:text=The%20brain%20can%20be%20divided.

21. Hockenbury, Nolan and Hockenbury, *Psychology*.

22. Eric R. Kandel and A.J. Hudspeth, "The Brain and Behavior," *Principles of Neural Science* (New York: McGraw-Hill Medical, 2012).

23. Mark F. Bear, Barry W. Connors, and Michael A. Paradiso, *Neuroscience: Exploring the Brain* (Burlington, MA: Jones and Bartlett Learning, 2016).

24. Kandel and Hudspeth, "The Brain and Behavior."

25. Hockenbury, Nolan and Hockenbury, *Psychology*.

26. *Ibid.*

27. Kandel and Hudspeth, "The Brain and Behavior."

28. *Ibid.*

29. Robert O. Collins, and John L. Adams, *Prefrontal Cortex: Developmental Differences, Executive and Cognitive Functions and Role in Neurological Disorders* (New York: Nova Biomedical, 2013).

30. Yusuke Moriguchi and Kazuo Hiraki, "Developmental Relationship Between executive Function and the Prefrontal Cortex in Young Children," in *Prefrontal Cortex: Developmental Differences, Executive and Cognitive Functions and Role in Neurological Disorders*, ed. Robert O. Collins and John L. Adams (New York: Nova Biomedical, 2013).

31. F.L. Stevens, R.A. Hurley, and K.H. Taber, "Anterior Cingulate Cortex: Unique Role in Cognition and Emotion," *Journal of Neuropsychiatry* 23, no. 2 (2011).

32. Bear, Connors, and Paradiso, *Neuroscience: Exploring the Brain*.

33. Endel Tulving and Hans J. Markowitsch, "Episodic and Declarative Memory: Role of the Hippocampus," *Hippocampus* 8, no. 3 (1998).

34. David A. Gallo and Mark E. Wheeler, "Episodic Memory," in *The Oxford Handbook of Cognitive Psychology* (New York: Oxford University Press, 2013).

35. Hockenbury, Nolan and Hockenbury, *Psychology*.

36. B. Preilowski, "Memory of an

Amnesiac (and a Half a Century of Memory Research)," *Fortschritte Der Neurologie · Psychiatrie* 77, no. 10 (2009).

37. Maguire, Gadian, Johnsrude, Good, Ashburner, Frackowiak, Frith, "Navigation-Related Structural Change."

38. Yashuo Zhu, Hui Gao, Li Tong, ZhongLin Li, Linyuan Wang, Chi Zhang, Qiang Yang, and Bin Yan, "Emotion Regulation of Hippocampus Using Real-Time fMRI Neurofeedback in Healthy Human," *Frontiers in Human Neuroscience* 13 (2019): 242.

39. James P. Herman, "Limbic System Mechanisms of Stress Regulation: Hypothalamo-Pituitary-Adrenocortical Axis," *Progress in Neuro-Psychopharmacology and Biological Psychiatry* 29, no. 8 (2005).

40. Alberto A. Rasia-Filho, Renata G. Londero, and Matilde Achaval, "Functional Activities of the Amygdala: An Overview," *Journal of Psychiatry and Neuroscience* 25, no. 1 (2000).

41. Anthony Wright, "Limbic System: Amygdala (Section 4, Chapter 6)," *Neuroscience Online: An Electronic Textbook for the Neurosciences*, Department of Neurobiology and Anatomy, University of Texas Medical School at Houston, 2019, https://nba.uth.tmc.edu/neuroscience/m/s4/chapter06.html.

42. Ibid.

43. R. Adolphs, Daniel Tranel, H. Damasio, and A. Damasio, "Impaired Recognition of Emotion in Facial Expressions Following Bilateral Damage to the Human Amygdala," *Nature* 372, no. 6507 (1994).

44. Chandra Sekhar Sripada, Mike Angstadt, Patrick McNamara, Andrea C. King, and K. Luan Phan, "Effects of Alcohol on Brain Responses to Social Signals of Threat in Humans," *NeuroImage* 55, no. 1 (2011).

45. J. Paul Hamilton, Amit Etkin, Daniella J. Furman, Maria G. Lemus, Rebecca F. Johnson, and Ian H. Gotlib, "Functional Neuroimaging of Major Depressive Disorder: A Meta-Analysis and New Integration of Baseline Activation and Neural Response Data," *American Journal of Psychiatry* 169, no. 7 (2012).

46. Larry Cahill and James L. McGaugh, "Modulation of Memory Storage," *Current Opinion in Neurobiology* 6, no. 2 (1996).

47. Rasia-Filho, Londero, and Achaval, "Functional Activities of the Amygdala."

48. Wright, "Limbic System: Amygdala."

49. Tyler J. Torrico and Sunil Munakomi, "Neuroanatomy, Thalamus," PubMed, 2020, https://www.ncbi.nlm.nih.gov/books/NBK542184/#:~:text=The%20thalamus%20is%20a%20mostly.

50. Nicholas D. Child and Eduardo E. Benarroch, "Anterior Nucleus of the Thalamus: Functional Organization and Clinical Implications," *Neurology* 81, no. 21 (2013).

51. Torrico and Munakomi, "Neuroanatomy, Thalamus."

52. James E. Jan, Russel J. Reiter, Michael B. Wasdell, and Martin Bax, "The Role of the Thalamus in Sleep, Pineal Melatonin Production, and Circadian Rhythm Sleep Disorders," *Journal of Pineal Research* 46, no. 1 (2009).

53. Bear, Connors, and Paradiso, *Neuroscience: Exploring the Brain*.

54. Amee D. Baird, Sarah J. Wilson, Peter F. Bladin, Michael M. Saling, and David C. Reutens, "Neurological Control of Human Sexual Behaviour: Insights from Lesion Studies," *Journal of Neurology, Neurosurgery, and Psychiatry* 78, no. 10 (2007).

55. Bear, Connors, and Paradiso, *Neuroscience: Exploring the Brain*.

56. Henk J. Groenewegen, "The Basal Ganglia and Motor Control," *Neural Plasticity* 10, no. 1–2 (2003): 115.

57. Tomáš Sieger, Tereza Serranová, Filip Růžička, Pavel Vostatek, Jiří Wild, Daniela Šťastná, Cecilia Bonnet, et al., "Distinct Populations of Neurons Respond to Emotional Valence and Arousal in the Human Subthalamic Nucleus," *Proceedings of the National Academy of Sciences* 112, no. 10 (2015).

58. Saori C. Tanaka, Kenji Doya, Go Okada, Kazutaka Ueda, Yasumasa Okamoto, and Shigeto Yamawaki, "Prediction of Immediate and Future Rewards Differentially Recruits Cortico-Basal Ganglia Loops," *Nature Neuroscience* 7, no. 8 (2004).

59. Groenewegen, "Basal Ganglia and Motor Control," 117.

60. V. Rajmohan and E. Mohandas, "The Limbic System," *Indian Journal of Psychiatry* 49, no. 2 (2007).

61. Ibid.

62. Y. Soudry, C. Lomogne, D. Malinyaud, S.-M. Consoli, and P. Bonfils,

"Olfactory System and Emotion: Common Substrates," *European Annals of Otorhinolaryngology, Head and Neck Diseases* 128, no. 1 (2011).

63. Bear, Connors, and Paradiso, *Neuroscience: Exploring the Brain*.

64. Kandel and Hudspeth, "The Brain and Behavior."

65. Hayden Basinger and Jeffery P. Hogg, "Neuroanatomy, Brainstem," PubMed (2019).

66. Kandel and Hudspeth, "The Brain and Behavior."

67. Eelco F.M Wijdicks, *Recognizing Brain Injury* (New York: Oxford University Press, 2014), 61.

68. Jerome Siegel, "The Neurobiology of Sleep," *Seminars in Neurology* 29, no. 4 (2009).

69. Basinger and Hogg, "Neuroanatomy, Brainstem."

70. Ibid.

71. Kandel and Hudspeth, "The Brain and Behavior."

72. Wijdicks, *Recognizing Brain Injury*.

73. Bear, Connors, and Paradiso, *Neuroscience: Exploring the Brain*.

74. Kandel and Hudspeth, "The Brain and Behavior."

75. Ibid.

76. Bear, Connors, and Paradiso, *Neuroscience: Exploring the Brain*.

77. Ibid.

78. Ibid.

79. Ibid.

80. Tyler LeBouef, Zachary Yaker, and Lacey Whited, "Physiology, Autonomic Nervous System," *StatPearls [Internet]*, StatPearls Publishing, 2023.

81. Christina Caron, "This Nerve Influences Nearly Every Internal Organ. Can It Improve Our Mental State, Too?" *The New York Times*, June 2, 2022.

82. Hanson and Mendius, *Buddha's Brain*, 60.

83. Bear, Connors, and Paradiso, *Neuroscience: Exploring the Brain*.

84. Michael Schemann, "Control of Gastrointestinal Motility by the 'Gut Brain'—the Enteric Nervous System," *Journal of Pediatric Gastroenterology and Nutrition* 41, Supplement 1 (2005).

85. Marilia Carabotti, Annunziata Sciracco, Maria Antonietta Maselli, and Carola Severi, "The Gut-Brain Axis: Interactions between Enteric Microbiota, Central and Enteric Nervous Systems," *Annals of Gastroenterology* 28, no. 2 (2015): 203.

86. Bear, Connors, and Paradiso, *Neuroscience: Exploring the Brain*.

87. Hockenbury, Nolan and Hockenbury, *Psychology*.

88. Bear, Connors, and Paradiso, *Neuroscience: Exploring the Brain*.

89. Shaozheng Qin, Erno J. Hermans, Hein J.F. van Marle, Jing Luo, and Fernandez Guillen, "Acute Psychological Stress Reduces Working Memory-Related Activity in the Dorsolateral Prefrontal Cortex," *Biological Psychiatry* 66, no. 1 (2009).

90. Agnese Mariotti, "The Effects of Chronic Stress on Health: New Insights into the Molecular Mechanisms of Brain–Body Communication," *Future Science OA* 1, no. 3 (2015); Peter C. Konturek, T. Brzozowski, and S.J. Konturek, "Stress and the Gut: Pathophysiology, Clinical Consequences, Diagnostic Approach and Treatment Options," *Journal of Physiology and Pharmacology* 62, no. 6 (2011).

91. Qinghua Chang, Liu Renguang, and Zhongyuan Shen, "Effects of Slow Breathing Rate on Blood Pressure and Heart Rate Variabilities," *International Journal of Cardiology* 169, no. 1 (2013): 6–8.

92. Go K. Pal, S. Velkumary, and A. Madanmohan, "Effect of Short-Term Practice of Breathing Exercises on Autonomic Functions in Normal Human Volunteers," *Indian Journal of Medical Research* 120, no. 2 (2004).

93. Serge Brand, Edith Holsboer-Trachsler, Jose Raul Naranjo, and Stefan Schmidt, "Influence of Mindfulness Practice on Cortisol and Sleep in Long-Term and Short-Term Meditators," *Neuropsychobiology* 65, no. 3 (2012).

94. Britta K. Hölzel, James Carmody, Mark Vangel, Christina Congleton, Sita M. Yerramsetti, Tim Gard, and Sara W. Lazar, "Mindfulness Practice Leads to Increases in Regional Brain Gray Matter Density," *Psychiatry Research: Neuroimaging* 191, no. 1 (2011).

95. Margaret E. Kemeny, "The Psychobiology of Stress," *Current Directions in Psychological Science* 12, no. 4 (2003).

96. Sami Elzeiny and Marwa Qarage, "Stress Classification Using Photoplethysmogram-Based Spatial and Frequency Domain Images," *Sensors* 20, no. 18 (2020).

97. Mark W. Chapleau and Rasna Sabharwal, "Methods of Assessing Vagus Nerve Activity and Reflexes," *Heart Failure Reviews* 16, no. 2 (2011).

98. Adam D. Farmer, Holly A. Randall, and Qasim Aziz, "It's a Gut Feeling: How the Gut Microbiota Affects the State of Mind," *The Journal of Physiology* 592, no. 14 (2014).

99. G.B. Rogers, D.J. Keating, R.L. Young, M.-L. Wong, J. Licino, and S. Wesselingh, "From Gut Dysbiosis to Altered Brain Function and Mental Illness: Mechanisms and Pathways," *Molecular Psychiatry* 21, no. 6 (2016): 738–48.

100. Ido Lurie, Yu-Xiao Yang, Kevin Haynes, Ronac Mamtani, and Ben Boursi, "Antibiotic Exposure and the Risk for Depression, Anxiety, or Psychosis: A Nested Case-Control Study," *The Journal of Clinical Psychiatry* 76, no. 11 (2015).

101. Hockenbury, Nolan and Hockenbury, *Psychology*.

102. Suzi Tortora, "2010 Marian Chace Lecture," *American Journal of Dance Therapy* 33, no. 1 (2011): 10.

103. Bear, Connors, and Paradiso, *Neuroscience: Exploring the Brain*.

104. Hockenbury, Nolan and Hockenbury, *Psychology*.

105. Bear, Connors, and Paradiso, *Neuroscience: Exploring the Brain*.

106. Hockenbury, Nolan and Hockenbury, *Psychology*.

107. Ibid.

108. Mary J. Allen, Sarah Sabir, and Sandeep Sharma, "GABA Receptor," accessed July 26, 2020, https://www.ncbi.nlm.nih.gov/books/NBK526124/#:~:text=Gamma%2Daminobutyric%20acid%20(GABA).

109. Brady, Siegel, Albers, and Price, *Basic Neurochemistry*.

110. Ibid.

111. Roy A. Wise, "Dopamine, Learning and Motivation," *Nature Reviews Neuroscience* 5, no. 6 (2004): 483–94.

112. Bear, Connors, and Paradiso, *Neuroscience: Exploring the Brain*.

113. Ibid.

114. Bear, Connors, and Paradiso, *Neuroscience: Exploring the Brain*.

115. Felix Sommer and Fredrik Bäckhed, "The Gut Microbiota—Masters of Host Development and Physiology," *Nature Reviews Microbiology* 11, no. 4 (2013).

116. Qinhong Huang, Liao Canming, Fan Ge, Jian Ao, and Ting Liu, "Acetylcholine Bidirectionally Regulates Learning and Memory," *Journal of Neurorestoratology* 10, no. 2 (2022).

117. Juhee Haam and Jerrel L. Yakel, "Cholinergic Modulation of the Hippocampal Region and Memory Function," *Journal of Neurochemistry* 142, Suppl 2 (2017).

118. Hockenbury, Nolan and Hockenbury, *Psychology*.

119. Bear, Connors, and Paradiso, *Neuroscience: Exploring the Brain*.

120. LeBouef, Whited, Yaker, "Physiology, Autonomic Nervous System."

121. Hockenbury, Nolan and Hockenbury, *Psychology*.

122. Bear, Connors, and Paradiso, *Neuroscience: Exploring the Brain*.

123. Kemeny, "The Psychobiology of Stress."

124. Hockenbury, Nolan and Hockenbury, *Psychology*.

125. Shazia R. Chaudhry and William Gossman, "Biochemistry, Endorphin," accessed April 5, 2022, https://www.ncbi.nlm.nih.gov/books/NBK470306/.

126. Sandra Manninen, Lauri Tuominen, Robin I. Dunbar, Tomi Karjalainen, Jussi Hirvonen, Eveliina Arponen, Riitta Hari, Iiro P. Jääskeläinen, Mikko Sams, and Lauri Nummenmaa, "Social Laughter Triggers Endogenous Opioid Release in Humans," *The Journal of Neuroscience* 37, no. 25 (2017).

127. Kandel and Hudspeth, "The Brain and Behavior."

Chapter 4

1. Meredith Monk, "'The voice is my river': Meredith Monk Reflects on 6 Decades of Music-Making," by Tom Huizenga, *NPR: The Composer Interview*, August 1, 2024, https://www.npr.org/2024/08/01/nx-s1-5020631/meredith-monk-interview-career-retrospective.

2. Noam Chomsky, "On Certain Formal Properties of Grammars," *Information and Control* 2, no. 2 (1959).

3. D. Marr, *Vision: A Computational Investigation into the Human Representation and Processing of Visual Information* (San Francisco: W.H. Freeman, 1982).

4. F.J. Varela, E. Thompson, and E.

Rosch, *The Embodied Mind, Revised Edition: Cognitive Science and Human Experience* (Cambridge: MIT Press, 2017).

5. J.J. Gibson, *The Ecological Approach to Visual Perception* (Boston: Houghton Mifflin, 1979).

6. Andy Clark, *Being There: Putting Brain, Body and World Together* (Cambridge: MIT Press, 1997).

7. Lawrence Shapiro and Shannon Spaulding, "Embodied Cognition," in *The Stanford Encyclopedia of Philosophy*, ed. Edward N. Zalta and Uri Nodelman. https://plato.stanford.edu/archives/sum2024/entries/embodied-cognition.

8. G. Lakoff and M. Johnson, *Metaphors We Live By* (Chicago: University of Chicago Press, 1980); G. Lakoff and Johnson, M. *Philosophy in the Flesh: The Embodied Mind and Its Challenge to Western Thought* (New York: Basic Books, 1999).

9. J.J. Gibson, *The Ecological Approach to Visual Perception*.

10. R.A. Brooks, "Intelligence without Representation," *Artificial Intelligence* 47, no. 1–3 (1991).

11. A. Clark and D.J. Chalmers, "The Extended Mind," *Analysis* 58, no. 1 (1998).

12. Linda B. Smith and Esther Thelen, eds., *A Dynamic Systems Approach to Development*, CogNet, 1993; Esther Thelen and Linda. B. Smith, eds., *A Dynamic Systems Approach to Development: Applications* (Cambridge: MIT Press, 1993); T. Van Gelder, "The Dynamical Hypothesis in Cognitive Science," *Behavioral and Brain Sciences* 21, no. 5 (1998).

13. M.M. Wanderley, B.W. Vines, N. Middleton, C. McKay, and W. Hatch, "The Musical Significance of Clarinetists' Ancillary Gestures: An Exploration of the Field," *Journal of New Music Research* 34, no. 1 (2005).

14. A.F. Winters, "Emotion, Embodiment, and Mirror Neurons in Dance/Movement Therapy: A Connection across Disciplines," *American Journal of Dance Therapy* 30, no. 2 (2008).

15. E. Hutchins, *Cognition in the Wild* (Cambridge: MIT Press, 1995).

16. T. Martin and D.L. Schwartz, "Physically Distributed Learning: Adapting and Reinterpreting Physical Environments in the Development of Fraction Concepts," *Cognitive Science* 29, no. 4 (2005).

17. Clark and Chalmers, "The Extended Mind."

18. Hutchins, *Cognition in the Wild*.

19. Clark and Chalmers, "The Extended Mind."

20. A.J. Sellen and R.H.R. Harper, *The Myth of the Paperless Office* (Cambridge: MIT Press, 2003).

21. D. Kirsh, "The Intelligent Use of Space," *Artificial Intelligence* 73, no. 1–2 (1995).

22. E. Hornecker and J. Buur, "Getting a Grip on Tangible Interaction: A Framework on Physical Space and Social Interaction," *Proceedings of the SIGCHI Conference on Human Factors in Computing Systems* (April 2006).

23. Linda B. Smith, Chen Yu, and Alfredo Pereira, "From the Outside-In: Embodied Attention in Toddlers," in *European Conference on Artificial Life*, pp. 445–54 (Berlin, Heidelberg: Springer Berlin Heidelberg, 2007).

24. Varela, Thompson, and Rosch, *The Embodied Mind*.

25. J.K. O'Regan and A. Noë, "A Sensorimotor Account of Vision and Visual Consciousness," *Behavioral and Brain Sciences* 24, no. 5 (2001).

26. A. Chemero, "Radical Embodied Cognitive Science," *Review of General Psychology* 17, no. 2 (2013).

27. H. De Jaegher and E. Di Paolo, "Participatory Sense-Making: An Enactive Approach to Social Cognition," *Phenomenology and the Cognitive Sciences* 6 (2007).

28. Ibid.

29. M. Auvray, C. Lenay, and J. Stewart, "Perceptual Interactions in a Minimalist Virtual Environment," *New Ideas in Psychology* 27, no. 1 (2009).

30. E. Thompson and M. Stapleton, "Making Sense of Sense-Making: Reflections on Enactive and Extended Mind Theories," *Topoi* 28 (2009).

31. Keith Davids, Paul Glazier, Duarte Araujo, and Roger Bartlett, "Movement Systems as Dynamical Systems: The Functional Role of Variability and Its Implications for Sports Medicine," *Sports Medicine* 33 (2003).

32. Akito Miura, Shinya Fujii, Yuji Yamamoto, and Kazutoshi Kudo, "Motor Control of Rhythmic Dance from a Dynamical Systems Perspective: A

Review," *Journal of Dance Medicine & Science* 19, no. 1 (2015).
33. Davids, Glazier, Araujo, Bartlett, "Movement Systems as Dynamical Systems."
34. Glenna Batson, "Teaching Alignment."
35. Karl M. Newell and David E. Vaillancourt, "Dimensional Change in Motor Learning," *Human Movement Science* 20, no. 4–5 (2001): 695–715.
36. Davids, Glazier, Araujo, and Bartlett, "Movement Systems of Rhythmic Dance."
37. Ibid.
38. Smith and Thelen, eds., *A Dynamic Systems Approach to Development*.
39. Zheng Yan and Kurt Fischer, "Always Under Construction: Dynamic Variations in Adult Cognitive Microdevelopment," *Human Development* 45, no. 3 (2002).
40. Smith and Thelen, eds., *A Dynamic Systems Approach to Development*.
41. Ibid.
42. Ibid.
43. Miura, Fujii, Yamamoto, and Kudo, "Motor Control of Rhythmic Dance."
44. N. Bernstein, *The Co-ordination and Regulation of Movements* (New York: Pergamon, 1967).
45. Pil Hansen, Karen Kaeja, and Ame Henderson, "Transference and Transition in Systems of Dance Generation," *Performance Research* 19, no. 5 (2014).
46. Ibid.
47. Shea and Morgan, "Contextual Interference Effects."
48. Elizabeth Limons and John B. Shea, "Deficient Processing in Learning and Performance," in *Advances in Psychology*, Vol. 55, ed. Ann M. Colley and John R. Beech (Amsterdam: North-Holland, 1988).
49. Dylan Van Der Schyff, Andrea Schiavio, Ashley Walton, Valerio Velardo, and Anthony Chemero, "Musical Creativity and the Embodied Mind: Exploring the Possibilities of 4E Cognition and Dynamical Systems Theory," *Music & Science* 1 (2018).
50. Ibid.
51. Denise Purvis, "Creating Thinking: Immersive Dance Theater as 4E Cognition in the Wild," *Journal of Dance Education* 21, no. 3 (2021).
52. Gabriele Wulf and Rebecca Lewthwaite, "Optimizing Performance through Intrinsic Motivation and Attention for Learning: The OPTIMAL Theory of Motor Learning," *Psychonomic Bulletin and Review* 23, no. 5 (2016).
53. Ibid.
54. Schmidt, Lee, Winstein, Wulf, and Zelaznik, *Motor Control and Learning*.
55. Wulf and Lewthwaite. "The OPTIMAL Theory of Motor Learning."
56. Ibid.
57. Ibid.
58. P. Knapp, "Rethinking Traditional Modes of Teaching and Learning Classical Dance Using Optimal Theory with the Students of the 2nd Cycle Dance Course at PALLC°—Performing Arts School & Conservatory," Master thesis, Escola Superior de Dança, Instituto Politécnico de Lisboa, 2022.
59. Ibid.
60. Rick D. Parsons and Kimberlee S. Brown, *Teacher as Reflective Practitioner and Action Researcher* (Belmont, CA: Wadsworth/Thomson Learning, 2002).
61. Knapp, "Rethinking Traditional Modes of Teaching and Learning Classical Dance."
62. Wulf and Lewthwaite, "The OPTIMAL Theory of Motor Learning."

Chapter 5

1. Twyla Tharp and Mark Reiter, *The Creative Habit: Learn It and Use It for Life* (New York: Simon & Schuster, 2003).
2. Martha Graham, "Martha Graham Speaks," *Dance Observer*, April 1963: 53, cited in Susan Foster, *Reading Dancing* (Los Angeles: University of California Press, 1986).
3. Maria N. Ayala and Denise Y.P. Henriques, "Differential Contributions of Implicit and Explicit Learning Mechanisms to Various Contextual Cues in Dual Adaptation," *Plos One* 16, no. 7 (2021).
4. Karen Schupp, "The Transgressive Possibilities of Foregrounding Somatic Values," *Research in Dance Education* 18, no. 2 (2017).
5. Brodie and Lobel, *Dance and Somatics*.
6. Rosen, *The Yoga of Breath*.
7. Irmgard Bartenieff and Dori Lewis, *Body Movement: Coping with the*

Environment (New York: Routledge, 1980).

8. N. Romita and A. Romita, *Functional Awareness: Anatomy in Action for Dancers* (Oxford: Oxford University Press, 2023).

9. Rolf Gates and Katrina Kenison, *Meditations from the Mat: Daily Reflections on the Path of Yoga* (New York: Anchor, 2002).

10. Mabel Todd, *The Thinking Body* (Perth: The Gestalt Journal Press, 2008).

11. N. Postman and C. Weingartner, *Meaning Making: Teaching as a Subversive Activity* (El Dorado, AR: Delta, 1969).

12. Glenna Batson and Margaret Wilson, *Body and Mind in Motion: Dance and Neuroscience in Conversation* (Chicago: University of Chicago Press, 2014).

13. Ibid.

14. Schmidt, Lee, Winstein, Wulf, and Zelaznik, *Motor Control and Learning*.

15. Ibid.

16. James, *Principles of Psychology*.

17. Wickens, "The Structure of Attentional Resources."

18. Wulf and Lewthwaite, "The OPTIMAL Theory of Motor Learning."

19. Lynn Anne Blom and L. Tarin Chaplin, *The Moment of Movement* (Pittsburgh: University of Pittsburgh Press, 1988).

20. Ibid.

21. Raymond W. Gibbs, Jr., *Embodiment and Cognitive Science* (New York: Cambridge University Press, 2006).

22. Batson and Wilson, *Body and Mind in Motion*.

23. Shea and Morgan, "Contextual Interference Effects."

24. Glenna Batson, "Teaching Alignment: From a Mechanical Model to a Dynamic Systems One," in *The Body Eclectic: Evolving Practices in Dance Training*, ed. Melanie Bales and Rebecca Nettl-Fiol (Champaign: University of Illinois Press, 2008).

25. Gibbs, *Embodiment and Cognitive Science*.

26. Ibid.

27. Integrated Movement Studies, "November Newsletter," email, 2023.

28. Hanson and Mendius, *Buddha's Brain*.

29. John Martin, *America Dancing: The Background and Personalities of the Modern Dance* (New York: Dance Horizons, 1936).

30. Emily S. Cross, Antonia F. de C. Hamilton, and Scott T. Grafton, "Building a Motor Simulation de Novo: Observation of Dance by Dancers," *NeuroImage* 31, no. 3 (2006).

31. Lidewij Niezink and Katherine Train, "When Kinesthetic Empathy Goes Viral: How the Jerusalema Dance Helped the World," *Psychology Today*, November 3, 2020.

32. Batson, "Teaching Alignment."

33. K. Anders Ericsson, Ralf T. Krampe, and Clemens Tesch-Römer, "The Role of Deliberate Practice in the Acquisition of Expert Performance," *Psychological Review* 100, no. 3 (1993).

34. Bilodeau, Bilodeau, and Schumsky, "Some Effects of Introducing and Withdrawing Knowledge of Results."

Chapter 6

1. Langston Hughes, "The Negro Artist and the Racial Mountain," *The Nation*, June 23, 1926.

2. Gibbs, *Embodiment and Cognitive Science*.

3. A.L. Blom and L. Chaplin, *The Intimate Act of Choreography* (Pittsburgh: University of Pittsburgh Press, 1982).

4. Hanson and Mendius, *Buddha's Brain*.

5. Martha Graham, *Blood Memory: An Autobiography* (New York: Doubleday, 1991).

Chapter 7

1. Kate Bush, "Running Up That Hill (A Deal with God)," EMI Records, 1985.

2. Hanson and Mendius, *Buddha's Brain*.

3. Hanson and Mendius, *Buddha's Brain*, 151.

4. Hanson and Mendius, *Buddha's Brain*.

5. Nyama McCarthy-Brown, *Dance Pedagogy for a Diverse World: Culturally Relevant Teaching in Theory, Research and Practice* (Jefferson: McFarland, 2017).

6. Ibid.

7. Paulette Beete, "Jawole Willa Jo Zollar," *American Artscape Magazine*, 2011, https://www.arts.gov/stories/

magazine/2011/4/what-innovation/jawole-willa-jo-zollar.

8. Eddy, "Somatic Practices and Dance."

Chapter 8

1. #TeamEBONY, "Choreographer Camille A. Brown: The Body Speaks," *Ebony*, November 14, 2016, https://www.ebony.com/camille-a-brown-harlem-school-arts/.

2. Selma Jeanne Cohen, *The Modern Dance: Seven Statements of Belief* (Middletown, CT: Wesleyan University Press, 1966).

3. "Mission and History," Dance Film Association, accessed February 28, 2024, https://www.dancefilms.org/about/.

4. *Threshold*, Malia Bruker and Ilana Goldman, 2021.

5. Bessel Van der Kolk, *The Body Keeps the Score: Brain, Mind, and Body in the Healing of Trauma* (New York: Penguin, 2014).

6. Andrea Olsen, *The Place of Dance: A Somatic Guide to Dancing and Dance Making* (Middletown, CT: Wesleyan University Press, 2014).

Chapter 9

1. *Pina*, directed by Wim Wenders (IFC Films, 2011), 1:43:00.

2. Peggy Hackney, *Making Connections: Total Body Integration Through Bartenieff Fundamentals*.

3. Rosen, *The Yoga of Breath*.

4. Chip Hartranft, *The Yoga-Sutra of Patanjali*.

5. Rosen, *The Yoga of Breath*.

6. Todd, *The Thinking Body*.

7. Hanson and Mendius, *Buddha's Brain*.

8. Gibbs, *Embodiment and Cognitive Science*.

9. Cross, Hamilton, and Grafton, "Building a Motor Simulation de Novo."

10. Knapp, "Rethinking Traditional Modes of Teaching and Learning Classical Dance"; Wulf and Lewthwaite, "The OPTIMAL Theory of Motor Learning."

11. "Palliative Care," World Health Organization, August 5, 2020, https://www.who.int/news-room/fact-sheets/detail/palliative-care.

12. Jennifer Im, Susanna Mak, Ross Upshur, Leah Steinberg, and Kerry Kuluski, "'Whatever Happens, Happens.' Challenges of End-of-Life Communication from the Perspective of Older Adults and Family Caregivers: A Qualitative Study," *BMC Palliative Care* 18 (2019): 1–9.

13. Ibid.

Bibliography

Adams, J.A. "A Closed-Loop Theory of Motor Learning." *Journal of Motor Behavior* 3, no. 2 (1971).
Adams, J.A., and B. Reynolds. "Effect of Shift in Distribution of Practice Conditions Following Interpolated Rest." *Journal of Experimental Psychology* 47, no. 1 (1954): 32–36.
Adolphs, R., Daniel Tranel, H. Damasio, and A. Damasio. "Impaired Recognition of Emotion in Facial Expressions Following Bilateral Damage to the Human Amygdala." *Nature* 372, no. 6507 (1994): 669–72.
Allen, Mary J., Sarah Sabir, and Sandeep Sharma. "GABA Receptor." Accessed July 26, 2020. https://www.ncbi.nlm.nih.gov/books/NBK526124/#:~:text=Gamma%2Daminobutyric%20acid%20(GABA).
Auvray, M., C. Lenay, and J. Stewart. "Perceptual Interactions in a Minimalist Virtual Environment." *New Ideas in Psychology* 27, no. 1 (2009): 32–47.
Ayala, Maria N., and Denise Y.P. Henriques. "Differential Contributions of Implicit and Explicit Learning Mechanisms to Various Contextual Cues in Dual Adaptation." *PLOS One* 16, no. 7 (2021): e0253948.
Baird, Amee D., Sarah J. Wilson, Peter F. Bladin, Michael M. Saling, and David C. Reutens. "Neurological Control of Human Sexual Behaviour: Insights from Lesion Studies." *Journal of Neurology, Neurosurgery, and Psychiatry* 78, no. 10 (2007): 1042–049.
Bartenieff, Irmgard, and Dori Lewis. *Body Movement: Coping with the Environment*. New York: Routledge, 1980.
Basinger, Hayden, and Jeffery P. Hogg. "Neuroanatomy, Brainstem." PubMed (2019).
Batson, Glenna. "Teaching Alignment: From a Mechanical Model to a Dynamic Systems One." In *The Body Eclectic: Evolving Practices in Dance Training*, edited by Melanie Bales and Rebecca Nettl-Fiol, 134–52. Champaign: University of Illinois Press, 2008.
Batson, Glenna, and Margaret Wilson. *Body and Mind in Motion: Dance and Neuroscience in Conversation*. Chicago: University of Chicago Press, 2014.
Bear, Mark F., Barry W. Connors, and Michael A. Paradiso. *Neuroscience: Exploring the Brain*. Burlington, MA: Jones and Bartlett Learning, 2016.
Beete, Paulette. "Jawole Willa Jo Zollar." *American Artscape Magazine*, 2011. https://www.arts.gov/stories/magazine/2011/4/what-innovation/jawole-willa-jo-zollar.
Bernstein, N. *The Co-Ordination and Regulation of Movements*. New York: Pergamon, 1967.
Bilodeau, Edward A., Ina McD Bilodeau, and Donald A. Schumsky. "Some Effects of Introducing and Withdrawing Knowledge of Results Early and Late in Practice." *Journal of Experimental Psychology* 58, no. 2 (1959).
Blackburn, Jack. "Tragers Psychological Integration—An Overview." *Journal of Bodywork and Movement Therapies* 7 (4): 233–39.
Blom, Lynn Anne, and L. Tarin Chaplin. *The Intimate Act of Choreography*. Pittsburgh: University of Pittsburgh Press, 1982.
Blom, Lynn Anne, and L. Tarin Chaplin. *The Moment of Movement*. Pittsburgh: University of Pittsburgh Press, 1988.

Bibliography

Brady, Scott T., George J. Siegel, R. Wayne Albers, and Donald L. Price. *Basic Neurochemistry: Molecular, Cellular and Medical Aspects*. Amsterdam: Academic Press, 2006.

Brand, Serge, Edith Holsboer-Trachsler, Jose Raul Naranjo, and Stefan Schmidt. "Influence of Mindfulness Practice on Cortisol and Sleep in Long-Term and Short-Term Meditators." *Neuropsychobiology* 65, no. 3 (2012): 109–18.

Brodie, Julie, and Elin Lobel. *Dance and Somatics: Mind-Body Principles of Teaching and Performance*. Jefferson: McFarland, 2012.

Brooks, R.A. "Intelligence without Representation." *Artificial Intelligence* 47, no. 1–3 (1991): 139–59.

Bruker, Malia, and Ilana Goldman. *Threshold*. 2021.

Buchanan, Patricia, and Beverly Ulrich. "The Feldenkrais Method®: A Dynamic Approach to Changing Motor Behavior." *Research Quarterly for Exercise and Sport* 72, no. 4 (2001): 315–23.

Bush, Kate. "Running Up that Hill (A Deal with God)." EMI Records, 1985.

Cahill, Larry, and James L. McGaugh. "Modulation of Memory Storage." *Current Opinion in Neurobiology* 6, no. 2 (1996): 237–42.

Carabotti, Marilia, Annunziata Scirocco, Maria Antonietta Maselli, and Carola Severi. "The Gut-Brain Axis: Interactions between Enteric Microbiota, Central and Enteric Nervous Systems." *Annals of Gastroenterology* 28, no. 2 (2015): 203–09.

Caron, Christina. "This Nerve Influences Nearly Every Internal Organ. Can It Improve Our Mental State, Too?" *The New York Times*, June 2, 2022.

Chang, Qinghua, Liu Renguang, and Zhongyuan Shen. "Effects of Slow Breathing Rate on Blood Pressure and Heart Rate Variabilities." *International Journal of Cardiology* 169, no. 1 (2013): 6–8.

Chapleau, Mark W., and Rasna Sabharwal. "Methods of Assessing Vagus Nerve Activity and Reflexes." *Heart Failure Reviews* 16, no. 2 (2011): 109–27.

Chaudhry, Shazia R., and William Gossman. "Biochemistry, Endorphin." Accessed April 5, 2022. https://www.ncbi.nlm.nih.gov/books/NBK470306/.

Chemero, A. "Radical Embodied Cognitive Science." *Review of General Psychology* 17, no. 2 (2013): 145–50.

Chen, Briana K., Nathen J. Murawski, Christine Cincotta, Olivia McKissick, Abby Finkelstein, Anahita B. Hamidi, Emily Merfeld, Emily Doucette, Stephanie Grella, Monika Shpokayte, Yosif Zaki, Amanda Fortin, and Steve Ramirez Chen. "Artificially Enhancing and Suppressing Hippocampus-Mediated Memories." *Current Biology* 29, no. 11 (June 3, 2019): 1885–894.

Child, Nicholas D., and Eduardo E. Benarroch. "Anterior Nucleus of the Thalamus: Functional Organization and Clinical Implications." *Neurology* 81, no. 21 (1993): 1869–876.

Chomsky, Noam. "On Certain Formal Properties of Grammars," *Information and Control* 2, no. 2 (1959).

Cicchella, A., T. Popotti, and J.B. Shea. "Effect of Different Spotting Heights on Ballet Pirouette Performance." *Acta Kinesiologiae Universitatis Tartuensis* 21 (2015): 19–30.

Clark, A., and D.J. Chalmers. "The Extended Mind." *Analysis* 58, no. 1 (1999): 7–19.

Clark, Andy. *Being There: Putting Brain, Body and World Together*. Cambridge: MIT Press, 1997.

Cohen, Bonnie Bainbridge. *Basic Neurocellular Patterns: Exploring Developmental Movement*. El Sobrante, CA: Burchfield Rose, 2018.

Cohen, Selma Jeanne. *The Modern Dance: Seven Statements of Belief*. Middletown, CT: Wesleyan University Press, 1966.

Collins, Francis. "What a Memory Looks Like." NIH Director's Blog. Last modified November 21, 2019. https://directorsblog.nih.gov/2019/11/21/what-a-memory-looks-like/.

Collins, Robert O., and John L. Adams. *Prefrontal Cortex: Developmental Differences, Executive and Cognitive Functions and Role in Neurological Disorders*. New York: Nova Biomedical, 2013.

Conrad, Emilie. "Continuum Movement." In *New Dimensions in Body Psychotherapy*, edited by Nick Totton, 142–152. Maidenhead, Berkshire, UK: Open University Press, 2005.

Costandi, Moheb. *Neuroplasticity*. Cambridge: MIT Press, 2016.

Craik, F.I.M., and R.S. Lockhart. "Levels of Processing: A Framework for Memory Research." *Journal of Verbal Learning and Verbal Behavior* 11, no. 6 (1972): 671.
Cross, Emily S., Antonia F. de C. Hamilton, and Scott T. Grafton. "Building a Motor Simulation de Novo: Observation of Dance by Dancers." *NeuroImage* 31, no. 3 (2006): 1257–1267.
Crosson, Bruce, Anna Bacon Moore, Kaundinya Gopinath, Keith D. White, Wieranga E. Christina, Megan E. Gaiefsky, and Katherine S. Fabrizio. "Role of the Right and Left Hemispheres in Recovery of Function During Treatment of Intention in Aphasia." *Journal of Cognitive Neuroscience* 17, no. 3 (2005): 392–406.
Dance Film Association. "Mission and History." Accessed February 28, 2024. https://www.dancefilms.org/about/
Davids, Keith, Paul Glazier, Duarte Araujo, and Roger Bartlett. "Movement Systems as Dynamical Systems: The Functional Role of Variability and Its Implications for Sports Medicine." *Sports Medicine* 33 (2003): 245–60.
De Giorgi, Margherita. "Shaping the Living Body: Paradigms of Soma and Authority in Thomas Hanna's Writings." *Revista Brasileira de Estudos da Presença* 5 (2015): 54–84.
De Jaegher, H., and E. Di Paolo. "Participatory Sense-Making: An Enactive Approach to Social Cognition." *Phenomenology and the Cognitive Sciences* 6 (2007): 485–507.
Del Rey, P., Wughalter, E., and M. Whitehurst. "The Effects of Contextual Interference on Females with Varied Experience in Open Sport Skills." *Research Quarterly for Exercise and Sport* 53, no. 2 (1982): 108–15.
Driver, J. "A Selective Review of Selective Attention Research from the Past Century." *British Journal of Psychology* 92 (2001): 53–78.
Eddy, Martha. "A Brief History of Somatic Practices and Dance Historical Development of the Field of Somatic Education and its Relationship to Dance." *Journal of Dance and Somatic Practices* 1, no. 1 (2009): 5–27.
Eddy, Martha. *Mindful Movement: The Evolution of the Somatic Arts and Conscious Action.* Chicago: University of Chicago Press, 2016.
Eddy, Martha. "Somatic Practices and Dance: Global Influences." *Dance Research Journal* 34, no. 2 (Winter 2002): 46–62.
Elzeiny, Sami, and Marwa Qarage. "Stress Classification Using Photoplethysmogram-Based Spatial and Frequency Domain Images." *Sensors* 20, no. 18 (2020): 5312.
Emslie, M. "Skinner Releasing Technique: Dancing from Within." *Journal of Dance and Somatic Practices* 1, no. 2 (2009): 169–75.
Ericsson, K. Anders, Ralf T. Krampe, and Clemens Tesch-Römer. "The Role of Deliberate Practice in the Acquisition of Expert Performance." *Psychological Review* 100, no. 3 (1993): 363.
Farmer, Adam D., Holly A. Randall, and Qasim Aziz. "It's a Gut Feeling: How the Gut Microbiota Affects the State of Mind." *The Journal of Physiology* 592, no. 14 (2014): 2981–988.
Feldenkrais, Moshe, and Elizabeth Beringer. *Higher Judo: Groundwork.* San Diego: Somatic Resources, 2010.
Feldman, A.G. "Functional Tuning of the Nervous System with Control of Movement or Maintenance of a Steady Posture—II. Controllable Parameters of the Muscles." *Biophysica* (1966): 565–78.
Feldman, A.G. "Functional Tuning of the Nervous System with Control of Movement or Maintenance of a Steady Posture—III. Mechanographic Analysis of the Execution by Man of the Simplest Motor Tasks." *Biophysics* 11 (1966): 667–75.
Fitts, P.M. "The Information Capacity of the Human Motor System in Controlling the Amplitude of Movement." *Journal of Experimental Psychology* 47, no. 6 (1954): 381–91.
Foster, Kimberley A., et al. "The Trager Approach in the Treatment of Chronic Headache: A Pilot Study." *Alternative Therapies in Health and Medicine* 10, no. 5 (2004): 40–46.
Foster, Susan Leigh. *Reading Dancing: Bodies and Subjects in Contemporary American Dance.* Berkeley: University of California Press, 1986.
Gage, Fred H. "Neorogenesis in the Adult Brain." *The Journal of Neuroscience* 22, no. 3 (2002): 612–13.

Gallo, David A., and Mark E. Wheeler. "Episodic Memory." In *The Oxford Handbook of Cognitive Psychology*. New York: Oxford University Press, 2013.

Gates, Rolf, and Katrina Kenison. *Meditations from the Mat: Daily Reflections on the Path of Yoga*. New York: Anchor, 2002.

Gibbs, Raymond W., Jr. *Embodiment and Cognitive Science*. New York: Cambridge University Press, 2006.

Gibson, J.J. *The Ecological Approach to Visual Perception*. Boston: Houghton Mifflin, 1979.

Ginot, Isabelle, Allegra Barlow, and Mark Franko. "From Shusterman's Somaesthetics to a Radical Epistemology of Somatics." *Dance Research Journal* 42, no. 1 (2010): 12–29.

Gintis, Bonnie. "Experiencing Osteopathy Through Continuum Movement." Cranial Academy Annual Conference, 2001. http://osteopathichistory.com/pdfs/Experiencing.pdf.

Graham, Martha. *Blood Memory: An Autobiography*. New York: Doubleday, 1991.

Graham, Martha. "Martha Graham Speaks." *Dance Observer*, April 1963: 53.

Greenhead, Karin, and John Habron. "The Touch of Sound: Dalcroze Eurhythmics as a Somatic Practice." *Journal of Dance & Somatic Practices* 7, no. 1 (2015): 93–112.

Groenewegen, Henk J. "The Basal Ganglia and Motor Control." *Neural Plasticity* 10, no. 1–2 (2003): 107–20.

Haam, Juhee, and Jerrel L. Yakel. "Cholinergic Modulation of the Hippocampal Region and Memory Function." *Journal of Neurochemistry* 142, Suppl 2 (2017): 111–21.

Hackney, Peggy. *Making Connections: Total Body Integration Through Bartenieff Fundamentals*. New York: Taylor & Francis Group, 1998.

Hamilton, J. Paul, Amit Etkin, Daniella J. Furman, Maria G. Lemus, Rebecca F. Johnson, and Ian H. Gotlib. "Functional Neuroimaging of Major Depressive Disorder: A Meta-Analysis and New Integration of Baseline Activation and Neural Response Data." *American Journal of Psychiatry* 169, no. 7 (2012): 693–703.

Hanna, Thomas. "Clinical Somatic Education." *Somatics* Autumn-Winter (1990): 4–10.

Hansen, Pil, Karen Kaeja, and Ame Henderson. "Transference and Transition in Systems of Dance Generation." *Performance Research* 19, no. 5 (2014): 23–33.

Hanson, Rick, and Richard Mendius. *Buddha's Brain: The Practical Neuroscience of Happiness, Love, and Wisdom*. Oakland: New Harbinger, 2009.

Harper, Susan. "Emily Conrad's Continuum." Accessed January 10, 2024. www.continuumteachers.com/about/emilie-conrad-continuum.

Hartranft, Chip. *The Yoga-Sutra of Patanjali: A New Translation with Commentary*. Boulder: Shambhala, 2003.

Hatfield, B.C., W.R. Wyatt, and J.B. Shea. "Effects of Auditory Feedback on Movement Time in Fitts Task." *Journal of Motor Behavior* 42, no. 5 (2010): 289–93.

Hayat, Hanna, Amit Marmelshtein, Aarom K. Krom, Yaniv Sela, Ariel Tankus, Ido Strauss, Firas Fahoum, Itzak Fried, and Yuval Nir. "Reduced Neural Feedback Signaling Despite Robust Neuron and Gamma Auditory Responses During Human Sleep." *Nature Neuroscience* 25, no. 7 (2022): 935–43.

Hebb, D.O. *The Organization of Behavior: A Neuropsychological Theory*. Mahwah, NJ: Psychology Press, 2002.

Herculano-Houzel, Suzana. "The Remarkable, Yet Not Extraordinary, Human Brain as a Scaled-up Primate Brain and Its Associated Cost." *Proceedings of the National Academy of Sciences* 109, no. supplement_1 (2012): 10661–668.

Herman, James P. "Limbic System Mechanisms of Stress Regulation: Hypothalamo-Pituitary-Adrenocortical Axis." *Progress in Neuro-Psychopharmacology and Biological Psychiatry* 29, no. 8 (2005): 1201–213.

Hick, W.E. "On the Rate of Gain of Information." *Quarterly Journal of Experimental Psychology* 4, no. 1 (1952): 11–26.

Hockenbury, Sandra E., Susan A. Nolan, and Don H. Hockenbury. *Psychology*. New York: Worth, 2015.

Hölzel, Britta K., James Carmody, Mark Vangel, Christina Congleton, Sita M. Yerramsetti, Tim Gard, and Sara W. Lazar. "Mindfulness Practice Leads to Increases in Regional Brain Gray Matter Density." *Psychiatry Research: Neuroimaging* 191, no. 1 (2011): 36–43.

Hornecker, E., and J. Buur. "Getting a Grip on Tangible Interaction: A Framework on Physical Space and Social Interaction." *Proceedings of the SIGCHI Conference on Human Factors in Computing Systems* (April 2006): 437–46.

Huang, Qinhong, Liao Canming, Fan Ge, Jian Ao, and Ting Liu. "Acetylcholine Bidirectionally Regulates Learning and Memory." *Journal of Neurorestoratology* 10, no. 2 (2022): 100002.

Hughes, Langston. "The Negro Artist and the Racial Mountain." *The Nation*, June 23, 1926.

Hutchins, E. *Cognition in the Wild*. Cambridge: MIT Press, 1995.

IADMS, and Glenna Batson. "Somatic Studies and Dance." 2009. www.iadms.com.

Im, Jennifer, Susanna Mak, Ross Upshur, Leah Steinberg, and Kerry Kuluski. "'Whatever Happens, Happens.' Challenges of End-of-Life Communication from the Perspective of Older Adults and Family Caregivers: A Qualitative Study." *BMC Palliative Care* 18 (2019): 1–9.

Jacobs, B.L., H. van Praag, and F.H. Gage. "Adult Brain Neurogenesis and Psychiatry: A Novel Theory of Depression." *Molecular Psychiatry* 5, no. 3 (2000): 262–69.

James, William. *Principles of Psychology*. New York: Henry Holt, 1890.

Jan, James E., Russel J. Reiter, Michael B. Wasdell, and Martin Bax. " The Role of the Thalamus in Sleep, Pineal Melatonin Production, and Circadian Rhythm Sleep Disorders." *Journal of Pineal Research* 46, no. 1 (2009).

Kaminski, J. "First Nations Pedagogy." 2013. https://firstnationspedagogy.com/FN_Pedagogy.html.

Kandel, Eric R., and A.J. Hudspeth. "The Brain and Behavior." *Principles of Neural Science*. New York: McGraw-Hill Medical, 2012.

Kemeny, Margaret E. "The Psychobiology of Stress." *Current Directions in Psychological Science* 12, no. 4 (2003): 124–29.

Keng, S.L., M.J. Smoski, and C.J. Robins. "Effects of Mindfulness on Psychological Health: A Review of Empirical Studies." *Clinical Psychology Review* 31, no. 6 (2011): 1041–056.

Kirsh, D. "The Intelligent Use of Space." *Artificial Intelligence* 73, no. 1–2 (1995): 31–68.

Kline, Morris. *Mathematical Thought from Ancient to Modern Times*. Oxford: Oxford University Press, 1972.

Knapp, P. "Rethinking Traditional Modes of Teaching and Learning Classical Dance Using Optimal Theory with the Students of the 2nd Cycle Dance Course at PALLC° - Performing Arts School & Conservatory." Master thesis, Escola Superior de Dança, Instituto Politécnico de Lisboa, 2022.

Konturek, Peter C., T. Brzozowski, and S.J. Konturek. "Stress and the Gut: Pathophysiology, Clinical Consequences, Diagnostic Approach and Treatment Options." *Journal of Physiology and Pharmacology* 62, no. 6 (2011): 591–99.

Kozel, Susan, Ruth Gibson, and Bruno Martelli. "The Weird Giggle: Attending to Affect in Virtual Reality." *Transformations* 31, no. 31 (2018): 1–24.

Lakoff, G., and M. Johnson. *Metaphors We Live By*. Chicago: University of Chicago Press, 1980.

Lakoff, G., and M. Johnson. *Philosophy in the Flesh: The Embodied Mind and Its Challenge to Western Thought*. New York: Basic Books, 1999.

LeBouef, Tyler, Zachary Yaker, and Lacey Whited. "Physiology, Autonomic Nervous System." *StatPearls [Internet]*. StatPearls Publishing, 2023.

Lee, D.N., and E. Aronson. "Visual Proprioceptive Control of Standing in Human Infants." *Perception & Psychophysics* 15 (1974): 529–32.

Lee, T.D., and R.A. Magill. "Can Forgetting Facilitate Skill Acquisition." In *Advances in Psychology*, Vol. 27. Amsterdam: North-Holland, 1985.

Lee, Timothy, and Heather Carnahan. "Motor Learning: Reflections on the Past 40 Years of Research." *Kinesiology Review* 10, no. 3 (2021): 1–9.

Lenneberg, E.H. *Biological Foundations of Language*. New York: Wiley, 1967.

Lewis, Marc D., and Rebecca M. Todd. "The Self-Regulating Brain: Cortical-Subcortical Feedback and the Development of Intelligent Action." *Cognitive Development* 22, no. 4 (2007): 406–30.

Limons, Elizabeth, and John B. Shea. "Deficient Processing in Learning and Performance."

In *Advances in Psychology*, Vol. 55, edited by Ann M. Colley and John R. Beech, 333–47. Amsterdam: North-Holland, 1988.

Lukoff, David, and Richard Strozzi-Heckler. "Aikido: A Martial Art with Mindfulness, Somatic, Relational, and Spiritual Benefits for Veterans." *Spirituality in Clinical Practice* 4, no. 2 (2017): 81.

Lurie, Ido, Yu-Xiao Yang, Kevin Haynes, Ronac Mamtani, and Ben Boursi. "Antibiotic Exposure and the Risk for Depression, Anxiety, or Psychosis: A Nested Case-Control Study." *The Journal of Clinical Psychiatry* 76, no. 11 (2015): 1522–528.

Magill, R.A. "Modeling and Verbal Feedback Influences on Skill Learning." *International Journal of Sport Psychology* 24, no. 4 (1993): 358–69.

Maguire, Eleanor A., David G. Gadian, Ingrid S. Johnsrude, Catriona D. Good, John Ashburner, Richard SJ Frackowiak, and Christopher D. Frith. "Navigation-Related Structural Change in the Hippocampi of Taxi Drivers." *Proceedings of the National Academy of Sciences* 97, no. 8 (2000): 4398–403.

Manninen, Sandra, Lauri Tuominen, Robin I. Dunbar, Tomi Karjalainen, Jussi Hirvonen, Eveliina Arponen, Riitta Hari, Iiro P. Jääskeläinen, Mikko Sams, and Lauri Nummenmaa. "Social Laughter Triggers Endogenous Opioid Release in Humans." *The Journal of Neuroscience* 37, no. 25 (2017): 6125–131.

Manning, Susan. "Modern Dance in the Third Reich, Redux." In *The Oxford Handbook of Dance and Politics*. Oxford: Oxford University Press, 2017.

Mariotti, Agnese. "The Effects of Chronic Stress on Health: New Insights into the Molecular Mechanisms of Brain–Body Communication." *Future Science OA* 1, no. 3 (2015).

Marr, D. *Vision: A Computational Investigation into the Human Representation and Processing of Visual Information.* San Francisco: W.H. Freeman, 1982.

Martin, John. *America Dancing: The Background and Personalities of the Modern Dance.* New York: Dance Horizons, 1936.

Martin, T., and D.L. Schwartz. "Physically Distributed Learning: Adapting and Reinterpreting Physical Environments in the Development of Fraction Concepts." *Cognitive Science* 29, no. 4 (2005): 587–625.

McCarthy-Brown, Nyama. *Dance Pedagogy for a Diverse World: Culturally Relevant Teaching in Theory, Research and Practice.* Jefferson: McFarland, 2017.

McPartland, Terence. "Moshe Feldenkrais and Modern Judo: The Strange Forgotten Tale of a Physicist Who Learned Judo." 2012. http://dcjudo.com/feldenkrais-and-judo.

Miura, Akito, Shinya Fujii, Yuji Yamamoto, and Kazutoshi Kudo. "Motor Control of Rhythmic Dance from a Dynamical Systems Perspective: A Review." *Journal of Dance Medicine & Science* 19, no. 1 (2015): 11–21.

Monk, Meredith. "'The voice is my river': Meredith Monk reflects on 6 decades of music-making." By Tom Huizenga. *NPR: The Composer Interview*, August 1, 2024. https://www.npr.org/2024/08/01/nx-s1-5020631/meredith-monk-interview-career-retrospective.

Monteiro, Nicole, and Diana Wall. "African Dance as Healing Modality throughout the Diaspora: The Use of Ritual and Movement to Work through Trauma." *The Journal of Pan-African Studies* 4, no. 6 (September 2011): 234–52.

Moriguchi, Yusuke, and Kazuo Hiraki. "Developmental Relationship Between Executive Function and the Prefrontal Cortex in Young Children." In *Prefrontal Cortex: Developmental Differences, Executive and Cognitive Functions and Role in Neurological Disorders*, edited by Robert O. Collins and John L. Adams. New York: Nova Biomedical, 2013.

Mullan, Kelly Jean. "Somatics Herstories: Tracing Elsa Gindler's Educational Antecedents Hade Kallmeyer and Genevieve Stebbins." *Journal of Dance & Somatic Practices* 9, no. 2 (2017): 159–78.

National Institute of Neurological Disorders and Stroke. "Brain Basics: Know Your Brain." Accessed September 26, 2022. https://www.ninds.nih.gov/health-information/public-education/brain-basics/brain-basics-know-your-brain#:~:text=The%20brain%20can%20be%20divided.

Newell, Karl M., and David E. Vaillancourt. "Dimensional Change in Motor Learning." *Human Movement Science* 20, no. 4–5 (2001): 695–715.

Ng, K., and S. Latorre. "How to Tie Your Shoes." WikiHow. Accessed July 28, 2023. https://www.wikihow.com/Tie-Your-Shoes.

Niezink, Lidewij, and Katherine Train. "When Kinesthetic Empathy Goes Viral: How the Jerusalema Dance Helped the World." *Psychology Today,* November 3, 2020.

Olsen, Andrea. *The Place of Dance: A Somatic Guide to Dancing and Dance Making.* Middletown, CT: Wesleyan University Press, 2014.

O'Regan, J.K., and A. Noë. "A Sensorimotor Account of Vision and Visual Consciousness." *Behavioral and Brain Sciences* 24, no. 5 (2001): 939–73.

Ottosson, Anders. "The First Historical Movements of Kinesiology: Scientification in the Borderline Between Physical Culture and Medicine Around 1850." *The International Journal of the History of Sport* 27, no. 11 (2010): 1892–919.

Oyeshile, Olatunji. "The African World-view, Science and the Quest for Development." *International Journal of African Culture and Ideas* 4 (2004): 99–107.

Pal, Go K., S. Velkumary, and A. Madanmohan. "Effect of Short-Term Practice of Breathing Exercises on Autonomic Functions in Normal Human Volunteers." *Indian Journal of Medical Research* 120, no. 2 (2004): 115–21.

Parsons, Rick D., and Kimberlee S. Brown. *Teacher as Reflective Practitioner and Action Researcher.* Belmont, CA: Wadsworth/Thomson Learning, 2002.

Polit, A., and E. Bizzi. "Characteristics of Motor Programs Underlying Arm Movements in Monkeys." *Journal of Neurophysiology* 42 (1979): 183–94.

Polit, A., and E. Bizzi. "Processes Controlling Arm Movements in Monkeys." *Science* 201 (1978): 1235–237.

Pölönen, Pasi, Otto Lappi, and Mari Tervaniemi. "Effect of Meditative Movement on Affect and Flow in Quigong Practitioners." *Frontiers in Psychology* 10 (2019): 474705.

Posner, M.I. "Orienting of Attention." *Quarterly Journal of Experimental Psychology* 32, no. 1 (1980): 3–25.

Posner, M.I., and S.E. Petersen. "The Attention System of the Human Brain." *Annual Review of Neuroscience* 13, no. 1 (1990): 25–42.

Postman, N., and C. Weingartner. *Meaning Making: Teaching as a Subversive Activity.* El Dorado, AR: Delta, 1969.

Preilowski, B. "Memory of an Amnestic (and a Half a Century of Memory Research)." *Fortschritte Der Neurologie · Psychiatrie* 77, no. 10 (2009): 568–76.

Purvis, Denise. "Creating Thinking: Immersive Dance Theater as 4E Cognition in the Wild." *Journal of Dance Education* 21, no. 3 (2021): 149–57.

Qin, Shaozheng, Erno J. Hermans, Hein J.F. van Marle, Jing Luo, and Fernandez Guillen. "Acute Psychological Stress Reduces Working Memory-Related Activity in the Dorsolateral Prefrontal Cortex." *Biological Psychiatry* 66, no. 1 (2009): 25–32.

Rajmohan, V., and E. Mohandas. "The Limbic System." *Indian Journal of Psychiatry* 49, no. 2 (2007): 132–39.

Rasia-Filho, Alberto A., Renata G. Londero, and Matilde Achaval. "Functional Activities of the Amygdala: An Overview." *Journal of Psychiatry and Neuroscience* 25, no. 1 (2000): 14–23.

Rogers, G.B., D.J. Keating, R.L. Young, M-L Wong, J Licino, and S Wesselingh. "From Gut Dysbiosis to Altered Brain Function and Mental Illness: Mechanisms and Pathways." *Molecular Psychiatry* 21, no. 6 (2016): 738–48.

Romita, N., and A. Romita. *Functional Awareness: Anatomy in Action for Dancers.* Oxford: Oxford University Press, 2023.

Rosen, Richard. *The Yoga of Breath.* Boulder: Shambhala Press, 2002.

Ross, Janice. *Anna Halprin: Experience As Dance.* Berkeley: University of California Press, 2007.

Saliers, Emily. "Closer to Fine." Elektra Records, 1995.

Santos, Edalmarys, and Chad A. Noggle. "Synaptic Pruning." In *Encyclopedia of Child Behavior and Development,* edited by Sam Goldstein and Jack A. Naglieri. Boston: Springer, 2011.

Schemann, Michael. "Control of Gastrointestinal Motility by the 'Gut Brain'—The Enteric Nervous System." *Journal of Pediatric Gastroenterology and Nutrition* 41, Supplement 1 (2005): S4–6.

Schmidt, R.A. "A Schema Theory of Discrete Motor Skill Learning." *Psychological Review* 82, no. 4 (1975): 225–60.

Schmidt, Richard, Tim Lee, Carolee Winstein, Gabriele Wulf, and Howard Zelaznik. *Motor Control and Learning*. Champaign: Human Kinetics, 2019.

Schneider, W., and R.M. Shiffrin. "Controlled and Automatic Human Information Processing: I. Detection, Search, and Attention." *Psychological Review* 84, no. 1 (1977): 1–66.

Schneider, W., S.T. Dumais, and R.M. Shiffrin. "Automatic Processing and Attention." In *Varieties of Attention*, edited by R. Parasuraman and R. Davis, 1–27. New York: Academic Press, 1984.

Schupp, Karen. "The Transgressive Possibilities of Foregrounding Somatic Values." *Research in Dance Education* 18, no. 2 (2017): 161–73.

Sellen, A.J., and R.H.R. Harper. *The Myth of the Paperless Office*. Cambridge: MIT Press, 2003.

Shapiro, Lawrence, and Shannon Spaulding. "Embodied Cognition." In *The Stanford Encyclopedia of Philosophy*, edited by Edward N. Zalta and Uri Nodelman. https://plato.stanford.edu/archives/sum2024/entries/embodied-cognition.

Shea, John B., and Robin Morgan. "Contextual Interference Effects on the Acquisition, Retention, and Transfer of a Motor Skill." *Journal of Experimental Psychology: Human Learning and Memory* 5, no. 2 (1979): 179–87.

Shea, John B., and Susan T. Zimny. "Context Effects in Memory and Learning Movement Information." *Advances in Psychology* 12 (1983): 345–66.

Siegel, Jerome. "The Neurobiology of Sleep." *Seminars in Neurology* 29, no. 4 (2009): 277–96.

Sieger, Tomáš, Tereza Serranová, Filip Růžička, Pavel Vostatek, Jiří Wild, Daniela Šťastná, Cecilia Bonnet, et al. "Distinct Populations of Neurons Respond to Emotional Valence and Arousal in the Human Subthalamic Nucleus." *Proceedings of the National Academy of Sciences* 112, no. 10 (2015): 3116–121.

Skinner, Joan, Bridget Davis, Robert Davidson, Kris Wheeler, and Sally Metcalf. "Skinner Releasing Technique: Imagery and Its Application to Movement Training." Accessed May 7, 2021. https://skinnerreleasingnetwork.org/wp-content/uploads/2020/11/-Imagery-and-its-Application.pdf.

Skinner, Joan, Bridget Davis, Robert Davidson, Kris Wheeler, and Sally Metcalf. "Skinner Releasing Technique." *Contact Quarterly* 5 (1979): 8–13.

Skinner Releasing Network. "About Joan Skinner." Accessed January 16, 2024. https://skinnerreleasingnetwork.org/welcome-to-srn/about-joan-skinner/#:~:text=Joan%20Skinner%20had%20a%20lifetime,The%20Thinking%20Body"%20in%201937.

Smith, Linda B., and Esther Thelen, eds. *A Dynamic Systems Approach to Development*. CogNet, 1993.

Smith, Linda B., Chen Yu, and Alfredo Pereira. "From the Outside-in: Embodied Attention in Toddlers." In *European Conference on Artificial Life*, 445–54. Berlin, Heidelberg: Springer Berlin Heidelberg, 2007.

Sommer, Felix, and Fredrik Bäckhed. "The Gut Microbiota—Masters of Host Development and Physiology." *Nature Reviews Microbiology* 11, no. 4 (2013): 227–38.

Soudry, Y., C. Lomogne, D. Malinyaud, S.-M. Consoli, and P. Bonfils. "Olfactory System and Emotion: Common Substrates." *European Annals of Otorhinolaryngology, Head and Neck Diseases* 128, no. 1 (2011): 18–23.

Sripada, Chandra Sekhar, Mike Angstadt, Patrick McNamara, Andrea C. King, and K. Luan Phan. "Effects of Alcohol on Brain Responses to Social Signals of Threat in Humans." *NeuroImage* 55, no. 1 (2011): 371–80.

Stall, Paula, and Manoel Jacobsen Teixeira. "Fibromyalgia Syndrome Treated with the Structural Integration Rolfing® Method." *Revista Dor* 15 (2014): 248–52.

Stallibrass, Chloë, Peta Sissons, and Colin Chalmers. "Randomized Controlled Trial of the Alexander Technique for Idiopathic Parkinson's Disease." *Clinical Rehabilitation* 16, no. 7 (2002): 695–708.

Stephens, James, and Susan Hillier. "Evidence for the Effectiveness of the Feldenkrais Method." *Human Kinetics* 9, no. 3 (2020): 228–35.

Stevens, F.L., R.A. Hurley, and K.H. Taber. "Anterior Cingulate Cortex: Unique Role in Cognition and Emotion." *Journal of Neuropsychiatry* 23, no. 2 (2011): 121–25.

Tanaka, Saori C., Kenji Doya, Go Okada, Kazutaka Ueda, Yasumasa Okamoto, and Shigeto Yamawaki. "Prediction of Immediate and Future Rewards Differentially Recruits Cortico-Basal Ganglia Loops." *Nature Neuroscience* 7, no. 8 (2004): 887–93.

#TeamEBONY. "Choreographer Camille A. Brown: The Body Speaks." November 14, 2016. https://www.ebony.com/camille-a-brown-harlem-school-arts/.

Tharp, Twyla, and Mark Reiter. *The Creative Habit: Learn It and Use It for Life. A Practical Guide.* New York: Simon & Schuster, 2003.

Thelen, E., and L.B. Smith, eds. *A Dynamic Systems Approach to Development: Applications.* Cambridge: MIT Press, 1993.

Thompson, E., and M. Stapleton. "Making Sense of Sense-Making: Reflections on Enactive and Extended Mind Theories." *Topoi* 28 (2009): 23–30.

Todd, Mabel. *The Thinking Body.* Perth: The Gestalt Journal Press, 2008.

Torrico, Tyler J. and Sunil Munakomi. "Neuroanatomy, Thalamus." Accessed Jul 24, 2023. In: StatPearls. Treasure Island (FL): StatPearls Publishing. PMID: 31194341.

Tortora, Suzi. "2010 Marian Chace lecture." *American Journal of Dance Therapy* 33, no. 1 (2011).

Tulving, Endel, and Hans J. Markowitsch. "Episodic and Declarative Memory: Role of the Hippocampus." *Hippocampus* 8, no. 3 (1998): 198–204.

Uttal, William R. *Mind and Brain: A Critical Appraisal of Cognitive Neuroscience.* Cambridge: MIT Press, 2011.

Van der Kolk, Bessel. *The Body Keeps the Score: Brain, Mind, and Body in the Healing of Trauma.* New York: Penguin, 2014.

Van Der Schyff, Dylan, Andrea Schiavio, Ashley Walton, Valerio Velardo, and Anthony Chemero. "Musical Creativity and the Embodied Mind: Exploring the Possibilities of 4E Cognition and Dynamical Systems Theory." *Music & Science* 1 (2018): 2059204318792319.

Van Gelder, T. "The Dynamical Hypothesis in Cognitive Science." *Behavioral and Brain Sciences* 21, no. 5 (1998): 615–28.

Varela, F.J., E. Thompson, and E. Rosch. *The Embodied Mind, Revised Edition: Cognitive Science and Human Experience.* Cambridge: MIT Press, 2017.

Veder, Robin. "The Expressive Efficiencies of American Delsarte and Mensendieck Body Culture." *Modernism/Modernity* 17, no. 4 (2010): 819–38.

Vertinsky, Patricia. "Transatlantic Traffic in Expressive Movement: From Delsarte and Dalcroze to Margaret H'Doubler and Rudolf Laban." *The International Journal of the History of Sport* (2009).

Wanderley, M.M., B.W. Vines, N. Middleton, C. McKay, and W. Hatch. "The Musical Significance of Clarinetists' Ancillary Gestures: An Exploration of the Field." *Journal of New Music Research* 34, no. 1 (2005): 97–113.

Wasserman, Judith. "A World in Motion: The Creative Synergy of Lawrence and Anna Halprin." *Landscape Journal* 31, no. 1–2 (2012): 33–53.

Wenders, Wim, director. *Pina.* IFC Films, 2011. 1 hr., 43 min.

Wickens, C.D. "The Effects of Divided Attention on Information Processing in Manual Tracking." *Journal of Experimental Psychology: Human Perception and Performance* 2, no. 1 (1976): 1–3.

Wickens, C.D. "The Structure of Attentional Resources." In *Attention and Performance,* edited by R.S. Nickerson. Hillsdale, NJ: Erlbaum, 1980.

Wickens, C.D., and J.G. Hollands. *Engineering Psychology and Human Performance.* Upper Saddle River, NJ: Prentice Hall, 2000.

Wijdicks, Eelco F.M. *Recognizing Brain Injury.* New York: Oxford University Press, 2014.

Winters, A.F. "Emotion, Embodiment, and Mirror Neurons in Dance/Movement Therapy: A Connection Across Disciplines." *American Journal of Dance Therapy* 30, no. 2 (2008): 84–105.

Wise, Roy A. "Dopamine, Learning and Motivation." *Nature Reviews Neuroscience* 5, no. 6 (2004): 483–94.

World Health Organization. "Palliative Care." August 5, 2020. https://www.who.int/news-room/fact-sheets/detail/palliative-care.

Wright, Anthony. "Limbic System: Amygdala (Section 4, Chapter 6)." In *Neuroscience Online: An Electronic Textbook for the Neurosciences*. Department of Neurobiology and Anatomy, the University of Texas Medical School at Houston, 2019. https://nba.uth.tmc.edu/neuroscience/m/s4/chapter06.html.

Wulf, Gabriele, and Rebecca Lewthwaite. "Optimizing Performance through Intrinsic Motivation and Attention for Learning: The OPTIMAL Theory of Motor Learning." *Psychonomic Bulletin and Review* 23, no. 5 (2016): 1382–414.

Yan, Zheng, and Kurt Fischer. "Always Under Construction: Dynamic Variations in Adult Cognitive Microdevelopment." *Human Development* 45, no. 3 (2002): 141–60.

Yang, G.Y., J. Hunter, F.L. Bu, W.L. Hao, H. Zhang, P.M. Wayne, and J.P. Liu. "Determining the Safety and Effectiveness of Tai Chi: A Critical Overview of 210 Systematic Reviews of Controlled Clinical Trials." *Systematic Reviews* 11, no. 1 (2022): 260.

Zhu, Yashuo, Hui Gao, Li Tong, ZhongLin Li, Linyuan Wang, Chi Zhang, Qiang Yang, and Bin Yan. " Emotion Regulation of Hippocampus Using Real-Time fMRI Neurofeedback in Healthy Human." *Frontiers in Human Neuroscience* 13 (2019): 242.

Index

Adams and Reynolds paradigm 49, 50
African and African Diasporic dance 14–15
Africanist somatic worldview 12–14, 31–32
aikido 16–18
Alexander, Frederick 24
Alexander Technique 24–25
Asian somatic practices 12, 16–18; see also yoga
attention 39–40, 42; automatic 40–41; controlled 40–41; selective 41
augmented feedback 53–56, 132; see also feedback
autonomic nervous system (ANS) 17, 75
autonomy 94–95, 103–107, 114

Bartenieff, Irmgard 28, 208
Bartenieff Fundamentals 28–29
Body/Mind Centering 34
body organization 125; task examples 146–149, 231
brain vs. mind 62–63
breath, in SomaLab 114–117, 135–136, 209; task examples 138–145, 148–150, 210, 213–215, 222, 230
Brown, Camille A. 185, 189
Buddha's Brain: The Practical Neuroscience of Happiness, Love, & Wisdom 127, 157
Bush, Kate 159

central nervous system (CNS) 42–44, 53, 65–74, 76, 82
circling 169, 183
closed-loop 44–45, 62, 191
Cohen, Bonnie Bainbridge 34
community practice/praxis 219–227
conceptualization 89, 113, 126, 137
conceptually-guided prompts 149–151, 153, 231
Conrad, Emilie 31–32

constitution 89–90
contextual interference 50–54, 59, 100, 123, 163
Continuum Movement 31
COVID-19 pandemic 17, 128, 188, 193–197, 199–200, 203–207
creativity 95, 101–102, 122
cultural relevancy 160, 162

Dalcroze, Émile Jacques- 20, 22
dance as archive 189, 205–207
deconstructive tasks 135–144
Delsarte, François 20, 23
distributed cognition 91
Duncan, Isadora 22
duetting: action/reaction—group activity 172; repertory informed—group activity 171
dynamical systems theory 26, 39, 85, 90, 93, 96–101, 107, 111, 113, 124, 126, 130, 131, 163, 164

Einstein, Albert 112
embedded cognition 92–93
embodied cognition 16, 87–91, 111, 185, 207; see also conceptualization; replacement; constitution
embodiment: in action 113, 125–127, 135, 137, 211–212, 231; visualized—group activity 168–169, 174
empathy 5, 160–162, 166, 172, 193, 228, 230
enactive cognition 93–96, 103, 104, 186
enteric nervous system (ENS) 75
expertise 56, 99, 100, 130, 131–132, 137, 169
extended cognition 91–93

facilitated phrase work task examples 154–156, 231–232
feedback 44–45, 103, 105, 116, 127, 164, 211, 212; augmented feedback 53–56, 132; feedback loops 88, 91, 124, 213
Feldenkrais, Moshe 18, 29, 33

257

Index

The Feldenkrais Method 26–27, 96
fight or flight 41, 67, 73, 76–78, 83, 205
First Nations' somatic worldview 13
Fitts's Law 46
focus: internal 16, 104, 120, 140; external 104–106, 120
4E cognition 39, 52, 84, 86–96, 97, 98, 100–104, 107, 115, 124, 126; *see also* embedded cognition; embodied cognition; enactive cognition; extended cognition
functionalism 87

German gymnastics 19
gifting 161, 169; gifting, expanded 170–171
Gindler, Elsa 21
Graham, Martha 30, 32, 112, 157
guided visualization task examples 140–142, 230
gymnastics *see* German gymnastics; Harmonic Gymnastics; Swedish gymnastics

Halprin, Anna 30–31
Hanna, Thomas 12, 33–34
Harmonic Gymnastics 20, 21
H'Doubler, Doubler 22, 30
Hick's Law 38
hospice caregiving 194, 195, 196, 200, 227–232
Humphrey, Doris 31, 115, 116

Ideokinesis 25–26, 117, 119, 125
imagery, visualization, and mental practice 119, 134–136, 140, 147, 150, 152, 156, 157, 168, 169, 210, 211, 212, 230
improvisation 20, 46, 50, 95, 96, 121, 122, 123, 130, 124, 126, 136, 144–146, 147, 150, 152, 178, 191, 211, 231; *see also* intuitive movement; self-guided movement
Individual Movement Inventory (IMI) 118–119, 164
information (exteroceptive, interoceptive) 41, 124
information processing 16, 25, 38–39, 46, 47, 86, 98, 101, 102, 103, 106, 113, 124, 163, 211
integrative tasks 101, 135, 137, 149–151, 166, 231
intention 15, 24, 32, 41, 44, 97, 98, 180, 211; intention/attention 113, 120–121, 127, 132, 134, 135, 210, 230
interference 40, 41, 122; contextual interference 50–53, 54, 55, 59, 100, 123, 163; retroactive interference 52
intuitive movement 113, 121–123, 135, 136, 211, 215, 218, 231; *see also* improvisation; self-guided movement

judo 18

kinesthesia *see* physical awareness
kinesthetic empathy 30, 80, 126, 128, 129, 228; *see also* movement empathy

Laban, Rudolf 21, 22, 28, 29
Laban Movement Analysis (LMA) 22, 24
Life/Art Process 30–31
limbic system 61, 66–68, 70, 76, 160, 161
Ling, Henrik 19–20

mass-spring model 44
meaning making 86, 88, 117, 118, 121, 123, 125, 136, 156, 181
meditation 16, 30, 77–78, 113, 181
memory 38–39, 42, 50, 52, 56–58, 66–68, 70, 76, 78, 82, 83, 89, 90, 92, 97, 99, 100, 137, 164
memory map 181–182
mirror neuron(s) 79, 80, 128–129
Monk, Meredith 85
motivation 37, 66, 70, 82, 103–104, 106
motor learning 6, 35, 36–37, 39, 45–48, 50–51, 70, 72, 85, 97, 111–112, 122, 123, 124; *see also* OPTIMAL theory of motor learning
movement empathy 80, 113, 114, 121, 127–130, 135, 137, 159, 160, 204, 212, 231; *see also* kinesthetic empathy

narrative medicine 228–229
neuroaxis 61, 62
neurogenesis 64–65, 67
neuroplasticity 63–64, 157
neurotransmitters: acetylcholine 83; dopamine 70, 82–83, 104; endorphins 83–84; epinephrine 76, 83; gamma-aminobutyric acid 82; glutamate 82; norepinephrine 76, 78, 83; serotonin 81, 83
non-patterning 113, 175

observation and embodied re-practice, group activity 167–168
ode to a woman, lost 188, 200–203, 205, 206
open-loop 45
OPTIMAL theory of motor learning 85, 94, 102–106, 107, 120, 126, 175, 220

parasympathetic autonomic nervous system (PANS) 73–75, 77–78, 145, 155
Parkinson's Disease 25, 26, 30, 70, 71, 82–83

Index

participatory sense-making 86, 94–95
pedagogy 104–105, 118, 123, 124, 137, 160, 162, 165
peripheral nervous system (PNS) 65, 72–74, 75, 82, 136
physical awareness (kinesthesia) 27, 34, 113, 116, 123, 124, 125, 135, 136, 151, 152, 172, 173, 201, 204, 211, 212, 230, 231
physical culture 18, 22
practice: distributed 48–51; massed 48–50; personal 134–158, 159; variability 50
pranayama 15, 115, 116, 209
progression 48, 165, 166, 178, 180
proprioception 41, 42, 53, 132, 135, 136, 173, 211, 213, 217, 218

qigong 16

reconstructive tasks 135–137, 144–149, 231
reflection/incorporation 113, 130–132, 135, 137, 212, 232
replacement 89
retention 48–49, 51, 52, 54, 56–58, 66
retrieval 52, 57–58, 66
Rhythm Runs Through It 188–193, 194, 198, 199, 200, 205
Rolf, Ida 27–28

schema theory of motor learning and control 45, 50
screendance 112, 188, 202–204
self-efficacy 103
self-guided movement 30, 113, 118, 121–123, 124, 130, 135–136, 160, 162, 163, 171, 211, 231; *see also* improvisation; intuitive movement
self-guided phrase work task examples 152–154
self-organization 98, 101–102
sensory-based improvisation tasks 136, 144–146, 147, 231
skill 37, 38, 40–41, 58, 59, 97–99, 113, 122, 123, 129, 159, 163, 166
Skinner, Joan 32
SomaLab for hospice caregivers 227–232
SomaLab framework and codified movement practice 113–133, 175–184: center work (free-form) 178; center work (structured) 178–180; community conversations 183; phrase work 180–181; reflection (memory map) 181–182; warm-up 176–177
SomaLab plus yoga and community practice 219–227
SomaLab plus yogic practices for ancers 213–219
SomaLab tasks *see* deconstructive tasks; integrative tasks; reconstructive tasks
SomaLab tools *see* breath; embodiment in action; intention/attention; movement empathy; physical awareness (kinesthesia); reflection/incorporation; visualization, and mental practice
somatic nervous system (SNS) 72, 73, 74, 76, 83
speed-accuracy trade-off 45–47
Stebbins, Genevieve 20, 21
subtle engagement 125, 138, 148, 153
Swedish gymnastics 19
sympathetic autonomic nervous system (SANS) 73–78, 83, 155

tai chi 16
targeted muscular engagement task examples 124, 142–144, 230
Taylor, Jill Bolte 60
Tharp, Twyla 111
theming 137, 165–166, 184
theory of mind 161
The Thinking Body 25, 117, 210
Todd, Mabel 25–26, 32, 117, 210
trauma 31, 63, 78, 188, 193, 195, 197, 204–205, 206, 207
Trager, Milton 29–30
transfer 58–59

vagus nerve 74–75, 78

Wigman, Mary 22

yoga 14–16, 20, 27, 37, 41, 103, 112, 114–115, 118, 120, 124–125, 138, 209–227
Yoga Sutras 15, 209

www.ingramcontent.com/pod-product-compliance
Lightning Source LLC
Chambersburg PA
CBHW052058300426
44117CB00013B/2185